BREAK, BREAK, BREAK

IAN DOUGLAS ROBERTSON

Prepared for publication by:

Authoraide Publications, LLC
1603 Capitol Ave, Suite 310 A275 Cheyenne, Wyoming 82001
Office: (307) 459-1803 | Fax: (307) 224-8450
Website: www.authoraide.com

To Alex, Prue, Zoe, and Aidan,
my beloved Australian family.

Break, break, break
At the foot of thy crags, O Sea!
But the tender grace of a day that is dead
Will never come back to me.

—Alfred, Lord Tennyson (1809–92)

Hugh Gorman was feeling stiff, and the bottom of his spine had gone numb. He got up, stretched, and took a few steps down the plane. He didn't go far. Passengers were overflowing into the aisle—legs dangling, arms protruding, heads swinging. He would only go the full length if nature called, which it did rather too frequently these days. He had been to the doctor about it, but it had been a total waste of a hundred dollars. "One of the hazards of getting old, I'm afraid, Mr. Gorman." He didn't need to pay a hundred dollars to be told about the hazards of growing old. He knew all about them. He wanted a solution, a pill to slow the flow, but all the doc said was, "I can give you something, but I can't promise it'll do any good." So, Hugh didn't bother.

Hugh had never felt old, not until now. At seventy, when others were complaining of aches, pains, and palpitations with a meal of pills lined up on their kitchen table for breakfast, he had felt just as he had done all his life. He still led an active life, waking up early and walking at least five miles a day when he had the time. Most graziers went everywhere in their pickups but he preferred walking. Of course, if the sheep were at some distance from the station, he'd have to take the old jeep or the pickup, but he invariably dumped it and went the last mile or two on foot. He found walking exhilarating, energizing—that's the word they liked to use nowadays.

There was nothing worse than being cramped up in a seat that was hardly wide enough to fit your buttocks and Hugh was a big man, not fat, just big-boned. When he was young, he could toss a hundredweight bag of wheat over his shoulder with one arm, no trouble. They once asked him if he wanted to train for the Irish

Olympic weightlifting team. He had the right build, they said, and he certainly had the strength, but he wasn't interested. One thing was lifting bags of wheat and barley as a necessity of life, another committing to a rigorous training programme. Besides, he'd never been the competitive type. He took things as they came, often letting circumstances determine the course of his life.

Hugh sat down again. He felt self-conscious standing in the aisle with blurry-eyed fellow passengers staring ghostlike at him. They had nothing better to do, he supposed. They were tired of watching films they'd already seen on Netflix. Hugh was a shy man, happy with his own company, and he'd had plenty of that over the years. He spent more time with dogs and sheep than with people and often had a better understanding of them too. He was the leader of the flock, and his whistled commands were undisputed.

He loved that feeling of freedom out on the station, alone in the middle of a vast expanse of land, but there was something soulless about it. It was wilder, bleaker, less intimate than Ireland. No shadowy *boreens* or whispering streams, no homely fields and familiar ditches, the inanimate remains of ancient civilizations and centuries of hard labour. There were times when he longed for those rounded hilltops and narrow country lanes inhabited by the spirits of his ancestors. Every shadow, every rush of wind, every shudder of a branch or stirring of a tree had meaning for him.

Australia was a fine place, good sheep farming land, beautiful in its way, but the spirits that populated it were not his spirits. They belonged to another race, a race whose language and culture he felt no affinity with. Not that he didn't admire the aborigines, he did. He admired their self-sufficiency, their determination to survive in a land dominated by an alien race, to hold on to their age-old traditions and beliefs. He often had such thoughts as he wandered the ditchless land and scanned the uninterrupted, unaffecting horizon.

The only person he had ever felt totally at ease with was Sheila, his third-generation Irish wife. She still had her Irish looks, her reddish hair and freckles, but she was as Australian as the rest of them. She did most of the talking and he was content to listen. She was happy too, if he nodded every so often—in the right places, of course. She used to get quite vexed if he nodded when a nod was not an appropriate response.

He had never felt particularly comfortable with his two sons. He had little in common with them. They were Australian, despite all the Irish blood that flowed in their veins. They could not understand him or where he came from. They thought like Australians and cared little about the land of their ancestors. All the poetry and romance that was so much a part of his soul was lost to them. He loved them, of course, and wanted the best for them; but he had no idea what they were thinking most of the time, and they always seemed to be after something, usually money, even though he paid them well while they had been working on the station.

Thinking about his sons always brought on a dismal cloud of melancholy. After they left the farm to "make their fortunes," he lost contact with them. They had their own lives, and he didn't want to constrain them in any way. When they did come home, he felt it was more to see Sheila than him. There were times when he blamed himself for the rift that had grown up between them. Should he have offered them a share in the station? He had talked it over with Sheila, and it was she who advised him not to. They both felt the boys were not mature enough to be partners. Even though they had been reared with sheep and knew almost as much as he did about the business, it was obvious to both of them that their heart wasn't in it. So, he never made the offer and now it was too late. He had lost any connection there may once have been between them, and he couldn't help feeling that when his time was up, he wouldn't be missed.

Brendan was a bit of a tearaway and couldn't be trusted with money. He'd use his allowance on drink, women, or poker. Hugh didn't mind his spending money on women. That was the privilege, nay, the duty of a healthy young man. It was the drink and the poker that worried him. He knew from bitter experience how someone can get hooked on either, or both. There was hardly a night when growing up back in Ireland that his father didn't roll in from the pub hurling foul language and whatever else came to hand at anyone who crossed his path. Fortunately, he never laid a hand on his mother, or there would have been hell to pay.

When they were very young, it was not uncommon for their father to take the belt to them on some trumped-up charge. Later, Hugh concluded it was just to vent his frustration at being a poor sheep farmer, not able to afford all the things that other farmers were slowly acquiring in the fifties. While they swanned into town in their shiny new jalopies, the Gormans still used the old ass and cart. Even when he was at the national school, most of his friends' fathers had an automobile. His father pooh-poohed it, claiming it was bought with borrowed money and said he wasn't going to take on a debt he couldn't pay back. But Hugh knew that if his father drank less and managed his affairs better, they too could have had a car.

The truth is Hugh couldn't wait to leave home. He stayed on more for his mother's sake than anything else. She had a kind, generous nature and had uncomplainingly put up with his father all those years. Of course, he wore her down in the end. On one of his journeys home, Hugh noticed how tired she was. "Is it Da?" he had asked.

"Ah, no," she had replied. She never had a bad word to say against him. "I'd just like a nice long holiday." Well, she never got that holiday. She died the following year.

His brother, Rory, called him one evening in December and told him that she hadn't long to live, but he didn't believe him or just didn't want to. When it happened, he got home too late to say goodbye. He wouldn't have made it to the funeral either if they hadn't put it off for a day. That was probably the saddest day of his life, barring the day Sheila died. But that was different. He had nursed her, fed her, cleaned her, shared her agony. In vain, he had endeavoured to keep up her spirits, but they both knew it was a losing battle. It was a relief when one day she finally gave up the ghost. At least, he had been holding her hand when she dragged out her last expiring breath.

After the funeral of his mother, even though he had already been thirty years in Australia, it was easier going back to Esperance. His father had sunk into old age and was a virtual recluse. Even the pub was no longer able to coax him out of his cocoon. After nearly half a century of kicking against the pricks, the old man found he couldn't do without her. It was ironic really.

Hugh didn't make it to his father's funeral. It was a bad time of the year on the station, and he wasn't prepared to leave the lads alone to do the shearing. They were sure to make a hames of it. He sent a long letter home, apologising and extolling his father's rare virtues. The letter moved him more than he had expected. Perhaps he had underestimated or even ignored those qualities that must have once attracted his mother to the old sod. Paddy Gorman could spin a yarn better than most and was a crack hand with the fiddle, which he played with such ease you'd swear he was born with it resting on a shoulder and the bow attached to his right hand. But Hugh couldn't ignore the fact that there was a cruel, self-pitying, often scathing side to him, which made him a hard man to love.

Hugh wasn't quite sure why he was going home now. Home? Yes, he still called it home after fifty years down under. He had lived two-thirds of his life in Australia but still referred to Ireland as home. "Does that mean the place you are born into will always be your home?" he pondered. What does a nomad call home then? It was difficult for him to grasp the notion of homelessness. Could the Gorman sheep station never be his true home? Why not? He loved the place in a way. And it was his, or more precisely theirs, his and Sheila's. When her parents died, they were able to buy out her brother, who was busy making his fortune elsewhere, by taking out a hefty loan from the bank. Fortunately, he had a good name with the Commonwealth Bank, and Bob Mulhern, the manager, knew he was good for it.

If he'd stayed in Ireland, he'd have had to share the farm with Rory and Joan, and it wasn't big enough to support one family, let alone three. One of them, he most likely, as the younger brother, would have had to seek work elsewhere. And he would never have got the money together to buy a place of his own. He would have had to work for someone else, pinching and scraping to make ends meet. God forbid, but he might even have been driven to the drink like his father.

Hugh closed his eyes and dropped off to sleep. It was a disturbed sleep, mixed with images of the dying Irish sun sparkling off golden leaves in autumn and the heat rising from the land in the Australian summer, drying everything to a tinder. He saw his mother by the fire reaching for the teapot, her hair going prematurely grey and her skin dry like parchment from overexposure to the elements.

The truth is life in Australia had been so much easier than it would have been in Ireland. Not that he hadn't worked hard, he had, but hard work was rewarded there. He had had a good life. No regrets. And in many ways, it was not all that different from what he had been used to. Esperance was a small town that had had its ups and downs. At one point, it had been "the gateway to the goldfields." When he arrived there in the early seventies, it had a population of around three thousand. Since then, it had grown considerably, but it had not lost it small town charm, despite the influx of tourists all the year round, keen to see the Pink Lake and the Cyclops Wave and enjoy the miles of golden sandy beaches.

He just wished he could banish that longing for home. It was like a stigma in his side that would bleed at the slightest provocation. He had almost resigned himself to the idea that there was nothing he could do but live with it. The wound would close over but would never completely heal. A call from Rory or a letter from Joan, reminding him of that other life, the one he had left behind, would scuff the scab and set the blood flowing.

He had tried many ways of curing himself of these overwhelming bouts of homesickness. He convinced himself that he could not have had such a good life in Ireland. He would never have met Sheila. He would have been tempted by the booze like his father. He would have fought with Rory and Joan. The arguments he put forward were endless, but he knew they were all just attempts at self-deception and self-consolation. Ireland was his first love, and you never get over your first love, they say. It still didn't answer the question though. Why was he going back now? There was no wedding, no christening, no funeral. Or was there? He hoped not.

If the truth were told, it was because he knew his days were numbered. How many years could he expect to live? Ten? Fifteen at the outside. He didn't need to work. He had been a slave to the station for most of his life. It was time to let go. Besides, he had a good foreman, who over the years had become like a son to him, the kind of son he wished he had had. If he could, he would have left the station to him, but he didn't want his natural sons cursing him in his grave till their dying days.

The boys were not coming back. That was for sure. They'd sell the place. Get a packet for it and then slowly blow it, at least Brendan would. With any luck, Niall would plough it into his business and buy himself another plane or two. Niall was a good lad but fiercely independent. Too busy to visit his old man, even though he could have flown himself down to Esperance any time he wanted, but that would have meant losing a bob or two.

It was Joan's letter that finally persuaded him to buy the ticket for Ireland. She implied that if he left it too long, he might get too old to make the journey. He didn't believe that. However frail he was, he'd make it somehow. It was the mention of Rory's failing health that did it. He would never have forgiven himself if Rory passed without him saying goodbye. Joan made light of it, but he knew that the years of three packs a day had played havoc with his lungs. There was a suggestion that he might have lung cancer, but it wasn't stated clearly. Maybe she just didn't want to use the dreaded C word. Then, she said, "Isn't it time you came home now, Hugh?" Did she honestly believe he'd go back to Ireland to live out the rest of his life?

Through the aeroplane window, he could see the lights of Dubai below. They'd make a two-hour stop there and then fly to Dublin via Amsterdam. At least he'd get a chance to stretch his legs, maybe even treat himself to a massage.

■

As he boarded the plane for the last stretch of the journey home, he could see the sun peeping above the horizon. It reminded him of dawns in Australia, the most beautiful time of the day, in his opinion. So full of hope and promise. What hope?

What promise? Sure, wasn't it all downhill now, as the fellow says.

On the last leg of the journey, the young man beside him woke up. He must have been in his early twenties, tousled light brown hair, bearded cheeks and a pleasant carefree smile. Hugh had guessed he was on his world tour, just after college, before knuckling down to a nine-to-five job.

"Visiting relations?" the young man said.

"What's left of them," said Hugh.

"You're Irish then?"

"I suppose you could say so, though I've lived most of my life in Australia."

"You wouldn't know it. No trace of Strine."

Hugh laughed. If anything, his accent had become more anglicised than Australianised, but he wasn't about to apologise for it. He supposed it was further proof that he had not fully integrated into Australian society and culture. Perhaps he should have made more of an effort. Yet, it had not been a question of resistance but a lack of desire or need perhaps. He had been content with his Irishness and was not about to change it now.

"And yourself?" said Hugh, glancing at the young man who had begun looking at his mobile phone. He wondered whether people these days ever noticed their surroundings. They were always immersed in their mobiles. What in God's name were they looking at, anyway?

"Third generation. I'm curious to see what my great-grandfather needed to get away from."

"Ireland is no longer the backward place it was then. It has a thriving economy, low unemployment, great opportunities for the youth."

"Why did you leave?"

Hugh thought for a moment, though he knew the answer. "I wanted to get out, mainly to get away from my father and make a better life for myself."

"Good enough reasons, I suppose. Why Australia?"

"I saw a notice in the local paper. They were looking for hardworking young men who had experience working with sheep. The pay was good, and there seemed to be a good future there. I had no idea then that I'd marry the boss's daughter and eventually own the place."

"You made a good move then?"

"I suppose you could say so."

"Do I detect some doubt in your voice?"

"No. No regrets. It's just you end up not belonging anywhere."

"Right," said the young man musingly. "I can empathise with that."

Hugh wondered whether he could.

As they travelled further west, with the dawn at their tail, he wondered which would arrive first, the plane or the dawn. In fact, it was nine o'clock when they touched down in Dublin airport, though it was hard to believe it, as it was a dark dull day with a heavy fog-like drizzle. Even the lights were still on everywhere.

As he descended the stairs from the plane, Hugh was overcome by a confusing mix of emotions. On the one hand, he had a desperate desire to search out the familiar, to feel the emotion that he had felt so often back in Australia. On the other, he couldn't help feeling that he didn't belong here. Everything was different, the way people dressed and behaved. Even the accents seemed more sophisticated and anglicised than in the past. Then, he heard a strong Dublin accent from one of the porters and realised things hadn't changed all that much. He felt excited and at the same time apprehensive. Why the apprehension? Was he afraid of being disappointed? Was he afraid that he might be persuaded to stay?

He wouldn't have recognised Joan, if she hadn't called out his name when he appeared at the gate with his suitcase. In fact, he had to look twice to make sure it was her and not some old woman calling another Hugh. His beautiful sister was an old woman, grey hair, grey clothes, grey everything, except her voice that was just as sprightly as he remembered.

"God, you're looking grand, young fellow. Sure, you could pick up a young thing no problem. Here, give us a kiss and make all the girls jealous."

Hugh could see no jealous girls eyeing him but that was Joan. She still thought like a sixteen-year-old. Girls must always be fancying boys and boys girls. When she was young, she had had all the eligible young men in the townland and beyond after her until Mikey Keogh won her heart. She could have done better but at least Mikey was not a boozer or a womaniser.

"You must be exhausted. Come on now, young fellow. We'll have you home in no time. I've even got your old room ready. Margaret is away in Dublin and seldom comes down. These high-flying youngsters. She has three children of her own now, but sure you know that. And runs a law practice in her spare time. I don't know how they do it."

They ran across the road to the carpark, sheltering as best they could under one umbrella. Joan took some time locating her car, but they eventually found it behind a concrete column.

Soon they were hurtling down one of the motorways. Without the sun to orientate him, he hadn't a clue in which direction they were going.

"I'm glad you came to pick me up, Joan. If I'd hired a car, I'd have surely got hopelessly lost."

"Oh, they're building new roads all the time. Sure, soon the whole country will be nothing but one big road. It's handy enough though. It used to take four hours from the airport. Now we can do it in two. How are you feeling, Hugh? Are you glad to be home?"

Hugh hesitated. He wasn't sure how to answer. What he had seen so far was not home. Only the green fields and the drizzle were familiar to him. "To be honest with you, Joan, I can't feel a thing at the moment, most likely the jet lag."

"Oh, it won't take long for you to be as right as rain."

He smiled at the expression, which he hadn't heard since the last time he was in Ireland. It was funny, he thought, that the Irish should consider rain 'right' when they were always complaining about having too much of it. It would have made more sense in Australia, where rain was such a precious commodity.

"I have a surprise for you," she continued. "But don't ask me what it is because it's a surprise."

Hugh smiled. Joan's surprises were usually not surprises at all. So, he gave it no further thought.

"Now, tell me about the boys. Are they well?"

"I hardly see them."

"Ah, sure that's the way. We oldies are of no interest to them. I suppose it's normal. They have their life to lead. So, are you lonely out there on your own with Sheila gone?"

Just like Joan to be so direct, he thought. "It's not easy, as you no doubt know yourself."

"Ah, for a woman, it's different. We always find someone to look after."

"Rory, eh? Is he in a bad way?"

"Oh, sure he is, Hughie. He won't see the year out."

Hugh had to fight back a spasm of emotion that threatened to erupt into tears. Another sign of old age, maudlin sentimentality. "Poor ould Rory," he said after he had recovered a steady voice. "Sure, the fags did for him."

"Oh, they did all right. Even now, when he's on oxygen most of the day, I see him sneaking a drag."

"Well, let him. It won't make a hap'ort of difference now. I'm glad I came."

Hugh looked over at Joan and saw that she was crying silently. She and Rory had been close. He had given her the family home and built a small bungalow on the edge of the farm for himself and the parents. Since he became ill, he had moved back in so that Joan could look after him. How many people had she nursed in their last months or years? First, their mother, then their father—the old grouser—then Mikey and now Rory. She had been there for them all. He felt guilty that he hadn't been around for any of them. Excuses had been easy to come by, but he knew they were just excuses.

At some point, they turned off the new main road and quickly things became familiar to him. The old landmarks were still there; the bridge under the disused railway, the old barracks, the crumbling castle, still smothered in ivy. He remembered walking these roads in the days before they were tarmacked, driving the sheep to market or a pig to the boar. Did he really walk barefoot summer and winter? No, in winter he had a pair of tough old boots his mother insisted he wore. They were grand days all right. Though it rained just as much then, he supposed, the sun always seemed to be shining. He wondered how Mat was. As children, they had been practically inseparable.

As they moved higher into the hills, the roads got narrower. They weren't even wide enough for two asses and carts to pass each other, let alone a couple of lorries, but no one except locals used these byroads, and they were used to pulling into a gateway to let another car pass. As they went by a familiar house, he asked about the occupant, whether they were still alive or not. Most were long gone and the house either sold or taken over by a son or grandson, who would only know him by hearsay.

"They're always askin' after you, you know."

"Who's that now, Joan?"

"All the people in the townland. You're a bit of legend around these parts."

Hugh laughed. "Is that so? I can't imagine why."

"Well, there's tales of you takin' on lads twice your size that were tormenting you. You were fairly handy with your fists, as I remember."

"I didn't enjoy it, I can tell you. But they had what was coming to them."

"Oh, they don't think bad of you for it. Just the opposite. They've turned you into a kind of local hero. That and your strength. They say you could throw a hundredweight bag of barley onto a lorry with one arm."

"I'm sure it's just an exaggeration. I certainly couldn't do it now."

"Perhaps not, but you haven't an ounce of fat on you. How do you do it?"

"Well, for a start, I don't have the temptation of Sheila's meals anymore."

Joan looked over at him, perhaps expecting to see tears in his eyes, but he hadn't. It hadn't been easy, but he had steeled himself to her loss.

"She was a lovely woman, Hugh. I'm sorry I didn't get to know her better."

"She was tough, Joan. The Australians are like that. No nonsense about them. None of our romantic nature. We were brought up with ghosts and spirits, angels and devils. They gave up that boloney centuries ago."

"Sure, weren't we brought up in the dark ages? Things are different now. It's all about new cars, new houses, a career, and all that. To be honest with you, though, I can't say they're any the happier for it."

The wrought-iron gate at the end of the lane was open. Hugh noticed that it needed a coat of paint. If he stayed long enough, he'd make sure to give it a lick.

The lane seemed to have more potholes in it than ever. There were signs everywhere of neglect. Of course, neither Joan nor Rory was up to doing the repairs and the kids no doubt couldn't give a damn, just waiting for them to die so that they could sell the place. It made him angry but that was life, he supposed. And he was no one to talk. Where had he been when his parents needed him?

The house seemed smaller than he remembered and the windows narrower. How could any light get in? Perhaps it didn't. But he never remembered it being dark inside.

Joan beeped the horn as they drove into the yard. Rory would be anxious to see them. Hugh expected him to appear at the door but he didn't, not even at the kitchen window.

"Leave your cases. You can get them later."

Hugh had to duck as he entered the front door. They didn't cater for tall men in the old days. It was indeed dark inside and smelt of must and soot.

The kitchen was warm at least. They still kept the Aga burning day and night. On the opposite side was a fireplace that had been put in some years after he had left. Some blackened logs lay cold in the grate. Rory sat in an armchair beside it, with layers of blankets over him to keep him warm. Hugh could tell at a glance that he was on his last legs. His face was hollow and the skin sallow and sagging. He didn't even have the strength to get up to greet him.

"Jaysus, if it isn't the man himself," Rory wheezed. "For the love of God, I'd swear you're not a day older than the last time you were over. Do you have some sort of a pact with the devil or what?"

Hugh didn't know what to say. In normal circumstances, he would have returned the compliment, but it would have been hypocritical in this case. Hugh took his hand, which was cold and lifeless. He tried to smile but it was more a grimace, as he fought back the emotion that was welling up inside him. It was the end then. Slowly, they would all fade away. My god, what had been the point of it all?

"Sit down there now, boy, and tell me what's happening down under. You got out of this place when the going was good. If I'd had any sense, I'd have gone over with you."

"Ah, no. You did right staying put. There's nowhere like home."

"That's what you say. I'm fed up with the place. The cursed rain and the cold. I'd give anything for a bit of your sun."

Hugh thought of the Western Australian sun and had to admit it was hard to beat. It gave you life and hope.

"The thing is, Hugh boy, you have the best of both worlds. You can live with your memories of childhood and enjoy the fruits of your new life in Australia. Do you think I remember my childhood? It's buried under a pile of banal events that are of no value to man or beast. Now, amn't I right, Hugh?"

Hugh was not able to answer at once. He had never seen it quite like that. Perhaps Rory was right. Perhaps he should make the most of those mawkish moments of homesickness.

Joan asked Hugh to light the fire, which he did. It helped to brighten the place up. Even Rory seemed less bunched up in his chair. Hugh would like to have walked the fields with him, roam the boreens and up to the top of the hill, but he knew he would have to do it alone. Perhaps it was better that way. It would give him time to think, to consider what life would be like in Ireland. He had heard of some spending six months in one country and six in the other, but that would be torture, he decided. No, it had to be one or the other.

Rory had run out of breath long before lunch, and he was only able to utter a word or two before his lungs collapsed in on him. Hugh helped him to the table, but he only picked at his food.

Joan talked about the neighbours as if he knew them all. He didn't bother telling her that he had no idea who she was talking about. Then, he asked what he had wanted to ask for some time but had been afraid to.

"How's Mat?" he said, catching his breath.

"Powerful. Sure, he's just like yourself. I don't know what you boyos ate in your youth, some sort of elixir of life, by the looks of it. He often comes up. He's looking forward to your visit. I wouldn't be surprised if he don't come by this evening."

Hugh heaved a sigh of relief. He had never had many friends in his life. In Australia almost none. Many acquaintances, but no friends. Friends need to understand each other, and to understand someone you need to know where they come from. Mat and he came from the same place.

"And Bridie?"

"In grand health. The two of them play golf almost every day, so they do."

"Golf?" Hugh couldn't help laughing. It just didn't seem the kind of thing a country lad like Mat would do but times had changed. The thought of their fathers playing golf was as laughable as the idea of the queen of England going to church in an ass and cart.

"Oh, sure everybody plays golf now. It's not cheap, mind, but everybody has money these days."

"What about you—money-wise, I mean?" Hugh knew it was cheeky of him to ask, but he needed to know that they were all right financially.

"Ah, we manage, don't we, Joan?" said Rory.

Joan didn't answer.

"And who's looking after the sheep?"

"What sheep? We sold them a long time ago. Sure, who's going to look after them? I can't walk more than a few yards without chasing me breath."

"So, what do you do for money?"

"We have a small bit put aside, and we let the fields to some neighbours," said Joan.

Hugh could tell that the small bit was not much, but she was too proud to say things were tight.

After lunch, Rory was put to bed. It had been an exhausting morning for him. He was so keen to talk, but the ventilator had to be used on a number of occasions. Hugh wondered which would give out first, his heart or his lungs.

Joan too liked to rest after lunch. She would sit in the small sunroom they had constructed on the south side of the house, many years ago, when they still had money. She made herself a cup of tea and asked Hugh to join her, but he declined and took his case upstairs to get settled in.

It was strange being back in his old room. Almost at once that happy-go-lucky feeling that he had taken so much for granted as a child came back to him, the freedom to do anything, or almost anything, after he had done his chores. He would set out across the fields with no clear destination, probably ending up at Mat's place, where he would often stay the whole day. Wherever he went there was something exciting going on. If it wasn't to watch them cutting barley or shearing sheep or stooking hay, he'd be out picking blackberries to sell to the man from the jam factory who came round in his van with two oil barrels strapped to the back. It was a way to make a few pence to spend on gob stoppers or acid drops. But those days were long gone, even before he left for Australia.

He slowly unpacked his things. He had decided to travel light, just one change of underwear, some old togs for walking around the farm and the set of decent clothes he came in. He didn't want to assume he would stay long. When he had finished, he lay down on the bed and contemplated the damp stains on the ceiling. He remembered lying awake in the long summer evenings making up stories about the shapes that had formed on the white plastered ceiling. Were they the same stains? No, surely not. Yet, if he lay there long enough, he could probably make out the strange creatures that inhabited a child's mythological world. He laughed. He was beyond that now. His overactive imagination had been smothered by the ever-pressing realities of life. Yet, he wished he could regain that infinite world of the imagination, which was so much more exciting and fulfilling than reality ever was.

He dozed off for a while. When he woke up, he felt disoriented. It was the smell coming through the open window that told him where he was, that distinct scent of rain on grass. He went over to the window and saw that the rain had stopped and the sun was trying to burn through the clouds. It would be a weak sun but sun nonetheless. If Joan would let him, he'd go for a walk across the fields, maybe ending up on Connick Rock.

As he was putting on his old clothes, he had a flashback to the time he was going out with Maggie McQuilty. When his parents had gone into town on some business or other, he'd skive off work early and pick Maggie up by the ditch at the bottom of the graveyard. They'd run across the field hand in hand screaming their heads off, scattering the sheep in all directions. He gallantly carried her across the stream so that she wouldn't get her feet wet. Not that there was much gallantry in it, just unadulterated lust. He could remember her still, her bright green eyes looking down at him, the burning heat of her panting breasts as they pressed into his chest. How quickly those carefree days had passed, giving way to the need to give battle with life.

By the time they reached the house, they were both aching with desire but things were different back then. They would play titillating games, half-naked on the bed, she teasing him with her lithesome body and wet lips, he begging her to let him enter her. She may have had the desires of a normal teenage girl, but she was also a good Catholic and Ireland in the sixties was not the England of free sex and promiscuity.

Joan knew that he and Maggie had been soft on each other and had always regretted that their relationship had come to nothing. Yet, she had discreetly, and half playfully, kept him informed of her life; her marriage to Tom Kehoe, who had had a successful second-hand car business down in Cork, and their three children, who had all studied at Cork University and were now married with a host of their own children. Hugh thought about it for a moment and wondered what would have come of their passion if he'd stayed.

From the top of the stairs, he could hear a chorus of snoring from the parlour. He tiptoed in and saw Joan lopsided on the armchair in the sunroom and Rory in the bed they had fixed up against the wall next to the kitchen. He crept through into the hall, found a pair of Wellington boots that fitted him and went out into the yard. He stopped and looked up into the sky and watched the giant balls of cotton wool scudding by. He opened his arms, as if to welcome them, and breathed in deeply. There was nothing so wholesome as the Irish air, nourishing almost, as if it alone could provide all the sustenance his body and soul needed.

As he walked across the grass fields, climbed over gates, and cut through small copses of oak trees, he was aware how far away Australia was, not just in terms of distance but in his mind. It was almost as if it didn't exist, as if he had never emigrated and spent most of his life there. When he reached Connick Rock, he found the stone he and his mother liked to sit on and watch the shadows of the clouds scudding over the fields and ditches. Sometimes in the distance you could see a rainbow with a crock of gold at its end. As a child, he remembered thinking how he would one day go and search for that gold so that he would have the money to buy a place of his own. In the end, he had to go to Australia to find the end of the rainbow.

It was still more or less as it had always been, a patchwork of small fields in myriad shades of green and brown. It was as if nothing had changed. He expected to see his father or Rory marching across a field, the sheep swirling in circles at the behest of the dogs. In the far corner of their land, he saw a flock of sheep that must have belonged to one of the neighbours and the owner in among them.

That evening, Mat called to say he couldn't come over, as he had a big client from one of the Arab countries—the United Arab Emirates or one of those. Mat had made it big making chipboard. After struggling at the beginning, it had taken off in the boom period, and now he was exporting all over the world. His son Robert had taken over the business, so Mat was able to take a back seat, but like himself he could not hand it over entirely.

"I'm really sorry now, Hugh, but Robert would like me to be there. He's great on the factory floor, but he feels a bit intimidated when it comes to big clients. Ali Karayana, I think his name is.

He's Pakistani, in charge of materials for a construction company out there. Very nice lad. Speaks English better than I do. How's the form anyway?"

"Grand. It's nice to be back."

"Joan tells me you're thinking of staying for a while, maybe even permanently."

"Just wishful thinking on her part. I'd like to stay, for a while at least, but I can't leave the station for too long."

"The station?"

"The sheep farm."

"Oh right. Well, look. I'll call over for you tomorrow, and we can play a round of golf. You do play golf, I suppose."

"It's that game where you hit a small white ball with a long stick, isn't it?"

Mat laughed. "Ah, sure it doesn't matter. You can't be any worse at it than I am. Bridie is the expert. She has a whole row of cups lined up on the mantelpiece. Don't worry. She'll go easy on us. Anyway, they have a very good restaurant, where we can have a decent dinner afterwards. And it's on me, so leave your wallet at home."

"I'll look forward to that."

"I'd best be going. I don't want to keep Ali waiting. If this deal goes through, it could be worth a few grand."

That evening, they had an early supper, and Hugh helped get Rory to bed. Rory could hardly do anything for himself now. Hugh was able to help him to the toilet, but he was deadweight and even he had difficulty keeping him from falling over. Apparently, Joan just used a potty but even that can't have been easy. A trained nurse would not be able to cope, let alone a seventy-seven-year-old. It became clearer to Hugh by the minute that, like it or not, he was going to have to stay on until—he didn't like to say it—until Rory passed. And then, what would happen to Joan? Would she survive without someone to look after, alone in that dreary old house? She wouldn't want to come back to Australia with him—that was for sure—but she might have to.

By the following evening, Hugh was looking forward to a bit of normality. Rory needed constant attention. If it wasn't to go to the toilet, it was to deal with a pain in some part of his body, not to mention the need to have the ventilator yoked up all the time. Hugh knew that sooner or later, Rory would have to go into hospital.

Mat rolled into the yard in his Range Rover at around eight. There was a great deal of hand-shaking and hugging. It had been a long time. Bridie didn't look a day over fifty, though he knew she must be going on sixty-five. Mat was in right form too, though there was some evidence of an incipient potbelly, but nothing that anyone would put any pass on.

The golf club was like something he had only seen on TV when US presidents were interviewed before teeing off. He couldn't believe the opulence. Most of the cars in the carpark were SUVs or what he would class as top-of-the-range cars. There was a kind of swagger to the members too, as if they felt superior to the ordinary hoi polloi. He knew Ireland had changed, but this was not what he expected.

The golf course was truly beautiful, rolling hillocks of grass, with small ponds, natural or artificial he was not sure, scattered here and there. In the distance, he could see the sea, not clearly, but enough to make out a ship cruising off the south coast. Bridie proved herself as good, if not better than Mat had said, but was very willing to give Hugh advice on how to hold the club and hit the ball, so that at the end of the course, he felt he had actually improved. He even toyed with the idea of joining a golf club back in Esperance.

The meal was superb too, a lot better than anything he could find in Esperance. The waiters were polite and friendly, not fawning as some of the waiters were in Australia. No doubt the bill would be steep, but he wasn't going to try and pay. Mat had insisted it was his call.

Mat talked about his business and Hugh briefly mentioned his, though he assumed they would not be interested in sheep and barley. To his surprise, Mat showed great interest, or pretended to, and wanted to know everything about life on the station, sheep prices, and the meat market in general. For a moment, Hugh wondered whether he was thinking of investing in a sheep station, but he quickly realised that it was just Mat's thirst for knowledge, particularly when it had to do with business.

Hugh went home that night feeling as if he hadn't had such a good time for years. He had felt totally at ease with Mat and Bridie. He was sure it had to do with the fact that, apart from being exceptional people, they understood him. Each knew where the other was coming from. That night he slept better than he had done since Sheila died.

He was woken up next morning by noises downstairs and Joan's voice calling for help. He threw on some clothes and rushed down. Rory had fallen out of bed, and Joan was trying desperately to get him back in. If he hadn't been there, God knows how long Rory would have lain there, gasping for breath, until Joan managed to call in a neighbour to help. It could very well have been the end of him. Hugh knew that there was no way he could leave Joan alone with Rory. He would have to stay or else hire a full-time nurse.

The ordeal had shaken Rory badly. Back in bed, he began to tremble all over, even though he was well covered in blankets. Hugh put it down to shock. They had the ventilator on all the time. The doctor said it would help to calm his nerves. Rory didn't feel like breakfast, but they did manage to get him to take sips from a cup of sweet milky tea.

Hugh knew his bedside manner left a lot to be desired, but he made an effort to be as attentive as he could to Rory's needs. Joan talked nonstop. He wasn't sure whether Rory found this soothing or not. If he were in his situation, he would have preferred an attentive presence rather than an incessant voice.

At about midmorning, Rory fell asleep, which gave Joan and Hugh a chance to take a breather. Joan suggested they have a cup of instant coffee in the kitchen. Hugh accepted willingly.

"You know he'll have to go into hospital, don't you?" said Hugh, as he watched Joan pour the boiling water into the mugs.

"Ah, no, Hugh. I couldn't do that to him."

"You can't look after him alone, however much you might want to."

"But sure, don't I have you now to help me."

Suddenly, Hugh felt trapped. It was no longer going to be a free choice, stay or leave. He was going to have to stay.

"Neither of us is a nurse, Joan. He needs specialist attention."

"I didn't tell you everything, either in my letter or when you arrived. I didn't want to upset you and you only after setting foot in the country after fifteen years. He only has a month to live. He's in the fourth stage of terminal cancer."

"How can they be so sure?"

"Experience, I suppose."

"And you, Joan, what are you going to do when he's gone? You can't live here alone. You'll go mad knocking around in this creaky old place full of family ghosts."

Joan chuckled. "But they are at least familiar ghosts and fairly benign at that. We get on well enough. Besides, I don't want to think about it. I'll face that when the time comes."

"Would you consider coming back to Australia with me?"

A look of horror tensed her face. "Sure, I've never been farther from home than Dublin in me whole life. What would I do in Australia?"

"We'd be together at least, and I have some very nice neighbours. I might even become a little more sociable with you around."

"I love you dearly, little brother, but I'd hate to live out me last days in exile."

"What'll you do?"

"God will provide. I'll insist Margaret and the children visit more often."

"Well, I hope they damned well do."

"There's no need to get angry now, Hughie. Margaret has her life to lead, like we had ours."

Hugh knew there was no point in continuing the discussion. She was not going to make any decisions now. Perhaps she'd change her mind when Rory was gone. It was hard for her to anticipate how lonely life would be without him.

"Now, let's not talk about death but life."

"Life," said Hugh with a huff, "what's left of it."

"We both have our health, you and I. There's no reason why we can't enjoy life for a few more years."

"I'm sorry, Joan. It's just everybody seems to be dying."

"Not everybody. Sure, aren't Mat and Bridie like two young-sters? And Maggie looks as young as she ever did."

"Maggie? When did you see her?"

"Just the other day. She called in to see how Rory was. You know Tom is dead, don't you?"

"I had no idea."

"Did I not tell you? He died of a heart attack about a year ago. He was going on eighty-four."

"Was he so much older than Maggie?"

"You wouldn't have known it when they got married but it showed later. Fourteen years makes a big difference. Oh, she's grand. He left her well-heeled. She built herself a little bungalow, next door to Deirdre's place, you know, the house Leonard built for her."

"Why didn't she move in with her? That would have made more sense."

"She wanted her independence, her own space, as they say. Oh, she's into everything, helps organise the local fete and is on the committee for the blind. She even took part in the panto last year. She's very talented. A lovely voice."

"What age is she now?" He didn't know why he asked because he knew exactly how old she was.

"Two years younger than yourself."

"She was always a live wire, the heart and soul of the party."

"You'll get a chance to see her in the flesh tomorrow. I've invited her over for lunch. She said she was desperate to see you."

Suddenly, Hugh felt flustered. Did he really want to see her? He was old. She was old. How could they pick up after all these years?

"I'm not sure it's such a good idea, Joan, what with Rory in the state he is."

"Not a bit of it. Rory will be fine by tomorrow, and Maggie will help to cheer him up. He won't have to do any talking anyway. She'll do it all for him."

He supposed it could be quite amusing to see her after so many years. Would she remember those lazy summer after-noons snogging by the river, talking nonsense, and all those times upstairs on the bed making love? If she was still the same Maggie, she'd probably make a joke of it in front of Joan and embarrass them all. He'd have to make it clear to her that he didn't want her to bring up the past. But then again, what the hell did it matter? There wouldn't be a word about in the hundred year, as Paddy Roche used to say.

The thought of meeting Maggie after all those years took his mind off worrying about Rory. He felt strangely young again. Could he actually be attracted to a woman of seventy? "Stupid thought," he said aloud. Yet, there was a quickening of his pulse every time she entered his mind.

Rory ate a little lunch, some chicken stew and potatoes, which Joan knew he was fond of. Hugh suggested he got up for a while and helped him out into the garden. It was a lovely summer's day with a warm breeze blowing in from the southwest. Hugh set out the deck chairs, and they all sat around a small table and had tea and scones, which Joan had made with strawberry jam and whipped cream. Hugh had forgotten how delicious they were.

"I haven't been outside for months, Hugh. It'll do me the world of good," said Rory croakily.

"There's nothing as fresh as Irish air," said Hugh, sucking in a chestful of it.

"Do you know? You might be right. I feel my lungs opening up already."

Hugh wasn't sure whether it was the right thing to do, but he got Rory to lean on his shoulder and they went for a snaillike walk around the garden, along the gravelled path that was now overgrown with weeds. With many stops, they made it the whole way around.

"I'll sleep well tonight anyway," said Rory, as they reached the entrance to the garage. "I feel as if I'm after running the marathon."

Hugh had to virtually carry Rory into the kitchen and sit him down in his chair near the fireplace.

"I'm a bit worried about you falling out of bed, Rory," said Hugh, as he lit the fire. "I saw a few boards out the back that I can nail together to make a side to it."

"A sort of cot, you might say."

Hugh knew what Rory was implying. "Better than falling out of bed."

"But sure, what can we do? Aren't we nearly in our dotage? From the cradle to the grave. By rights, it should be from the cradle to the cradle and then the grave."

Hugh laughed at Rory's attempt at humour, but it was too close to the bone to be funny.

Rory was in exceptional spirits, at least so Joan said. She hadn't seen him so cheerful in months. She said it was because they were all together again after so long.

Hugh then set about making Rory's bed safe. He had to construct a side that was strong enough to prevent him rolling out but could be removed and put back easily. He just hoped he could find the right tools and materials.

To his surprise, the shed at the back had everything he wanted. Rory had always been the handyman of the family and liked to have a full set of tools and ample materials. "You never know what you might need to knock together," he would say. He remembered watching in admiration as his elder brother would fashion something out of wood. The result was pure art. Apparently, he had built the lodge at the end of the lane virtually singlehanded. Maybe Mikey gave him a hand when his back wasn't playing up. Poor ould Mikey, there was always something wrong with him. If it wasn't his back, it was the migraines.

Over the years, Hugh had become quite a good handyman himself, more out of necessity than desire or aptitude. He always found it easier and less time-consuming to do a job himself rather than arrange for someone to do it. It also cost a tenth of the price. So, with a bit of trial and error and a lot of planing and cutting, he fixed up a simple side to the bed that was easy to put in and take out.

"Oh, you'll have me well boxed in now all right, Hughie," said Rory with a gruff laugh that immediately turned into a rasping cough.

That night after a light supper, they watched the news, but it meant little to Hugh. It was all about some strike or other. He supposed they had some justification for it, but more often than not, they were simply cutting off their nose to spite their face. If the factory closed down, as the company claimed it would, they'd all be out of a job. *Sometimes*, he thought, *people don't know when they're well off.*

Everyone slept well that night, Joan because she didn't have to worry about Rory, Rory because he felt secure in the bed, and Hugh because he was light-years away from the station.

■

As it was Sunday morning, Hugh was sure Joan would want to go to mass, as they always did when they were children.

"What time is mass?" said Hugh as he entered the kitchen.

"You're not thinking of going to mass, are you?"

"I thought you'd be going."

"I haven't been this long while. I don't like leaving Rory on his own."

"How about we all go?"

Joan gave Hugh a reproachful look. "For God's sake, Hugh, can't you see Rory isn't up to it? Getting him into the car and then into the church would be a terrible ordeal for him."

"Better than sitting around here. If we see he's getting tired, we can always leave."

"I didn't know you were religious, Hugh. I thought you'd forsaken the church long ago."

"I'm not much of a believer, it's true, but the church used to be the centre of our lives."

"No longer, I'm afraid."

"Maybe it's for the better."

"I don't think so, Hugh. It kept the community together. It was a focal point, a place where we all came together, even if it was only on Sunday."

"A place to gossip and natter."

"If you want to call it that. But what is gossip but an interest in others. It isn't always malicious."

"So, how about it then so? Shall I bring the car round?"

"God, you know, Hugh, I don't even know what time mass starts."

"Give Deirdre a call. She'll know."

"You're right. I will. You help Rory get dressed. God, I hope he can still get into his suit. He hasn't worn it for years."

Rory took the tray off Rory's lap. "Get up, old man. We're off to mass."

"What the divil are ye talking about, Hugh? I'm not stirring out of this bed. What if I can't breathe or start choking with a cough?"

"We'll have that yoke in the boot of the car, and if necessary, I'll bring it into church. I'm sure the priest won't mind."

"Well, the truth is, Hugh, I'd love to go to mass. There's something very reassuring about the inside of a church, especially when you're not stretched out in a coffin."

It took Hugh some time to get Rory dressed. Joan's worry that the suit would be too small was proved unfounded. In fact, it hung off him as if it belonged to a much bigger man. He had lost a lot of weight, it seemed. On the way to the car, Rory tried walking without Hugh's help and found he could, though rather unsteadily. Even getting into the car was less of a trial than they had anticipated.

Hugh was surprised to see so few cars outside the church. "Do you think we're too late?" he said. "Everybody seems to have left."

"Ah no," said Joan. "Young people don't go to mass anymore. Only oldies like us."

The church was surprisingly full when they entered. The pew that they used to sit in was free so they went there. Quite a few heads turned as they walked down the aisle.

An elderly man and his wife got up and came over to them. "By the Jaysus, if it isn't Hugh Gorman himself."

Hugh smiled but without recognition.

"Johnny Walsh, do you not recognise me?"

"Johnny, my god! You're looking well."

"Not the half as well as yourself."

Johnny and he had been in National School together. They had knocked around a bit but had never been close friends. His father had had the garage on the edge of the village.

"You haven't lost the ould brogue anyway. I thought you'd be a thoroughbred Aussie by now."

"No, Johnny. When you're born and bred an Irishman, you don't lose it all that easy."

"Well, I hope you'll come for a pint with me sometime. In fact, I'll give you a call and we can arrange it. I want to hear all about the outback."

Hugh laughed. He wondered what Johnny imagined Australia was like. He would be surprised at what Esperance had to offer.

Having made the effort to go to church, Rory insisted on having Holy Communion as well. The priest, a placid young man in his early thirties, facilitated matters by coming to Rory with the host. Hugh was amazed at the effect it had on him. It was as if the spirit of God had truly entered him. His face brightened up and a bit of colour returned to his ashen cheeks. *Faith is a wonderful thing*, he thought, and regretted losing it, along with everything else, but it was too late to get it back now.

As usual, the congregation gathered outside after mass. Everyone was curious to meet Hugh, even those who knew him only by hearsay.

"It's an honour to meet you, Mr Gorman," said a smart young man in a green jersey and striped tie. "I've heard a lot about you."

"All lies, no doubt," said Hugh.

The man pumped his hand with great vigour. Was he trying to see if that formidable strength he was supposed to have had was still there?

"No. I can see that it's all true. You're a grand pillar of a man, so you are. I hope we'll be seeing you around these parts more often."

"I'd like to, but Australia is a long way away and duty calls."

"Ah, duty. Sure, it'll be the ruin of us all. Sometimes we don't even know where our real duty lies."

"True enough," said Hugh, thinking of his own situation.

Most of the parish wanted to shake Hugh's hand. He felt like some minor celebrity returning to his place of birth. He would have enjoyed it if he had felt he deserved it, but there was nothing he had done in his life that he believed merited celebrity status. If he had lived all his life in the village, he would be no more than just another old man. *But let them think what they like of me*, he thought, *if it gives them pleasure.*

Hugh could see that Rory was tiring, so they made their excuses and went back to the car.

"I haven't been to mass this good while, Hugh. And I wouldn't have gone now if it hadn't been for you. It may be my last time, on me feet anyway. No doubt I'll visit the place on me back soon enough."

"Stop that talk now, Rory," said Joan from the back of the car. "We'll come again next Sunday, if you're up to it."

"The Holy Communion did you good," said Hugh. "You can't beat the faith."

"Right enough, Hughie. God is good, but He wouldn't have afflicted me with this chest if He hadn't already decided me fate. Me time is up, I'm afraid."

"Look," said Hugh enthusiastically. "How about we go for a spin in the car? Down to the coast. You don't have to get out. We'll just open the windows and let the sea breeze in. What do you say?"

"Jaysus, Hughie. I wouldn't say no to that."

"Well, you men can do what you like, but I have lunch to prepare," said Joan tetchily.

Hugh thought taking Rory for a ride in the car would give her some respite from her nursing duties, but it was clear she didn't want to let him out of her sight for one minute as long as he was home. *Making up for lost time*, he thought, but he knew that there was no recovering lost time. Still, it wasn't going to make him change his mind. He needed some time alone with Rory. There were certain things that had been left unsaid between them, things that had bothered him, but he had never sought answers to. Then, it hadn't seemed important. Now, it did.

"We have Maggie coming over, and I want it to be a very special dinner," Joan continued, as if the boys were determined to spoil it for her.

"Why is that now, Joan?" said Rory flippantly. "When did Maggie become someone special?"

Hugh could tell by the crooked smile on Rory's face that they were in on it together. Maggie was the bait to snare him into staying in Ireland. Well, he wasn't going to be caught that easily. He hated plots, even if they were intended for his good. He remembered as children how Rory and Joan were always up to something, while he, the baby, was left out. Their plots usually ended in fiascos, like the time they arranged a surprise party for their father's birthday. He came home from the pub stinking drunk and more or less threw their presents back in their faces. If it hadn't been for their mother, they would have ended up in the fire.

Unlike Joan and Rory, he gave up on his father early on and made no attempts to resolve things between them. They had a belligerent and antagonistic relationship. Yet, it was one they both felt strangely at ease with. They knew where they stood, in opposite corners of a boxing ring, waiting for the bell, which Hugh knew would sound sooner or later unless he got out.

It was agreed that they drop Joan off at home and the "boys" would go down to the coast, on condition that they returned in good time for lunch. Hugh promised to be back by one at the latest. But by the look on Joan's face, she didn't believe him. Nothing had changed. At seventy-three, he was still the baby of the family, the one who couldn't be entirely trusted, the one who always did his own thing, regardless.

"Well, you'd better be," she said, as she got out of the car, brandishing the sharp edge of her hand. That hand, he remembered, had given him quite a few clouts in its day, but it was obvious to both of them that it had failed to knock the rebel out of him.

Hugh had always looked up to Rory. He was the sensible one of the family, the one who invariably did the right thing. Rory had had many opportunities to marry but had always put the family first. He had had a strange, almost servile relationship with the old man, while he had been the intransigent one, the one to say no, the one who would question his father's old-fashioned notions. Yet, strangely enough, the old man respected Hugh for it, and despite Rory's subservience, he was the preferred son. It must have cost the old man dearly when he decided to emigrate, though he would never admit it, though they all knew that Hugh would never come back, except on holiday, and even then rarely.

The road down to the coast was no longer familiar to Hugh, even though he must have taken it hundreds of times in the past. He relied entirely on Rory to keep him on the right track. When the Gormans eventually got a car, a second-hand Popular with a humped roof, he was in his early teens and had no desire to spend much time with his parents, but he did occasionally go with them to the beach.

They were not happy memories. His father would be in a grumpy mood, complaining about everything—the wind and the sand. Even the sandwiches his mother had carefully prepared to suit his demanding tastes would never meet his approval. Nothing was ever right. The tea was too cold. The scones too dry. They all wished he hadn't come and wondered why he had.

His mother would spread the green tartan rug in some sheltered spot—as sheltered as was possible on an Irish beach—and unpack the tea things from her picnic basket. They would then sit around and shudder, with sand blowing into everything, making the sandwiches a lot crunchier than they were intended to be. His mother would do her best to cheer everybody up by extolling the beauty of the sea, the wholesome taste of salt on the sea breeze, the squawking of the seagulls that wheeled overhead, but she was unable to lift the cloud of despondency from off the old man. In the end, with a grunt of disgust, he would take his mug of tea and a handful of cake and go and sit in the car until it was time to go home.

With the old man in the car, they could at least ignore his presence and begin to enjoy themselves. After tea, they would roll up their trouser legs and paddle in the shallow sea or run along the beach splashing each other. Swimming was out of the question. It was always far too cold, and none of them knew how to swim anyway.

His mother desperately wanted it to be a fun occasion and would organise games of rounders or *tigh*. As a child, he had the feeling that she was enjoying herself but later he realised that she must have been worrying all the time about the old man griping away in the car. She would sometimes beckon to him, but he just sat there moping. He didn't even bother signalling back. Hugh often wondered what was going through his father's head on these occasions. Or was he just thinking of getting home so that he could go down to the pub?

Divorce was not an option back then, but she probably would never have left him. What could she have done on her own, anyway? In those days, the cards were stacked against a woman. She was reared with one aim in mind, to be an unpaid servant—some would say slave—to some man, who would usually treat her as such. Of course, they didn't call it slavery or servitude, but it amounted to the same thing.

As they crossed the county to the sea, Hugh had to admit that Ireland was truly a beautiful country—the undulating fields of green grass, the outcrops of deciduous trees down in a valley or on top of a hill, water flowing incessantly. As far as he could see, the country was thriving; fields of fattening cattle, acres of ripening barley, enormous round bales of hay waiting to be stacked for the winter. Why was he unable to appreciate it back then? Or had things changed so much?

"They'll be cutting the barley soon," said Rory. "Let's hope the weather holds."

To Hugh, the fields seemed pocket-size. "It's great farming country all right. There's money to be made if you do it right."

"Sure enough, as long as you have the right-sized spread. Ours was always too small to make a decent living."

As a farmer, Rory had not been all that imaginative, Hugh thought. Sheep, hay, and barley, that's all he had ever done, and Mikey just went along with whatever Rory did. But they had been content with that. Rory had never had any great desire for wealth, not that anyone with a limited imagination could become rich on a hundred-and-fifty-acre farm.

"Tell me, Rory. Why did you never marry Josie? Weren't you courting for a good few years?"

Hugh turned his head briefly in Rory's direction and immediately regretted he had brought up the subject. It was clear he had scratched an old wound.

"The time was never right, Hugh boy. And in the end, she got tired of waiting for me."

"So why did you leave it so long?"

"I wasn't going to inflict the old man on her."

"But you built the bungalow for the parents."

"And where were Joan and Mikey and the children going to live? Mikey hadn't a place of his own. His brother Jimmy had the farm above."

"By rights, the house was yours, not Joan's. Mikey should have found somewhere else to live."

"Sure, he hadn't two brass farthings to rub together. I couldn't toss them out."

"So, you sacrificed yourself."

"I wouldn't call it that, Hughie. I probably wouldn't have made much of a husband anyway, or father, for that matter."

"So, Josie married someone else."

"Oh, she did. A grand lad from up the country she met at a dance in the village hall. It was the best thing. She had four lovely children."

"…that could have been yours."

"A lot of things could have been, Hughie, but weren't to be. I was happy enough on me own. I loved Joan's two girls, and they loved me. I was like a second daddy to them. I was content to be an overindulgent uncle."

"What was it like living with the old man when he got old?"

Rory didn't answer at once. Perhaps he was trying to remember. "It wasn't easy."

"I can imagine."

"He had no respect for me. I did my best to please him, but nothing was ever good enough. We had what you might call a challenging relationship."

"One of the reasons I left was so that I wouldn't end up murdering the old fart. I don't know how you stuck it."

"It wasn't easy, I can tell you. I put up with him for Mam's sake. It would have been hard for her living with him on her own. I was a comfort to her."

The more Hugh heard, the clearer it became that Rory had sacrificed everything, even his own happiness, for their mother. He, Hugh, could never have done that. Was it selfishness on his part? Or foolishness on Rory's? Rory must have had regrets but, on the other hand, didn't we all?

As they ascended a small incline, the sea slowly came into view. They passed some white thatched cottages a few hundred yards in from the beach, most likely holiday homes now. Hugh wound down the window with gusto, letting in a blast of sea air.

"Hold your horses there now, Hughie. They say fresh air is good for you, but it's also bloody cold."

Hugh laughed and wound up the window a bit.

There was one other car parked near the beach. If this was Esperance, Hugh thought, the place would be packed and you'd end up having to pay through the nose for a parking space.

"So, shall we go for a walk along the beach, old man?"

Rory looked suddenly anxious. "God, Hugh, I don't think I'm able for it."

"Of course, you are. That walk round the garden yesterday did you a power of good."

"I don't know whether I'm up for another marathon so soon. You go on. I'll just sit here and admire the view."

"Do you want to stretch out on the sand? Joan may have a rug in the boot."

"Lying down is easy enough, Hughie. It's getting up that's the difficulty."

Hugh was not going to listen to his objections. He went around to the other side of the car and started tugging at Rory, despite his protests.

"Easy there now, boy. You better keep a good hold on me. I don't want to fall flat on me back."

It was a struggle carrying Rory over the soft sand, especially going up the side of the dune to the beach. Neither could get a grip, and despite some valiant efforts to stay on their feet, they ended up in a heap on the sand.

After some fretting, Rory too was able to see the funny side of it. "Jaysus, Hughie, you were never able to take no for an answer, were you? At least, the sand is soft."

"Come on now, old man. I don't want to hear any more of that gab out of you. We're near the top."

Hugh lifted Rory up, and they managed to reach the crest of the dune. From the top, Hugh could see a dip in the sand protected from the wind.

"There's a grand spot for you to do a bit of sunbathing and get some colour back in your cheeks."

"Are you sure you're going to be able to get me out? Otherwise, you might as well get a shovel and bury me in it here and now. Not that it's all that bad a spot to spend eternity."

Hugh helped Rory down into the hollow and laid him with his back against the side of the dune.

"Are you all right there now, lad?"

"Not bad at all. Jaysus, that sun is hot. They'll be thinking I'm after spending a month on the Costa de Sol with the tan I'll be having."

"How are you feeling?" asked Hugh, looking down at his brother, who seemed to be half the size of the brother he once knew. His clothes hung baggily off him as if he had been on hunger strike for weeks.

"Battered but comfortable enough. And now we're here, I'm going to make the most of it. You wouldn't find a spot as beautiful as this out in Australia, I'd warrant, and damned near deserted to boot."

"Ah, there are some lovely places out there too." He thought of the golden sands of Esperance that stretched for miles along the coast. They weren't deserted but they weren't too crowded either, even in summer.

"Lookat, Hughie, I'm grand here. You go for a trot along the beach. I'll be with you in spirit."

"Are you sure you don't want to come with me?"

"There was a time I could race you to the end of that stretch of beach and beat you every time but no longer. You have an open field in front of you."

Hugh remembered how he was always trying to catch up with his elder brother. He wanted to be like him. He even tried to cultivate his kind gentle spirit, but it was beyond his capabilities, and now that he had finally overtaken him, it gave him no satisfaction at all.

"All right so. I won't be long."

Hugh set off at a run down the dune to the hard sand packed down by the pounding waves. The wind rushed through his hair, blowing away all thoughts of past, present and future. All that remained was the roar of the waves. They at least had not changed. Nor had the sand or the straggling dark brown seaweed that littered the beach and swirled below the surface of the water like winged eels.

On reaching the water's edge, the waves crashing to the shore, he remembered a poem by Tennyson he had had to learn by heart at school. It seemed somehow appropriate. He tried to recall the words. "Break, break, break, at the foot of thy crags, oh sea!" He wasn't sure exactly what came next. It didn't mean much to him back then. He just liked the sound of the words. How could children understand such sentiments? Old age is so far away.

Thank God we don't know how near it is, he thought.

There is something eternal and immutable about the sea, he mused, but he supposed that even that changed. Man was destroying everything; continents of plastic in the oceans, fish depletion, polluted seas. When he was young, there were times when you could literally pick the mackerel out of the sea with your bare hands. No more. What would be left in a century or so? At least he would not be around to see it but it upset him, nonetheless. Man would end up alone on a deserted planet with the ants and the rats, the sole survivors of man's eradication process. But he wasn't going to think about that today. Today, he was going to float on the wind—he could feel the sleeves of his jumper flapping like the sails of a kite—and imagine that life was still worth living.

In the distance, he could see a family with two small children playing by the water. The children would run up to the charging waves and race back up the sand screaming, the waves licking at their heels. A little one with long wavy blond hair would rush into her mother's arms then, almost as quickly, sprint back to defy the waves once more. Though the family couldn't have been more than two hundred yards away, their voices were syncopated by the wind, as it snatched them up and scattered the sound in all directions.

Hugh thought of his own grandchildren, two lovely little girls, Eileen and Helen. At least, Niall had kept the tradition of giving them Irish names. He hardly saw them. They talked on Skype sometimes, but they were growing up without him. In years to come, they would wonder what kind of an old fellow Grandpa Hugh was. No one would be able to tell them for sure. They would make something up, hopefully not too far from the truth, as they perused old photos of a tall gaunt man with a penetrating stare and an inscrutable smile. He vowed that when he went back, he'd make a point of flying up to see them, maybe tell them a few yarns about Ireland. But what would they mean to them? He might as well tell them stories from Fiji or the Falkland Islands.

Halfway along the beach, he turned and waved to Rory. He wasn't sure whether he could see him, but he thought he could make out a white hand flashing an indecipherable Morse in the bright sun.

The sea always fascinated Hugh, perhaps because it frightened him. And there wasn't much that scared him. It was probably its vastness. He was a landlubber through and through, but when he got the chance, he would go out on a friend's yacht and feel the pulse of the sea as it heaved and sighed under the hull of the boat. But here on the Irish shore, he felt safe, happy to imagine the adventures of more daring seafarers than himself.

He looked at his watch. Time to get back. He wanted to prove to Joan, this once at least, that her opinion of him was unfounded. He was, or had become, a man of his word.

He took off his shoes, rolled up the bottoms of his trousers, and began to trot over the waves. The water was cold but exhilarating, just as he remembered it. If he weren't under pressure of time, he would strip naked and wade out as far as he could, let the waves wash over him, cleanse him of morbid thoughts. Instead, he just dug his toes into the sand and felt the rasping sensation rise pleasurably from the soles of his feet to the base of his spine. He picked up a long piece of slimy seaweed and dragged it along the sand, as he used to do as a child, erasing his footsteps as he went. In time, he thought, there would be no trace of him, on sand or soil. That was the way it was, and the way it should be.

Hugh found Rory dozing, his head resting on a moulded pillow of sand. He stood over him contemplating the depleted figure of his brother. Old age was not an enviable state. He didn't want to wake him. He seemed so content lying there soaking up the sun. Was it possible that he could beat the cancer? It wouldn't have been the first time. Miracles had happened. It was unlikely, though, and there was no point in indulging in such hopes. At least, his visit had brought some joy to his beloved brother.

Rory must have felt Hugh's shadow over him because he woke up with a start. He was momentarily dazzled by the sun and had to shade his eyes with a hand. "Oh, you're back, Hugh. Did you have a good walk?"

"A walk down memory lane."

"I hope there were things worth remembering."

"Strangely enough, yes. I always thought my memories of Ireland would be inextricably bound up with the old man, but I've found I can somehow erase him from the picture. You know, like you can do with digital photos these days."

"What's that now, Hugh?"

"It's a computer programme called Photoshop. Are you familiar with it?"

"Never heard of it."

"It's basically a way of adding or subtracting whatever you want from a photo. It can be very handy."

"The result, though, is not the truth. It presents a false picture of reality."

"Maybe, but a more acceptable version of it."

"I'm too old for tampering with reality. I take it as it comes."

"Yes, but what is reality, Rory? What we see? What we imagine we see? Or what we want to see?"

"Jaysus man, are we going to have a philosophical discussion or what?"

"Why not? I seem to remember you were very keen on philosophy in the past."

"Oh, I read a few books, but I can't say they did me any good."

"You never know."

"Look, Hughie, get me out of this hole before I start sizzling. Give me your hand, will you?"

Hugh took the hand offered him and, with his arm behind Rory's back, helped him to his feet. Getting out of the dip was not as easy as getting in, but with a bit of slipping and sliding they managed to get to the top of the dune.

When they got into the car and Rory was once again comfortable in the front seat, he said, "All of the above."

Hugh looked at him with a quizzical frown.

"Reality. We all see it different. You see it different from the way I do and so on. Our memories, experiences, and emotions, even our imagination, have created multiple layers over our version of reality so that we all have a unique perception of the world. That's why no book, no painting, no work of art is ever the same."

Hugh was taken aback. He had had no idea that Rory had such profound thoughts.

"But however hard we try to blot out the past, Hugh, with Photoshop or whatever you call it, you'll find, I think, that's it's impossible to obliterate it entirely. We can paint over it, shove it into a dark corner, but it will always be there, waiting to appear at the most unexpected and possibly most unwanted moments. Though we may think otherwise, memories are indelible, to the healthy mind, anyway."

As always, he thought, *Rory has a much better grip on reality than I did.* He had always wanted to superimpose his own ideal on it, but all he was doing was creating an impossible utopia. As the wise man said, "You can fool yourself part of the time but not all the time."

He started the car and set off up the narrow road. Soon, they were on the bigger highway that would take them back to Connick. All the time, Hugh was thinking how his memories, emotions, and experiences had shaped his view of reality. It was almost too complex to contemplate. How accurate was his memory? How many things, good and bad, had he omitted? How reliable were his emotions? He had known love. He had also known hatred and anger. How could they be measured and apportioned a place in his view of reality? And his imagination, the worst deceiver of all! Adding, subtracting, distorting, embellishing. He had no idea what reality was anymore.

They arrived back at the farm a little later than he had promised, but Joan seemed not to mind. She was happy to see them. Rory again managed to walk unaided to the kitchen. But by the time he got to his armchair by the fireplace, his chest was heaving in an effort to catch his breath. Hugh quickly set up the ventilator and handed Rory the mouthpiece. He wondered whether he had pushed his brother too hard. On the other hand, what was the point in just letting him get weaker and weaker until he became totally bedridden? They had to make the most of that little strength he still had before it was too late.

Hugh remembered how on special occasions they would have a drink before lunch, not a good idea when his father was around, but his father was thankfully not around, so they could do whatever they wanted.

"How about a drink, old man?" Hugh said to Rory, as he lit the fire.

"You mean alcohol?"

"Well, I wasn't talking about Lucozade."

"Jaysus, sure I doubt there's any in the house."

"Well, if there isn't, I can always drive up to the village and get some."

Joan heard and turned to face him, her large hands lodged defiantly on her hips. "You'll do nothing of the sort. I don't want you boys two sheets in the wind with Maggie coming. I want this to be a civilised dinner. We can open a bottle of wine when she comes but not before. I think we have a couple of bottles somewhere in the larder."

"Let's hope they're still drinkable. Wine doesn't last forever, you know."

"If it's off, we can have a glass of sherry. I'm sure that's still all right."

Hugh sighed. "All right, Joan, but to be honest with you, I was hoping for a bit of Dutch courage."

"What would you want that for? Sure, it's only Maggie, not the queen of Sheba."

"I'd almost prefer it to be the queen of Sheba. At least then, I'd know where I stood. Now don't tell me you're not trying to hook us up together."

"Now why would I do such a thing? I thought you'd like to see each other after so long now that the both of you have lost your better halves. You have a lot of catching up to do."

"No doubt, but half a century and three continents have created a bit of a rift between us."

"Ah, stop moaning, will you, and give me a hand. I want you to set the table in the dining room."

Hugh gave Rory a long-suffering look and shrugged his shoulders in resignation. Joan had become just like their mother.

"You do know how to set a table, I suppose?"

"I think I'll just about manage it." Hugh assumed that the good cutlery and plates were where their mother used to keep them. He went into the dining room, and sure enough, they were there in the sideboard just as they had been fifty years ago. As a child, setting the table for Sunday lunch had been one of his duties. Did Joan remember that? Their mother had been very particular about where each piece of cutlery should go, which on the right of the plate, which on the left, and so on. Everything had its position in his mother's world order. He put some wineglasses out and realised he hadn't found the little mats his mother used. He loved those mats but they had no doubt been replaced by now. He searched in the back of a drawer and found a box that appeared to have wine mats in it. To his surprise, they were his mother's, the ones with the pictures of Irish wild flowers on them.

When he had set the table, Hugh went into the kitchen to see if Joan needed his help. "Is there anything else I can do, Joan?"

"No, you'd only get in the way. You go and keep Rory company. No, on second thoughts, why don't you get the Hoover and sweep up a bit."

The place looked perfectly clean to Hugh, but Sheila used to say he had a blind spot when it came to dirt. Women, he concluded, were awful particular when it came to dirt. Or else they had magnifying glasses for eyes. Anyway, he did as he was told and hoovered the nonexistent dirt and even searched for some dust on the mantelpiece with a feather duster.

When he had put away the Hoover, he asked Joan what time Maggie was expected.

"Any moment now. Are you both dressed?"

"The last time I looked, yes."

"And your brother, is he in a fit state?"

"He looks grand to me."

"Just check his shirt is clean, and is he wearing a tie?"

Hugh looked over at Rory and saw that he wasn't. "I don't think he likes wearing a tie. He says it chokes him."

"Don't listen to him. Put a tie on him. There's one hanging on the bed in the parlour. The blue one with white spots. His executive tie."

Hugh couldn't help laughing. He had never thought of Rory as an executive, but if that's what Joan wanted, there was no arguing with her.

When Hugh came back with the tie, Rory made some mild protests. "I can't even breathe, and you want to harness me up to that choker. You might as well as put it around me neck and throttle me, be damned."

"The boss's orders."

"Jaysus, what's got into her? Anybody'd think we were expecting royalty."

"Just what I said."

"The match of the century."

"What match is that now, Rory?"

"You and Maggie."

"God, I thought you were talking about football. You know, Rory, I think Joan is making too much of this whole thing."

"Didn't I tell her you wouldn't want to be manipulated, but she wouldn't hear of it? She says you never knew what was good for you. And it appears nothing's changed. So, you'd better behave yourself with Maggie. Not that she would mind if you didn't. But Joan has this notion that because she has money from Tom that she's someone important."

At that moment, they heard a car crunching over the gravel at the front of the house.

"I think our guest has arrived," said Hugh, with a sudden unsettled feeling in his stomach.

"Oh god, she's arrived early," said Joan, flapping two sets of splayed sticky fingers in the air. "You'll have to go and let her in. I have my hands full."

"I could always take over what you're—"

"Go on now and open the door. She won't bite you. Lord, I didn't know you were such a yellowbelly."

There was no point in arguing. He would have to go. As he passed the mirror over the sideboard, he stopped briefly to check his appearance. *God, I look old*, he thought, and there was a tuft of unruly hair sticking up at the back that looked ridiculous, like a goat's horn, but as hard as he tried to rein it in it would just pop up again. "Well, I suppose she's not expecting to see a twenty-year-old stud with a slicked-back Elvis Presley hairstyle," he muttered and made his way apprehensively to the front door.

Maggie got there before him and rat-tat-tatted on the heavy wooden door with the brass knocker.

He hesitated before opening, trying to conjure up an image of what she would look like after so many years, a sagging wrinkled face and unbecoming grey hair but it blurred very quickly into someone unrecognisable. Finally, he steeled himself and opened the door with resolve.

He wouldn't have recognised her, it's true, but the woman before him was indeed a very elegant lady. She reminded him of Jane Fonda, with her short golden-brown hair. She was amply made up, wearing scarlet lipstick. She obviously kept fit or watched her diet or both because she had none of what he called the "OAP look," a slightly hunched back, wilting face and drooping eyes.

They were both a bit speechless, as each adjusted to the changes that had occurred to the other.

"God, you're looking grand, Hugh. To be honest with you, I had no idea what to expect. A bent old man with no hair or a tall upstanding man like yourself. It's not easy getting that kind of information out of Joan. Here, give us a hug. Sure, it's been such a long time." She put her arms around him and placed her chin momentarily on his shoulder. The palms of her hands felt soft as they pressed gently against his back.

Hugh didn't like perfume as a rule, but he liked what she was wearing—exotic, enticing. He had smelt it before on younger women and had felt distinctly aroused.

"Well, you're looking good, Maggie. You've looked after yourself, I can see."

"I may be a widow, but I'm damned if I'm going to remain inconsolable and wear widow's weeds for the rest of my life. I have a lot of living to do still."

"That's the spirit," said Hugh, placing his hand on her arm and ushering her through into the dining room.

Joan in the meantime had somehow managed to put on her best clothes and was standing like a lady-in-waiting ready to curtsey to her majesty. But as far as Hugh was concerned, this was just Maggie, the girl he had once courted, half a century before.

"Maggie! You're looking great."

"I do my best, Joan, but it comes at a price. Two hours in the hair salon and another couple at the beautician's, not to mention my personal trainer."

Hugh laughed. He realised that she hadn't changed. "You have a personal trainer. Now that's very sophisticated, I must say."

"Trying to stay young isn't easy, or cheap, I can tell you. Now, tell me how you keep so fit, you ould divil you?" said Maggie, knocking Hugh on the chest with her clenched fist, as if trying to stethoscope what was contained within.

"Clean living, I suppose."

Maggie burst out laughing. "You, clean living, who would have thought it? I seem to remember you had quite a fondness for the liquor when you were young."

"I had a wife that kept me on the straight and narrow. And a father who set a bad example. So, all in all, I was lucky, I suppose."

"Don't tell me you're a teetotaller?"

"Ah, no, nothing as bad as that. Which reminds me. Where did you say that wine was, Joan?"

Hugh found some bottles of wine on a shelf in the larder covered in a thick layer of dust and cobwebs. He opened one to test it and, to his surprise, found it was still drinkable.

Maggie insisted they sit in the kitchen so that Rory could remain in the chair that he was most comfortable in.

Hugh poured everyone a glass of wine.

Rory took a sip and spluttered. "Jaysus, Hugh, where did you get that? If nothing else, it'll raise the hairs on your chest, this will."

Hugh laughed. "You don't need any more of those, but it'll surely warm the cockles of your heart."

"It might even kill the cancer in me."

There was a heavy silence. The C word had been spoken.

They all solemnly took a sip of wine.

"Oh, this is lovely wine, Joan," said Maggie in an effort to delete the unspeakable word. "Where did you get it?"

"I think it may be Australian. Was it those bottles you brought with you the last time you were over, Hugh?"

Hugh looked at the label. "You're right. My god, you've had them lying around since then. Dalyup River Wines. It is—or should I say was—the only winery in the Esperance region. It closed in 2014. This is probably the last of it. A collector's item. So, make the most of it."

"We intend to, don't we, Rory?" said Maggie, clinking her glass against his.

"Oh, by the holies, we certainly do. It's great to have your man over after so long. I think he nearly forgot where he came from."

"I could never do that, Rory. Ireland will always be my home."

"And how long are you planning to stay, Hugh?" said Maggie, eyeing him wistfully.

That was indeed a difficult question, which could not be answered with the whole truth.

"I'm going to play it by ear. I have a good man looking after the station, but I can't stay away forever."

"You can always commute, Hugh," said Joan.

"It's a long ould commute now, Joan. But I won't commit to anything for the moment." He took a sip of wine and put another log on the fire. He needed to change the subject. He didn't want the reunion dinner with Maggie to deteriorate into a morose occasion. "So, Joan tells me you're into everything, Maggie. Is it true you were in the panto last year?"

"Oh, I love the theatre, Hugh. I wish I had discovered it sooner."

"It seems like you missed your vocation. I had forgotten how much like Jane Fonda you look."

Maggie chuckled with false humility. "You were always a terrible flatterer, Hugh Gorman. The truth is I admire her terribly. She's still gorgeous, even at her age, and she's a good few years older than me. But I don't have her talent. Besides, it's too late now. Tell me, Hugh, what do you do in your free time?"

"Well, free time is a precious commodity, something I don't have much of. When I do have a spare moment, I read or potter about the house. I like to be out on the land mostly."

"That explains why you're as fit as a fiddle so."

"I may be fit, but the ould fiddle is getting a bit creaky."

Everyone laughed, but no one was quite sure what Hugh was referring to.

Joan called them all to lunch, and Hugh helped Rory to the table.

Joan had surpassed herself as usual, a three-course lunch, with mushroom soup, a side of roast pork with all the trimmings, and a sherry trifle for dessert. Hugh hadn't had sherry trifle since he left Ireland. It was indeed a great treat.

By the end of the meal, Rory was looking exhausted. "I suggest we go into the kitchen for coffee and let Rory have a sleep," said Hugh decisively.

"No, no, I'm grand, Hugh."

"You're not grand. I shouldn't have taken you to the coast today. It was stupid of me."

"By Jaysus, you should have, boy. It's been one of the best days of me life, though I am feeling a bit jaded now, it's true. I wouldn't mind having a little kip in the chair. Just for a few minutes to get me strength back."

Hugh helped Rory to an armchair in the sunroom.

"Leave everything. I'll clear up later," said Joan.

"You will not," said Maggie resolutely. "All I need is an apron, and we'll have these washed up and cleared away in a jiffy."

Joan was happy for the help, and the three of them didn't take long to clear up. Hugh wasn't used to being around women, especially since Sheila had passed. He found it strangely pleasant. He had never much enjoyed the company of swearing, farting, spitting men. He found their vulgarity offensive. He put their boorishness down to an overstated demonstration of virility, an attempt to show other men they were not pussies. Hugh had always liked the gentleness of women, their sensitivity and concern for others. He often thought that if men were more like women, the world would be a much better place. *It is a pity*, he thought, *that so many women these days want to be like men.*

After they had finished washing up, Joan said she felt like a little nap too and suggested Maggie and Hugh have coffee or go for a walk.

Hugh had felt comfortable with Maggie as long as Joan was there, but he wasn't sure he wanted to be alone with her. It would be too much like a date. Besides, they had said all there was to say about the present. All they had to talk about now was the past or the future, and to talk about the past would be like digging up skeletons in a graveyard, and the future was too uncertain to be of any great importance.

Suddenly, Hugh was aware that Joan had left, and Maggie was preparing coffee for them. "You'll have a cup of coffee, Hugh?"

"I won't say no. Just a half spoon of sugar." His doctor had told him not to drink coffee, but it was his policy not to do everything his doctor told him.

"Watching your weight? I thought only women did that."

"That's the way I like my coffee," he said, unwilling to rise to the gibe.

Maggie brought the cups of coffee and laid them on the table in front of the fire. *She is indeed a handsome woman*, he thought. Surely she didn't have any designs on him. It was just wishful thinking on Joan's part. Joan was a born matchmaker. It was a pity she didn't find a better match for herself, but at least they had two lovely children, and she didn't ask for more than that.

"Did you ever regret going to Australia, Hugh?"

"Sometimes," he said vaguely.

"I was terrible upset when you left, you know. I would have come after you if I'd had the money."

Hugh wasn't sure whether she was being serious or just trying to tease him. Yet, despite the smile on her face, Hugh could tell that there was still some hurt there, even after fifty years.

"We never said a proper goodbye. You just upped and left. I had always thought we were an item."

Hugh hated that word *item*. It was somehow belittling, but perhaps that was her intention. What did it mean anyway? Were they an item? He wasn't sure. They certainly had something. They were both physically attracted to each other. There was no doubt about that, but he was not sure that he had ever been truly in love with her.

Maybe he hadn't taken her seriously at the time. Her demonstration of love and devotion he took for mere teenage passion. He knew she would find someone else and get over him eventually. She was a beautiful girl with many admirers. Yet, he may have underestimated the fact she had chosen him over all the other studs that swarmed around her.

"I'd have married you if you'd asked me," she said meekly.

Hugh didn't know what to say. He had been only twenty-three. Marriage was far from his mind back then. What was the point in bringing it up now? But he had learnt from Sheila when she had decided to do therapy that certain things need to be talked about in order to—what was the correct term?—"find closure."

"I cried every night for months after you left. I thought it was the end of the world. I had plenty of men after me, but it was you I wanted."

"I wouldn't have been able to make you happy, Maggie. I had nothing but the shirt on my back. It was sheer luck that I made a go of things in Australia."

"Do you think I would have cared? I would have followed you to the end of the earth, through jungle or desert, if it meant being with you."

"Tom gave you all the things I couldn't. You were much better off with him."

"Tom provided, Hugh, but I never loved him like I loved you."

"I'm sorry, Maggie." He didn't know what else to say. "I had no idea."

"Sure, didn't I tell you often enough?"

"People say things. Young people especially. I thought it was just a crush you had on me because I was in a higher class at school."

"God, you men, you don't understand anything. You're about as perceptive as jackasses."

"Who said jackasses aren't perceptive?"

"And just as stubborn, too."

"That I'll accept."

She looked at him with a half-smile. He could tell she was enjoying this little wrangle, as it reminded her of how things used to be.

"Do you know when I fell in love with you?"

"I have no idea."

"You mean you couldn't tell."

"It's been a long time."

"You see. Just what I was saying. Men. You have skins as thick as a rhinoceros and memories as feeble as a gold fish's. When I was five! Don't you remember? You and Mat came by the house to play with Joe. It was love at first sight. You had the most adorable chubby cheeks. I just wanted to pinch them."

Hugh put a hand to his face. "I'm glad you didn't. It doesn't sound much like fun."

"Oh, it would have been…for me…but I was too shy."

"You, shy?"

"Oh, you never understood me, Hugh Gorman. I was an extrovert outwardly, it's true, but inwardly I was a shy Maryellen. And I was never flighty."

Hugh smiled at the reference to a song he had heard sung many times in his childhood, "I'm shy, Maryellen, I'm shy."

"I seem to remember you hugging all the boys. You made me terribly jealous."

"That was my intention. And I see that it worked. But you were always so remote. I couldn't get through to you. So, you thought I was flirting when all I was trying to do was provoke some reaction in you."

"I think I had other things on my mind. Like how to get out before I murdered someone."

"You really felt that way?"

"I didn't trust myself. It was easier just to abscond."

"Well, you did that all right. I never gave up on you, though. If you'd come back and proposed to me, I'd have left Tom."

"Maggie, please. Don't talk nonsense now. You had a lovely family and a man that loved you. Why would you throw it all away for me? I wasn't worth it, I can tell you."

"You men don't understand a woman's heart. For us, love is not just a word you use in bed. You will always be number one in here." Maggie touched her heart with the painted tip of a slender finger.

This conversation was not what Hugh had anticipated. He imagined them laughing and joking about old times, not this. It was making him feel penitent, guilty, sad almost. By trying to avoid one crime, he had ended up committing another. Not that knowing the depth of her love would have changed anything. Perhaps it was better that he hadn't.

All he could do was say, "I'm sorry, Maggie," and look repentant.

"Sorry? For what? You lived your life and I lived mine. God knows how it would have turned out if you'd stayed."

"Not good, I'd say. You wouldn't have been able to save me."

"From what?"

"From myself."

"And Sheila was?"

"No. Exile was. I was able to deny the past. Australia gave me the chance to start over. To make a different man of myself. In Ireland, I would always have been a bitter loser, hating everything and everyone. In the end, I would have hated life. And you wouldn't have been able to halt the decline when that set in."

"I never knew things were that bad."

"Maybe they weren't, but it seemed like it at the time. I was stuck in a rut with no apparent way out. That notice in the local paper advertising a job in Australia saved my life and others too perhaps."

"I never knew you were the ambitious type."

"I wasn't. I just knew I didn't want a life here. I could have gone closer to home looking for a job, but I needed to get away, far away. That was the only way I knew how to save my soul."

"God, Hugh, I had no idea."

"Why should you? I've never been great at expressing my feelings, and I was even worse at it back then. I just followed my instinct and that told me to get out as soon as I could. I wasn't worried about you. I knew you'd find someone else."

"You're right. I did. And from what you're after telling me, you did the right thing."

Hugh looked longingly out of the kitchen window at the sun dipping in the early autumn sky, dimming and brightening through the tossing branches of a tall ash like a wonky street lamp.

"Maybe we've talked enough about the past. What's done is done. It's a lovely day out. Shall we go for a walk?"

"I don't have any boots, only the shoes I'm wearing."

"What size do you take?"

"38."

"I'm sure Joan's around that size. Come on. Let's rummage in the cupboard and see what we can find."

When they were suitably attired and out in the yard, neither of them took the lead.

"So, where are we going?" she said, eying Hugh mischievously.

"Well, we can walk up to the top of Connick Rock or walk down along the river, unless it's too overgrown with weeds."

"I like the idea of the river. There's something very restful about flowing water."

Hugh opened the gate into a field of cut grass. Swathes of fresh hay lay in wavy lines across the field. He loved the sweet smell of drying hay. It was almost intoxicating. He picked up a sprig and began to chew it. The flavour reminded him of lazy summer days lying in the sun by the side of a haycock waiting for the hand of his watch to approach five, the time he had arranged to meet Maggie up at the graveyard, their clandestine meeting point.

Their feet made a swishing sound as they padded through the damp grass that was already beginning to grow again after the mowing. What a fertile land it was! The rain kept the grass so green and lush.

In the distance, Hugh could just make out the old church, now abandoned, where Mat and he used to play among the gravestones. There were tales of it being haunted by tormented souls, one at least, the soul of a young girl who had died in horrific pain, so they said, possibly in a fire or maybe of consumption or possibly in childbirth. Paddy Whelan, who used to live in the cottage attached to the church, swore that he had seen her many times. He was sure she was trying to tell him that her soul was not at rest. He tried in vain to persuade the clergy to hold a mass to help her escape from purgatory, but they all thought it was just the delirium of an old man. That was Ireland, a land full of troubled spirits, with no one to put them to rest.

There was a light breeze and the sun was still strong. It was a perfect August day. Back in Australia, it would be winter, if you could call it that. It seldom went below zero, and most days were more like an Irish summer.

As they approached the river, he was mildly startled when he felt Maggie's hand thread through his arm and her hip touch his.

"You don't mind?" she said, looking askance at him. "I feel so much at ease with you. It's almost if it was only yesterday we were running down that field hand in hand."

So, she had the same memories as he. They shared a past, however long ago it was.

"No, not at all. After all, you were like a sister to me." As soon as he said it, he realised that it was not exactly what he meant.

"I think I was more than that to you. At least I hope so. Brothers and sisters don't usually do the kind of things we did."

Together they let out a roguish laugh.

"You know what I mean," said Hugh, correcting himself.

"I was only codding. Of course, I do. We more or less grew up together. We were that close, but my love for you wasn't sisterly, I can tell you."

The mower had gone along the edge of the river so they were able to walk by the bank to a shallow point where they could cross over to the other side, if they were to continue up to the church.

"It was here, I think, that you used to carry me across. You were such a chivalrous gentleman. A real knight."

"Definitely not in shining armour. Dirty old jeans and a ragged T-shirt, if I remember correctly. And I'm sorry to disappoint you, but it had nothing to do with chivalry."

"What do you take me for? You think I didn't know?"

They both laughed at their teenage decadence, something that would have shocked them as parents and horrified their parents even more.

"Well, I liked to think it was chivalry anyway. Are you going to carry me across today?"

"I'd say you're perfectly capable of making it across yourself without my help. You're wearing Joan's boots, if I'm not mistaken."

She gave him a look of feigned anger. "Now that's not very chivalrous of you. Or is it because I'm not the babe I used to be?"

"Neither. I'm not sure my back is up to it."

"Oh god, of course it is. You have a big strong back, Hugh Gorman. I'd swear you could still swing a hundredweight bag of barley on to a trailer if you had to. And I'm well below a hundredweight, aren't I? What's a hundredweight anyway?"

"About fifty kilos, I think. I hope you're more than that. Otherwise, you're the next thing to a skeleton."

"I'm a bit more than fifty kilos. I won't tell you how much, but I'm far from being a skeleton. But I think you're still up for it, Hugh Gorman."

"Let's just sit on the bank for a bit and watch the river flow by before I have to prove myself to you."

"I can wait," she said coyly.

Hugh found some loose hay and made a seat for them on a grassy patch near the side of the river.

"Who said you weren't chivalrous? A perfect gentleman!" she said, responding to his invitation to sit next to him.

They were so close he could feel the heat of her body. For some reason, he felt an urge to put his arm around her. She didn't seem to mind and took hold of his dangling hand.

"This is nice, Hugh. It's been some time since I had a man's arm around me."

"I'm sure you have plenty of admirers at your theatre club."

"Many," she said with a playful smile. "But none who'd want to put their arm around me. There is an old lad in his sixties who fancies me, but I prefer younger men."

Hugh gave her a hard stare to see if she was joking. He never knew with Maggie.

"I got you there," she said with a modest lowering of her eyes.

If she considered a man in his sixties old, what did that make him? Far too old to have his arm around a woman that was not his wife.

Hugh watched the water toppling over the slippery brown stones, the dark green river weed wavering like the mane of a young girl's hair. Now, as then, it made him think of a scene from the Russian version of Hamlet the English teacher had taken them to in his last year at school; Ophelia lying in the river where she had drowned herself. Hugh smiled at the thought of Maggie drowning herself in despair. She may have been heartbroken, but she got over him quickly enough.

"A penny for your thoughts," she said, jolting him out of his reverie.

"Oh, I was just thinking how life turns out. It could have been so different. Not necessarily better. In fact, it could have been a lot worse."

"We were both happy enough, I suppose. And life seems to have come full circle. The two of us sitting here, like in the old days."

He hoped he wasn't getting her hopes up. He didn't want to abandon her a second time. "I may not stay, you know."

She laughed and pinched his cheek.

"Ouch! So that's what you wanted to do to me when you were five. You must have been born with a sadistic streak in you."

She smiled and pinched him again. The truth is, it didn't really hurt. Her hands were too soft, and it was no more than a playful pinch.

"You don't have to worry about me, Hugh," she said, sounding serious for the first time. "I'm not a vulnerable young teenager anymore. I'm going to enjoy you as long as you're here. No false hopes."

He would like to have been able to please her, to pretend that they were lovers again, but so much had happened since then.

"Come on! Let's go to the church," she said gleefully. "I haven't been there for years."

They got up and took one step into the water.

"Hey, mister! Aren't you forgetting something?"

He turned and saw her poised, ready to jump into his arms.

"You're not serious!" he said frowning.

"Dead serious! If you don't carry me across, I'll drench you, so I will." She bent down ready to scoop up handfuls of water to throw at him.

"All right, jump on my back," he said, turning.

"And all these years, I thought you were a chivalrous man. You're a great disappointment, Hugh Gorman."

She is behaving like a child, he thought. Had she never grown up? Or had being with him made her revert to her pubescent self? He decided to humour her, though he wasn't sure why. "Come on then so. But I hope no one is watching us, or we're going to be the laughingstock of the townland."

"Stop worrying, Gorman, there's no one else in the whole county but the two of us. Come on now and pick me up."

He came reluctantly towards her as if approaching a tiger about to spring. She leapt forward and grabbed him around the neck with both arms, settling herself neatly in his embrace. She was a great deal lighter than he expected.

"Oh, this is exciting!" she yelled. "I'm not too heavy, I hope."

"Like a sack of barley," he said, grunting and pretending to drop her.

She let out a yelp. "Don't you dare, Gorman!" Then, she realised he was just messing and pretended to be angry. "I've a good mind to belt you one, Hugh Gorman. But you'd probably like that, so I won't."

Hugh laughed at her inverted logic and waded into the river. Hugh looked around to make sure no one was walking the fields, but all he could see was a flock of sheep looking curiously in their direction, wondering at the childish antics of these elderly humans.

He felt her breath on his face and breathed in her heady perfume. He hadn't been so close to a woman since Sheila passed. He suddenly realised that he was being aroused. A twinge of guilt spiked his heart.

But surely now that she was dead, he thought, *it couldn't be considered cheating*. Maybe she'd even want him to get to know another woman. She understood human needs.

"Now don't drop me, Gorman, or I'll kill you!" she screeched, as they reached the deepest part of the river.

He pretended to stumble and nearly did, only righting himself at the last moment. "God, that was a close one," he said drolly, letting his arms drop slightly. She let out another shriek that reminded him of how she used to scream at the slightest provocation. Though unintentional on his part, the result was that she grabbed on to him even more tightly.

When they finally reached the other side, she wouldn't let go before kissing him, not on the cheek but on the lips, nothing sexual, just a quick peck. He was quite taken aback by her forwardness and didn't know how to respond. So, he just let her slide gently out of his arms, hoping that his erection was not too obvious. They both demurely rearranged their clothes.

"Well, that was fun," she said with a bashful chuckle. "And you've proved you're still up to."

He wasn't sure whether she was referring to his ability to carry her across the river or his erection. He was hoping the former. One thing was being momentarily aroused and another taking a woman to bed.

They set off at a pace not befitting their age and were both panting by the time they reached the church. They could have gone around by the road and entered the graveyard through the wrought iron gate—the lock on the chain had been broken for as long as he could remember—but Maggie insisted they went over the ditch, as they used to "in the old days."

"You're going to tear that dress of yours," he warned.

"Ah, who cares? I've got plenty more. And I'm not likely to be doing this again all that soon."

Hugh went ahead and held back the nettles and briars as best he could. Eventually, they emerged from the undergrowth relatively unscathed. At least, she did. He had a scratch on one hand and a nettle sting on the other. He had forgotten how vicious briars and nettles could be.

He understood her desire to recapture the past, even if it was a mere travesty of their lost youth. They had experienced too much to recapture the thrill of that first kiss, the magnetic power that attracts two people together, the intoxication of being in love for the first time.

The branches of the surrounding trees had been trimmed and lay in a heap in the corner of the old graveyard. The grass had also been cut recently and tossed on top of the pile of branches.

Hugh noticed that there were some new gravestones, distinguishable by their unblemished whiteness. He looked at the names and found that they were all familiar to him, grown-ups he had known as a child, the parents or grandparents of his friends and schoolmates. They had lived, grown old, and died without his even being aware of it.

There was something solemn and at the same time peaceful about the graveyard. All his boyish exuberance had drained out of him, out of Maggie too, it seemed. Like him, she was examining the names of the dead, possibly conjuring up living images of them.

On one grave, someone had planted a rosebush, which thrived on the remains of the deceased beneath. Maggie had cupped one of its blooms in her hand and was breathing in its perfume. It was a dark velvety red, almost black. It reminded him of the velvet suit he had bought for Joan's wedding and how his father and Rory had laughed when they saw him wearing it, saying that he looked like a "first-class ponce."

It will be considered hideous today, he thought, but at the time it was the height of fashion, or so he believed.

"Come here, Hugh, smell this," Maggie said excitedly. "It's out of this world."

He bent down and inhaled the heavy honey-sweet scent. For a moment, he felt almost light-headed. It evoked memories of playing in gardens on summer evenings, the light fading into a prolonged dusk, with the dew beginning to fall, drawing out myriad scents that would permeate the night air and give it a mystical quality. "Amazing!" he said, almost to himself.

They sat down on a flat family gravestone. It was cracked and collapsing in places. The granite was weathered to a speckled dark grey and was almost completely covered in a thin layer of greenish brown moss that acted as a mantle for them to sit on.

"Have you ever thought where you want to be buried?" she said distractedly.

Hugh thought it was a rather morbid question and not at all fitting their juvenescent mood, but he considered it, nonetheless. He realised he had not made any provision for his burial, though he always assumed he would be buried next to Sheila in Esperance. "I'll let others decide that one," he said.

"Why? It's your last resting place. You're going to be there a very long time."

"Does it really matter where I'm buried?"

"I suppose not," she said, looking absentmindedly up at the sky. "I think I'd like to be cremated and scattered to the four winds. That way, I could wander the world forever."

"I'd prefer my ashes to be thrown into the sea."

"Then, you could find your way back to Ireland," she said musingly.

He hadn't considered that, but it was an engaging thought. Yet, somehow, he felt it was his duty to be buried next to Sheila, not that she would notice his absence, if he weren't there. Besides, it would be too much trouble for the boys to arrange his cremation. They were not the types to indulge in sentimental ceremonies that involved hiring a boat and casting ashes into tumbling waves. They were hard-assed Aussies, not an ounce of romanticism in them. He envisaged himself in an urn in some attic gathering dust, until some future owner found it and tossed it into the garbage bin. He felt the "Break, break, break" the waves resounding in his head.

The cottage beside the church was now just a ruin. The roof had fallen in and the stone walls were held together by a thick jacket of ivy. Hugh recalled Paddy Whelan with his furrowed brow and his wife, Patsie, who cleaned the church, when it was still functioning.

As a young lad, he would often pass by the cottage and chat to Paddy, who more often than not would be sitting on the doorstep of the cottage sucking away on the half-chewed stem of his briar. It would squeak and crackle like a piece of damp wood on a bonfire. He remembered the nauseating smell of mouse urine that issued from the house and the sound of the smelly creatures rustling in the shredded newspaper in their cage under the staircase. He never understood why anyone would want to keep a mouse as a pet, given there were so many wild ones around.

Patsie would appear with a slice of soda bread, plastered in homemade strawberry jam and farmyard butter. It always seemed so much tastier than anything he ate at home.

"I suppose Paddy Whelan is dead this long while," Hugh said at last.

"Not all that long. Sure, he was nearly a hundred when he died. He lived with his daughter Betty over beyond the village for years."

"He used to tell me about the ghost of a young girl who would appear to him."

"Ah, sure you wouldn't want to believe a word Paddy said. He had a very lively imagination."

"Maybe he was clairvoyant."

"I'm surprised at you, Hugh. I didn't think you'd believe in that kind of thing."

He got up and walked to the unmarked grave by the north wall. "It's a mystery, nonetheless, why this grave should be so far removed from all the rest and no gravestone on it," he said staring down at the raised mound of earth. She, if it was a she, must have been short, he noted. The grave couldn't have been more than five feet in length. "Some say she got pregnant out of wedlock and died in childbirth. Others claimed that her parents engineered her death because they couldn't live with the shame."

"A sad story whatever."

"So, it wouldn't be unreasonable to suppose that she was a troubled soul, like Paddy claimed."

"He could have just made it up."

Hugh would have liked the girl to appear before them to prove...to prove what? That Ireland still had spirits and ghosts. That all the yarns and stories of his childhood were not just figments of someone's imagination. That everything that kept him tied inextricably to this land was not a lie, a myth, a religion based on groundless faith and mumbo jumbo.

Silently, he tried to invoke the spirit of this young girl, to imagine her as Paddy had described her; her long flowing brown hair, her shapeless grey dress made of a rough homespun material, her bare tanned feet, cracked and sore. Paddy had said she was pretty but very thin, not more than sixteen at the most. Hugh knelt on the mound of clay and tried to will her to the surface, but all he could feel was the dampness seeping through the knees of his trousers. He clearly did not have Paddy's clairvoyance.

He started slightly when he felt a presence behind him. He looked around, hoping that it was the young girl. For a brief second, he thought it was. Only when his blurred vision came into focus did he see that it was Maggie.

"Were you praying for her salvation?" she said mirthfully.

"No, just wondering whether there are such things as troubled spirits."

"There are plenty of troubled spirits all right. One just hopes they find peace in the ground." She turned and strode out of the deep shade into the sunlight. "Come on now, Hugh. We should be thinking of the living not the dead. Do you know what time it is? Joan'll think we have eloped or something."

Hugh reluctantly got to his feet and threw a last glance at the grave, just in case the girl had heard him. He so wanted to believe in spirits and shades, in the existence of something beyond flesh and blood and ephemeral emotions. He wanted to believe that something remained beyond a pile of ashes or a heap of bones. As he left the shade of the laurel tree, it felt as if he were exiting a mausoleum, designed to commemorate a special loved one and keep her remains intact.

Back in the sun again, he felt strangely exhilarated. He looked at his watch. "You're right. It's nearly tea time. Shall we go by the road or across the fields?"

Maggie pretended to give the matter a lot of thought. "If we go by the road, it'll take much longer. I'd say we trip off down the field and across the river." She looked at him with a mischievous glitter in her eyes.

"Maggie, I'm an old man. You're going to do me back in."

"You had no trouble on the way here. And I could tell you got quite a thrill out of it," she added with an impish smile.

So, she had noticed his erection. Maggie had been a tease back then and she was still one now.

They decided to take more or less the same route back, down along the meadow and over the river. He carried her across again because that's what she wanted. This time she laid her head on his shoulder and didn't want to get down when they reached the other side.

"Could we not stay like this forever, Hugh?"

"I doubt my back or my legs would stand it."

She slapped his arm in feigned anger. "You're about as romantic as those sheep in the field below. Can't you at least pander to me?"

"I can do that all right, as long as you know that's all I'm doing."

"Oh, don't worry. I know you too well, Hugh Gorman. You wouldn't think twice about leaving someone heartbroken and going off to Australia."

Yes, it probably had been callous of him, but love wasn't strong enough to save him then and probably wasn't now, either.

This time she didn't kiss him on the lips, just placed her cheek on his, which he found even more rousing than the kiss. There was something exceedingly intimate and almost moving about the sedateness of it.

They walked up to the house hand in hand, just like the old days, not to roll around on his bed, but to have afternoon tea in the garden with Joan and Rory. That's what old people do, he supposed, though the thought of rolling on the bed with Maggie was not wholly distasteful to him. She was still an attractive woman, well preserved, probably more so than he. He remembered her as she was fifty years ago and that's how he saw her now, making some allowances for the normal wear and tear of life.

"Do you know what, Hugh?"

"I have no idea, but you're going to tell me anyway."

She punched him again on the arm. It was fortunate he didn't bruise easily, he thought, or else he would be black-and-blue by the end of the day with all her hitting and slapping.

"I want you to come to a rehearsal one evening."

"I'd love to. I'm told you have a beautiful voice."

"It isn't bad, but I want you to meet the crowd."

"Would they want to meet me?"

"And why wouldn't they? I've already mentioned you to one or two of them. I'll introduce you as my boyfriend. I think they might be impressed."

Hugh nodded his head in disbelief. "You're incorrigible, Maggie. Couldn't you at least say I'm an ex-boyfriend?"

"Ah, no. That would spoil the fun. They want to see a real boyfriend, not an ex."

"And what about this other lad who fancies you? What's his name?"

"Oh, Jerry? It'll do him good to know there's some competition."

"As you know, I'm not very sociable. But I suppose, if I'm going to be here for a while, it might do me good to get out of the house for a bit."

"Joan is a real saint. She's been through so much. I know I couldn't do it."

"We can all do it, if we have to."

"True enough, I suppose."

Hugh wondered whether she had had a hard time with Tom before he died, or was it a sudden death? It didn't seem the right time to ask her.

Joan stuck her head of the kitchen window when she saw them crossing the yard. "You two had a long walk. Did you have fun?"

They gave each other a questioning look and said, almost in tandem, "Yeah, great!"

"It's another lovely day, so we're going to have tea in the garden. Would you help Rory, Hugh? And, Maggie, could you carry out a tray for me?"

As they sat around the garden table drinking tea and eating scones, Hugh could tell Joan was dying to know what had gone on between them. She kept eyeing them to see if they were exchanging furtive glances. It made Hugh feel uneasy. He was being manipulated again. If anything was going to happen between him and Maggie, which it probably wasn't, he wanted it to be spontaneous, something that happened by accident rather than design. Had she and Maggie talked about it? Had she roped Maggie into conniving with her to keep him in Ireland? He didn't normally believe in conspiracy theories, but this one would not be beyond either of them.

After tea, Maggie got up to leave. "It's been lovely, Joan. And it was great seeing your man here again. He hasn't changed a bit. Still as stubborn as ever."

"That's my young brother all right."

"It's been great seeing you, Hugh," she said in a low voice he could hardly hear. She put both hands on his arms and leaned in to him without actually touching his cheeks. Her scent reminded him of the dark velvety red rose up in the churchyard.

■

Though initially overwhelmed by memories, retrieved scents and sounds, Hugh was slowly returning to the present reality, even getting used to those transformed faces, in some cases beyond recognition, that he had not seen change through time. He began to worry about the station again. Were things going to pieces with him not there? Was Ron as reliable as he had led him to believe, or would he take advantage of his absence?

On Tuesday, he couldn't hold back any longer and called Ron.

"Everything's going swimmingly, boss. No worries. Had a couple of stillbirths but nothing out of the ordinary. Now, you enjoy yourself, Mr. Gorman. No need to hurry back. By the way, how is your brother?"

"Not well, Ron. But thanks for asking."

"Sorry to hear that, boss. I know what it's like. My father was really broken up when his brother died. They were very close."

"I'm still hoping for a miracle, Ron, but they don't happen all that often."

"Right enough, Mr. Gorman, but no harm in hoping. Just give me a tinkle whenever you feel like it, and I'll get you up to speed."

Hugh felt reassured. He could now devote himself to Rory, for the time being at least.

Even though it required considerable effort on his part, Rory was keen to be taken out in the car. He often had a specific request, to go somewhere that had fond memories for him. Other times he was just happy to be driven to random parts of the country. They never went for more than an hour or two, and Hugh gave up asking if he wanted to walk when they got to their destination. The most he was capable of doing was going from the car to a bench, where they could sit and admire the view or drink a cup of coffee at some café with tables outside.

When they returned home, Rory would need a couple of hours to recover, often dozing in the armchair by the fire. Hugh lit the fire not because it was cold but because Rory "was feeling the cold more than he used to."

Mat called one evening and said he was sorry he hadn't been over, but things were going crazy at the factory. The order from the Emirates was phenomenal, and they had to work round the clock to meet the deadline.

"Look, why don't you play a round of golf with Bridie?' Mat suggested. "She'd love the company. She can come round and pick you up one afternoon."

"Thanks, Mat, a lovely idea, but I think I would be an insurmountable handicap."

Mat laughed. "No, not at all. She said she thought you were a natural and that you'd be competing with the best in no time."

"Thanks, Mat. To be honest with you, I want to spend as much time as I can with Rory and Joan."

"Sure, I understand. Look, as soon as things start easing off here, I'll pick you up and we'll go out for a pint. I'd like you to see the new house too. It's a bit bigger than we really need, but if you can't enjoy a bit of luxury in your old age, when can you?"

"I'd love to. But I understand from personal experience that work takes precedence."

"Unfortunately, you're right. Success has its drawbacks, mainly not having the time to appreciate it."

Maggie was going into town to a rehearsal on Thursday evening and asked Hugh to go with her. He didn't say yes at once. He said he'd think about it. He gave the convenient excuse that he felt he should spend as much time as he could with Rory and Joan. The truth was he hated being the focus of attention. The spotlight would be squarely and very dazzlingly on him, especially if Maggie carried out her threat to introduce him as her boyfriend. The young crowd would find it great *crach* that these two oldies were having an affair, taking bets on whether they were having it off or not.

Hugh decided to talk it over with Joan. She had been his confidante in his teens, and it seemed natural that she should be again. Rory was in bed, and they were sitting beside the fire having a nightcap, without the mind-numbing TV on for a change.

"Maggie's asked me to go with her to one of her rehearsals, but I'm not sure I should."

"Why not? It'll do you good. You've been here nearly a week. You must be fed up of the sight of us."

"Not at all. It's great to be able to spend time with Rory, though he's not as talkative as he used to be."

"It's not surprising. Even talking takes it out of him. But he's very glad you're home and things are all right between you, Hugh."

"And why shouldn't they be?"

"He felt there was possibly bad blood. The old man left you nothing in his will and…"

Hugh looked up from his glass with surprise. He had had no inkling of bad blood before this. "For God' sake, what did he have to leave anyway but the farm? And even if he had, he wouldn't have left it to me. Bad blood? What nonsense!"

"Well, you didn't come over for so long."

"You know what it's like running a farm, especially one the size of ours. We have over two thousand sheep, you know, not to mention all the wheat we grow."

"God, I had no idea it was so big. You did well for yourself out there all right. You must have made a fair amount of money over the years."

Hugh sensed that Joan was leading up to something, but he pretended not to notice. "Not too bad, I suppose. It was hard work, but Sheila and I built the place up and got it running efficiently. Her father didn't know the first thing about business. He handled the men very badly too. These days you have to treat employees with kid gloves or you're in for trouble."

"Look, Hugh, there's something I've been meaning to talk to you about, but I didn't want to bring it up in an email for fear of a misunderstanding. And I didn't want to mention in front of Rory either, the state he's in. It would upset him."

Hugh frowned. He had no idea what this could be about.

"It's about that loan I gave you. It was a lot of money back then and we'd hoped—"

"Joan, hold on there now. What loan are you talking about?"

"It's so long ago now you have most likely forgotten. You remember I came into a bit of money when Uncle Patty died."

"I seem to remember something of the sort all right. So, you think I resented that. You were always Uncle Patty's favourite. You were like a daughter to him. It was only right that you should get his money. The truth is we could have done with a bit at the time but I'm—"

"But you did get it. All of it."

Hugh suddenly went on the defensive. He hated being accused of something he hadn't done. "What are you talking about, Joan?"

Joan put out her hands to calm Hugh down. "Don't get upset, Hugh. We didn't need the money at the time, but you did. So, I gave it to Rory to send over to you. You were trying to buy out Sheila's brother, don't you remember?"

"Joan, I'm sorry, but I never got any money from Rory. We bought out Joe with our savings and a hefty loan from the bank that took us twenty years to pay off."

Joan pursed her lips into a conciliatory smile. "Look, Hugh, I don't want us to fight. It's just we could do with the money now, what with the doctor's bills and all, and that spell Rory spent in hospital took our last euro."

"If you want money, Joan, all you have to do is ask for it, but I don't like being accused of something I didn't do."

"Maybe you're after forgetting, Hugh. It's a long time ago and, well, we're only human."

"For God's sake, Joan. I'm not gone senile yet. I tell you again. I never got a loan from you. Would I tell you a lie?"

Joan didn't answer, but her silence indicated that she believed he would.

"I can't believe it. Is that what you think of me, Joan? I might have been looking out for myself when I was twenty, but would anyone blame me? No one else was going to." Hugh knew that his anger was getting the better of him, and in such a state, he was afraid of what he might do or say. "I'm going to bed. We can talk about it in the morning."

"I knew it'd upset you, Hugh. That's why I didn't bring it up any sooner. Money is such a delicate matter between siblings."

"Well, it shouldn't be. So, for the last twenty years you've been thinking I reneged on a loan. All you had to do was fucking well ask me!" With that, he slammed his glass down on the table, causing the wine to splash on to the table.

Joan sighed but made no attempt to stop him leaving the room.

That night, Hugh had difficulty sleeping. He kept turning over in his mind Joan's accusation. How could she think they had given him a loan that he had not paid back? Was it possible that the old man had wheedled the money out of Rory and then went and lost it on a game of poker? More likely, he had resented him getting the money and persuaded Rory to put it in a joint account, which he then polished off on drink and cards. Could he have sunk that low in his old age? He knew the old man was fond of the liquor and liked the odd game of poker, but he had always believed him to be honest. Then again, if the truth were told, he was capable of nearly anything.

He kept tossing and turning, turning it over in his mind. He even considered the possibility that he had been given the loan and had forgotten to pay it back, though he believed this highly unlikely.

He eventually got to sleep, but it was a troubled sleep. He woke up intermittently with an urge to go the toilet. Finally, he started awake when the sun burst through a slit in the curtains. He began thinking again. He felt badly about speaking harshly to Joan. He couldn't remember when last he had lost his temper, probably the time Brendan came home drunk, and they had nearly ended up strangling each other.

The whole situation was getting to him. He liked to be in control, not only of his life but of himself, and it was clear that he was losing his grip on both. Added to that was the frustration of not being able to do more for Rory, and then seeing Maggie and remembering those blithe, carefree days of his youth. She had stirred up thoughts and feelings that he believed were dead and buried long ago. He was even beginning to question the correctness of his decision to emigrate to Australia. What did this say about his life? It would nullify two-thirds of his existence. And now this. Did relationships all boil down to money in the end? He thought that what he had with Rory and Joan was beyond money. It wasn't as if he had ever consciously gone after money. Wealth had never been of any great importance to him. He had worked hard not to become rich but to make a success of his life and to please Sheila, who loved the station.

When he had arrived home, the first thing he did was offer to help them financially. Didn't that say something? Rory declined his offer, though he knew it was just pride on his part. There had always been rivalry between them, nothing that led to any great animosity, but it had always been there, nonetheless, under the surface. Rory had envied his dynamism and success with women. It was strange how in their late teens the tables had turned and the envied became the envier. And now it was all coming to a head. They desperately needed money and had to invent a way of getting it out of him without it seeming like they were asking for charity. Was that why Joan had been so keen to get him home? Surely, she wouldn't stoop to that. He was willing to give them as much money as they wanted—he had a fair amount put aside—but he was damned if they were going to get it by reclaiming a nonexistent loan or what they claimed was an unpaid one. He wasn't going to part with a penny piece until it was accepted as a gift. He had no intention of indulging their ridiculous pride.

■

He waited until he heard noises below before going down. Rory was awake but was having difficulty breathing. He looked more drained than ever. His eyes seemed to have retreated into their murky sockets, and his skin was sallow and drawn.

"Did you have a bad night?"

"I did," said Rory in a voice that was hardly audible.

"Shall I yoke you up the ould machine?"

"Leave it where it is, Hugh. I'm a gonner. Me lungs are collapsing."

"Well, you should be on the machine then so."

"What's the point?"

Rory's face pinched in momentary agony.

"I think we should ask Dr. O'Malley to come over. He may be able to give you something to ease the pain."

Rory pointed to a packet of painkillers he had on the table beside the bed.

"Well, they don't seem to be doing you much good. You need something stronger." Hugh realised that the time had come when only morphine could kill the pain, even if it killed him at the same time.

"What I'd like now, Hugh boy, is to be able to pass peaceably. The thought of dying of suffocation scares the shite out of me."

"Lookat. I'll call O'Malley as soon as it's a decent hour and get him to come out." Hugh looked at his watch. "I'll call him at nine."

"Thanks, Hugh."

Joan was in the kitchen making eggs and bacon. The sound and smell of sizzling bacon brought him back fifty years. Sheila had always been health conscious and was in an endless battle with cholesterol and the flab. Fatty bacon or meat was never allowed over the threshold of their house. Not that it did her any good. She ended up dying of a stroke at the age of sixty-five.

Hugh stood there for a while not wishing to startle her. Contemplating her bent back and thinning grey hair, he realised how old she was. It was such a pity that anything should come between them now.

She eventually turned, frying pan in hand, and saw Hugh standing there. "It's yourself. Just in time."

"What's the occasion?" he said, indicating the bacon and eggs.

"It's time you had a decent breakfast, young man, and I'm hoping that I may be able to coax your man inside to eat a bit. He's fading away."

"Give me his plate and I'll try and ease a bit into him."

"You're a good lad, Hugh. Sure, weren't you always the golden-haired boy?"

"If you say so, Joan. Would he like a bit of toast with that, do you think?"

"Oh god no, he's sure to choke on it. Cut up the bacon nice and fine and put a bit of egg on it and you might be able to coax it down him."

"I'm thinking of calling O'Malley after breakfast. Maybe he can give him something for the pain."

"He's taking painkillers."

"He needs something stronger. He may need to go into hospital. You know that, don't you? We can't give him the right treatment at home."

"No, Hugh. All he needs is love and care, and no nurse is going to give him that."

"We'll have to see what O'Malley says."

She gave him a look of obstinate displeasure. She wasn't going to give in, and Rory was too weak not to comply. The truth is he wasn't sure himself what was best for Rory.

Hugh took the plate into his brother, who showed no interest in food. "I'm too old to be spoon-fed, Hugh. I'd sooner die of malnutrition."

"Well, you will, if you don't eat. Can I tempt you with a couple of mouthfuls of bacon and egg?"

Rory made a grimace of disgust.

Hugh gave him a despairing look. Then, in a hushed voice, nodding towards the kitchen, he said. "Joan'll kill me if I go back to the kitchen with food still on the plate."

"Do me a favour, Hugh, and eat it yourself."

"Just one mouthful so I don't have to lie. Come on now."

Rory forced a half-smile. "Okay so."

Hugh eased a forkful of egg and bacon into Rory's mouth, which he chewed agonisingly slowly. However, it seemed to stimulate his appetite and he asked for more.

"Oh, Jaysus, you can't bate the eggs and bacon," said Rory croakily.

After he'd eaten five or six mouthfuls, he clamped his mouth shut, refusing another. So, Hugh took pity on him and finished the rest.

Joan looked in surprise at the empty plate when Hugh brought it back into the kitchen. "God, Hugh, he hasn't eaten so much in weeks." She gave him a suspicious look. "I hope you didn't eat it for him."

"Innocent," said Hugh, raising his hands in protest and hoping there were no remains of egg on the side of his mouth. "It was the bacon did the trick."

During breakfast, neither made any reference to the row they had had the previous evening. They were both too concerned about Rory.

There will be time later to sort things out, Hugh thought. Nevertheless, it was still on his mind. It explained so much—why their relationship had gone sour over the previous twenty or so years, why his offers to pay for their flights over to Esperance had been rejected with snide remarks like "I'm sure you can't afford it, Hugh" and "We wouldn't want to put you to any expense now," when they knew that he was a great deal better off than they were. He had never hidden from them that with the exception of 2007, the year of the great storm, he had made a lot of money out of the station.

Hugh looked at his watch. It was past nine. "Would you give me O'Malley's phone number, Joan?"

She threw him a slightly pugnacious glance. "Look, Hugh, I know you're the boss back in Sperance or whatever you call that place in Australia, but I know what's right for Rory. So, I'll decide whether to call O'Malley or not."

Hugh was taken aback. He hadn't expected such a confrontational response to his simple request. Was it wrong of him to have taken the initiative to call O'Malley? "I was only doing it for Rory. There's never a word out of him, but I can see he's suffering something terrible. He told me that the best thing that could happen to him was to pass away peacefully."

The muscles around Joan's mouth twitched, but she forced back the emotion. "Don't mind, Rory, Hugh. Sure, hasn't your coming home given him a new lease of life?"

"It's true he found the strength to rally for a few days, but it didn't last long. It wouldn't do any harm if O'Malley came out and saw him. If it's the money you're—"

"We're not paupers, Hugh," she said brusquely.

Money again, thought Hugh. It was clearly a subject he'd have to steer clear of. "I know, but can I at least talk to him? I need to find out something about Rory's medical history."

"What? When did you get your degree in medicine then?"

Hugh sighed inwardly. So, this was how it was going to be from now on. "I'm not claiming to know much about medicine, Joan, but I'd like to know from a medical expert what we're dealing with here."

"Go ahead so, but I can tell you all you need to know."

"Can I have his number then?"

Joan thumbed through the pages of a grubby notebook and finally located O'Malley's number. "Here you are," she said, begrudgingly handing him the notepad. "But don't do anything without asking me."

"I won't."

O'Malley was friendly enough, but it was clear he didn't want to reveal too much on the phone to a man he had never met. "I can see from my records that your brother has not been in for a checkup for some time. He should have been in three weeks ago. I think it's very important that we review his case as soon as possible. Now, I believe your sister, and he made the decision not to do another course of chemotherapy, and though it was not what I advised, I do understand. It can be unpleasant and in Rory's case perhaps futile. However, we will need to keep a close eye on him as the disease takes over vital organs. Ideally, he should be in hospital, but if I remember correctly, Joan and he decided on home treatment. Again, not what I would advise, but I can't force him. I'll call around at about three, if that's convenient?"

Hugh panicked. "Just a moment, Doctor. Let me just confirm that with my sister." He told Joan of O'Malley's suggestion.

She looked at him crossly. "Okay then."

"That's fine, Doctor. See you at three."

When he put the phone down, he felt he needed to under-stand why Joan was being so antagonistic. Did it all boil down to the money business? "I'm sorry, Joan, but you did ask me to come over. What do you expect me to do? Remain a passive bystander. He is my brother too, you know."

"I'm glad you finally realised that, but I invited you over to be with him, not to interfere. You were always like that. You can't leave well alone."

Hugh was once more stunned by Joan's insinuations. "I don't know what you're talking about, Joan. I've been away for fifty years. I've never interfered in anything."

"In the past, you were always over and writing regular. It was almost as if you hadn't left."

"And so?"

"It was wrong of you, Hugh, to give Ma notions."

"What in God's name are you talking about?"

"Don't deny it now, Hugh. I read it in a letter you sent to her. You were setting her against Da. And she always listened to you."

"I may have told her once or twice that she shouldn't put up with Da's bullying. You know as well as I do that he treated her very badly."

"Yes, but there was an understanding between them…until you got her thinking like Germaine Greer."

"What understanding, Joan? That he could bully her and treat her like dirt. The priests at the Christian Brothers had an under-standing with us too. Do what I tell you or I'll beat the shite out of you. That's what I call tyranny, not an understanding."

"All your liberal ideas may work in Australia, Hugh, but they don't here, or didn't then. The fights between Ma and Da were something terrible until the cancer got the better of her."

"I'm sorry, Joan, but you can't blame me. I simply spoke my mind. It was up to her to listen to me or not. She was a grown woman."

"Oh, it was very easy to give advice from the other side of the world. You didn't live here. You didn't have to put up with him, cursing you and then her for listening to you."

"And I suppose you and Rory just stood by and let him kick the shit out of her."

"Your father was a powerful man, Hugh. What could we do? When roused, he was like a bear with a thorn in his paw."

"Well, I would have beaten the living daylights out of him if I'd been here."

"I know you would, and what good would that have done?"

"He might have thought twice about doing it a second time."

"But sure, you know Rory. He wouldn't lift a finger to hurt a fly. The old man couldn't stand it that you still had influence over her from so far away."

"What do you mean 'still'?"

"Jaysus, Hugh, have you forgotten? You and Ma were as thick as thieves?"

"Come on now, Joan. Rory was always her favourite."

"She felt sorry for him, that's all, because he never had your confidence, your determination to make a new life for yourself. She wanted to make him feel loved at least, given that Da had no time for him."

"Sure, Da had no respect for anyone."

"Da had great respect for you, Hugh, but you were too much alike for him to admit it. He felt threatened."

"In more ways than one, no doubt."

"He was happy to see the back of you when you left for Australia."

"What? He said so."

"More or less. I'm telling you now because I know it won't upset you. Not long after you'd gone, he said, ''Tis good riddance to that lad. He'd only have torn the family apart.'"

"He was angry that I left. He wanted me to suffer like he had. He couldn't stand it that I was able to escape. He was just a damned loser, Joan. But for the drink and the cards he could have made a go of this place, like you and Mikey did."

"You never understood your Da, Hugh."

"What was there to understand? He was a miserable old sod with a cruel streak in him."

"Hugh, you're only thinking of the bad times. Don't you remember when you were a youngster how he'd rub your chest with his rough ould hands and say, 'This'll make the hairs grow,' and how he'd take you on his lap and get you to light his pipe for him?"

"It's a wonder he didn't turn me into a chain-smoker."

"There you go. You can only see the bad side of him. You and he used to be inseparable when you were a nipper. You'd go every-where with him. I'll never forget the day—I must have been about eleven—when he said to me, 'That brother of yours has a head on his shoulders, Joan, not like you and your brother. He could go to university and become a professor if he wanted.' But then some-thing happened between you…"

"You know what happened between us, Joan."

"I do not."

"I acquired an opinion, a mind of my own. I was able to com-pare him with other fathers. I no longer saw him as god almighty but a cruel tyrant."

"Did you never think that perhaps the first was closer to the truth?"

"He was no god and that's for sure. And Mam knew as well as I did that he was a terrible tyrant."

"Underneath, he was a sad man. Didn't he suffer from depression something terrible? Don't you remember those split-ting headaches that'd drive him mad? He'd sit in that chair where you're sitting now with his head in his hands trying to squeeze the pain out of him."

"It was no more than a hangover. You're trying to make excuses for him, Joan, like you all did until I put Mam straight."

"And what good did it do?"

"It gave her back her dignity."

"And was she any better off with 'dignity,' as you call it?"

"It couldn't have been any worse than it was and maybe at least it gave her a bit of satisfaction to speak her mind once in a while."

"It's too late now anyway. What's done is done. We need to think about Rory. And the last thing he wants is to die in hospital."

"In that case, we need to make sure that O'Malley gives us everything we need to make him comfortable at home."

"What do you mean, Hugh?"

"I mean painkillers. We haven't seen anything yet. When the time comes, he's going to need morphine and strong doses of it at that."

"Sure, O'Malley has been our doctor for years. I'm sure he'll give us a prescription for it."

"Only trained medical staff can administer morphine."

"I can give him an injection if he needs it. Sure, didn't I do the first year of a nurse's training?"

"You don't understand. Morphine is an illegal drug. It's against the law for anyone else, but someone with a medical licence to administer it."

Joan looked doubtful, but Hugh could see that it was beginning to dawn on her what looking after Rory in his final days would entail.

O'Malley came into the yard at exactly three. Hugh noticed he was driving a Range Rover. His fee was going to be steep.

However, he seemed friendly enough and had a good bedside manner. The important thing was that Rory was glad to see him and didn't mind being examined by him.

After he had finished, Joan made him a cup of tea, which she served in the kitchen so that they could talk freely about Rory.

"I can see no marked deterioration," said the doctor, pulling the cup and saucer towards him. "That doesn't mean he's any better. Without a CAT/MRI scan, I have no idea whether the cancer has spread and, if so, where to. Maybe seeing Hugh has had a beneficial effect on his general disposition, his psychological state, that is, but I cannot say the cancer is in remission. Are you sure now you don't want him to go into hospital? I can arrange for him to have a bed in the next day or two."

Joan's eyes started out of her head. "Absolutely not. If he goes into hospital, he'll never come out alive. He was born in this house, and he'll die in this house. We can look after him grand."

"Can you?" said the doctor sceptically.

"Hugh said you could give us a prescription for some morphine injections, if necessary."

"Well, I didn't…" said Hugh, vainly trying to defend himself.

"I'm afraid I can't do that, Joan."

"But you're not just our doctor, Sean. You're also a good friend."

"You'd be surprised how many doctors have been sued by so-called good friends for simply carrying out their wishes. I'm sure it doesn't apply in this case, but I can't take any chances. Besides, an overdose could kill him. It has to be very carefully administered."

Joan went silent, her features sagging. She looked as if she was about to break down. Whether it was real or just a ploy to get O'Malley's sympathy, Hugh was not sure. With Joan, both were possible.

O'Malley laid his hand lightly on Joan's shoulder. "I'm sorry, Joan. I know you did some basic training as a nurse, but you're not qualified and, even if you were, your licence would be long out of date. There are strict regulations, and they are there for a purpose, I assure you. Certain decisions can only be taken in consultation directly between doctor and patient. You'd be surprised how many would gladly get rid of a senile or bedridden relative. In many cases, it might be humane to do so; but in others, it could simply be expediency. In either case, it is against the law, as you can understand. Look, Joan. I will come out whenever you need me. Now that you have discontinued the treatment, the only thing you can do is pray for a miracle." O'Malley looked hastily at his watch. "I'd better be going. I have a few more patients to see before the day is out."

Hugh accompanied him to the door and offered to pay his fee. He seemed put out. "I'll get my secretary to send you the invoice, Mr. Gorman." Hugh didn't dare ask how much it would be or whether the bill could be sent to Esperance. Now that he had O'Malley's number, he'd call his secretary to arrange payment.

Rory got up briefly for lunch but ate little. He declined Hugh's offer to take him for a drive in the car, and pleading fatigue, he went straight back to bed. He said all he wanted was rest.

It turned into a rainy afternoon but Hugh was restless. He needed to get out of the house to clear his head. Ever since the row with Joan, he had had a tightening around the nape and temples as if a metal clamp was slowly crushing his skull. *Probably high blood pressure*, he thought, but he wasn't going to worry about that now.

He felt frustrated, on the one hand, and unsettled, on the other. He could do nothing for Rory except act as a glorified nurse, and Joan seemed set on digging up as much unpleasantness from the past as she could. For what reason, he was not sure. He assumed that she had been bearing a grudge against him for years, and it was all coming out now. But her behaviour was contradictory. At times, she gave every indication that she wanted to make him feel welcome. At others, she seemed bent on driving him away. In many ways, Joan was right, he knew. It was easy to be self-righteous from afar, and the truth was he had not been there to take care of his mother, to protect her from the tyrant, when she needed him. His half-hearted attempts to intervene from the other side of the world had failed totally and had possibly made things a great deal worse.

He found a set of oilskins and a pair of rubber boots and set off across the fields in no specific direction. It was a soft gentle rain, one that he always associated with Ireland. He held his head up to the sky and allowed the drops to wash over his brow on to his face in what he liked to think was a cleansing ritual, the hand of nature caressing his face with its own holy water. They could have been the tears of a loved one, once warm, now cold. Yet, there was something comforting about it. Even the constricting band around his head felt less tight.

A heavy mist had descended over the land, and he could no longer see the farmhouse below. He felt somehow cushioned against feeling, though he knew it was there inside him, only temporarily appeased. He was alone with the elements and the seagulls screeching, as they circled aimlessly overhead. He wondered what they were looking for in that desolate sky, not food certainly. It was almost as if they had lost their way and were stranded halfway between the murky hills and their natural element. Were they having second thoughts about coming inland but couldn't decide in which direction to go? What were they afraid of? What had they hoped to find?

He went over a ditch into a *rath*. Historians said it was an old Irish settlement, abandoned millennia before. As children, they believed it was the home of ghosts and the Little People. No farmer would dare knock down the ditches to incorporate it into a field. Disaster was sure to follow. And there were many tales of whole families being wiped out by a curse invoked by the Little People in retaliation for the destruction of their home.

He tried to find a way through the thick undergrowth of brambles and nettles but found it nearly impossible. Finally, he sat at the base of a tall oak tree and breathed in the pervasive eeriness of the place. A rabbit suddenly appeared a few metres away and stood there, ears cocked, silently watching him. Seeing there was no reaction from the creature in the yellow oilskins, the rabbit quietly went about its business without any apparent sign of fear.

He remembered as a teenager how he would take the rifle and go off in search of prey. He would invariably bring back a rabbit or a few pigeons and proudly present them to his mother, who would skin the rabbit or pluck the pigeons, to be made into a stew. He wouldn't kill a rabbit or even a pigeon now. Approaching the end of his, he knew how precious life was, even that of an animal or a bird that was in overabundance.

Such contributions to the family budget were always appreciated. The old man kept her short of cash, and she was always devising methods of making a little pocket money to fund her small luxuries, the Walnut Whorls she reserved for after Sunday lunch and her monthly visit to the hairdresser. She made her own dresses from patterns she would find in Woman's Own and jam with wild fruit and all the fruit they had in the garden at the back of the house—rhubarb, apples, blackcurrants, gooseberries. She would then sell the jam at fetes or to the neighbours. She was famous for her jams, made with only the purest of ingredients and never too sweet.

He found himself so immersed in past memories he almost forgot he was in the present. Yet, in his mind, past and present were always merging. Life was a series of links in a chain of events, each link playing a vital part in keeping the whole together. He rose stiffly from under the oak tree and said goodbye to the rabbit that seemed so comfortable with his presence. He wondered whether he would ever enter the rath again.

Almost involuntarily, he ended up on Connick Hill. He was drawn to this place like metal to a magnet. The landscape below bore no resemblance to that of his first day home. Now, it was sad and dismal like an old house whose occupants had died leaving everything as it was. The sheets of driving mist were like frayed curtains flapping in the wind gusting through a broken window. Even the sheep seemed set in stone; silent, motionless, like alabaster figurines scattered about haphazardly. It was a desolate landscape, accentuated by the droning lament of an inconsolable wind that rose and fell like a dirge, mourning the passing of those who had once occupied this land.

He decided it was time to return to the house. He was allowing the weather to get to him, or was it more than that? He had always had a love-hate relationship with Ireland and nothing had changed. He was like a man in love with a woman who would only be content with marriage, which he was constantly avoiding for fear of being tied down. So, he loved her one minute and hated her the next because she was forcing him to make a decision he wanted to put off indefinitely. Ireland and Maggie had been one and the same thing, he supposed. He hadn't been able to commit to either, and he would most likely be unable to commit now.

Joan was surprised when she heard him enter through the back door. "What are you doing out in this weather? You must be soaked."

"No. I'm grand. I borrowed Rory's waterproofs."

"Come on in then so and sit down while I put the kettle on. Rory was asking for you. I told him you were upstairs resting."

"I'll go in and see him after I've had the cup of tea."

Hugh lit the fire and stood with his back to it.

Joan brought a tray with tea, cake, and sandwiches. He remembered what it was like when his mother was alive. They never stopped eating, but for some reason never put on weight. Only the old man got stout, no doubt the result of too much beer and whiskey.

"Are you getting used to being home, Hugh?" said Joan, handing him a cup of tea and a plate with a sandwich on it.

Hugh had the feeling that Joan was being more affable. Was she having second thoughts about her accusations? "It's not easy, Joan. It's hard to bridge the gap."

"What do you mean?"

"Between what I was and what I am now, between life then and life now, between youth and old age. Some of the links seem to be missing."

"But you were born and bred here, Hugh. This is your home. And you are still the same as you always were. Things may have changed but you haven't."

"That's the thing, Joan. I have. You can't live in a country for fifty years and not be affected by it. Despite the ould brogue, the Australians have never treated me as a foreigner. They welcomed me with open arms into their home. Though I may never feel one hundred percent Australian, I've learnt to love and respect their culture."

"I always thought the Australians didn't have a culture."

Hugh laughed. "You'd be surprised, Joan. They may be a young nation, but they have developed a distinct character and culture of their own. And being a nation of immigrants, they are tolerant and friendly."

Joan looked sceptically at him over the top of her teacup. "I've never heard you singing the praises of the Australians before. I always thought you were rather disparaging."

"Well, I've had more time to think since Sheila died. Thinking is not always a good thing. It's possibly best to just get on with life. But a reckoning has to be made at some time so that you can depart feeling you've got things straight in your head."

"Well, have you?"

"It's an ongoing process," said Hugh ambiguously, borrowing a noncommittal phrase from some local politician.

"I see," said Joan, visibly disappointed, as if she should have known better than to expect a straight answer from Hugh. "So, are you going out with Maggie tomorrow?"

She made it sound like a date. "I'm thinking about it. As long as Rory is okay."

"Don't worry about him. You go out and have fun. I'll manage."

He couldn't stand it when Joan acted the martyr, especially as it was a role she had taken on voluntarily. Or was he being too hard on her? Had it been forced upon her by circumstances? She had always regretted not qualifying as a nurse but had ended up being a nurse in one way or another most of her life.

Life is so complicated, he thought. *You want one thing and end up doing another, and it may be what you wanted to do all along.*

"Do you like the cake, Hugh?"

"Lovely, Joan."

"I made it especially. Mam used to make it because she knew you liked it."

"You mean she made it just for me?"

"Mainly for you. She wanted to spoil you in the hope you wouldn't go away."

"But it didn't work."

"No."

"And are you trying to do the same?"

"I can only try," she said with a smile. "But I know from past experience it probably won't do much good."

"I'll bring in some tea and cake to Rory."

"That would be kind of you, Hugh."

She handed him the cake and tea, and he went into the parlour where Rory was dozing raucously. Looking at him lying there, propped up against two cushions, Hugh thought he looked like a whale he had once seen washed up on the sand near Rosslare harbour. It was still alive, panting urgently, desperately trying to draw air into its deflated lungs. It was destined to die as Rory was. There was no dragging him back out to sea, no more diving through the waves. He was beached for good. All that remained was the "Break, break, break" of the undying sea. Hugh could hear the bustle of the waves ending their short life in a hectic race to the shore. Break, break, break.

Possibly Rory wasn't fully asleep, for as soon as Hugh sat down, his eyes shuddered open. It took him some time to take in his surroundings. Hugh wondered where he had been in his dreams. Was he a young man again, out courting Josie? Was he cowering from the old man's abuse? Were they all together, as a family, on a day trip to the sea or the Galtee Mountains?

"I've brought you a cup of tea, Rory. And some of Mam's sponge cake."

"Joan is pulling out all the stops, I see. She may tempt you to stay yet."

"She has a hard job on her hands."

"There's a lot to be said for Connick, Hugh. And this is your home, after all."

"The thing is, Rory, I'm not sure it is anymore."

"Where does your heart lie, Hugh boy? That's the question you have to ask yourself. Who knows, you might hook up with Maggie again."

"I don't think so. That was over long ago, before it even started, in fact."

"What do you mean?"

"It was just a flirt with Maggie. Sure, you know that yourself."

"Not for Maggie it wasn't. She was inconsolable when you left."

"Histrionics, Rory, no more."

"No. It was genuine. I should know."

"How's that?"

Rory hesitated before answering but then charged ahead, as if it didn't really matter anymore or perhaps because it was time for things to come out into the open. "I offered myself in your place." He said it without any attempt to soften the blow, but Hugh could tell by the circumspect look in his eyes that he was unsure what reaction he would get.

"You what?"

"I asked her to marry me, seeing as how you weren't going to have her. I thought she might take me, as a sort of consolation prize, like, you know?"

Hugh's initial reaction was astonishment, which turned almost instantly into mirth. "And what did she say?"

"That no one could replace you. You were the only one she would ever truly love. That's what she said."

"Ah, sure they all say that. But it doesn't take long for them to find someone else."

"You may be right, Hugh, but she was well and truly knocked about when you left."

It took Hugh some time to take in what Rory had done. Did he honestly believe she would accept? Had he just asked her on the off chance? "So, how long were you going out?"

"For about a year."

"But she married Tom only a couple of years after I left."

"It was before you two got together. I took her to the show bands up at the dancehall."

Hugh was even more astounded by this piece of information. "You mean you were going together before me?"

"I thought you knew."

"What, when I was doing that Mickey Mouse course in agriculture down in Limerick?"

"You were away for nearly a year. When you came back, she couldn't stop talking about you. Just the mention of your name would send her all googly."

"All googly?"

"You know, all starry-eyed. It wasn't difficult to understand that I'd lost her to you."

"How come you never told me?"

"What was the point? Love is a mysterious thing. Well, not in this case. You were the big handsome man, the apple of everyone's eye. I was no better than a cripple beside you."

"I've never heard such nonsense in all my life. If you'd only told me, I'd never have gone near her."

"I thought you knew."

"How could I know? At one of the dances up at the hall, she was all over me. She was even flirting with me in front of you, and you never opened your mouth. Why didn't you say something? Weren't you angry? I'd have gone mad."

"Ah, no, Hugh. Disappointed maybe. I was very fond of her. She was a very attractive woman."

"Oh, she was that. Still is, in fact."

"She is all right. She's looked after herself. They say she gave ould Tom a bit of a runaround before she finally agreed to marry him."

"Sounds like Maggie. Look, Rory, I'm sorry if I took her off you. If I'd known…"

"What was there to know? We never did anything but snog behind the dancehall anyway. She was very good at that. Can I ask you something, Hugh, just out of curiosity, like? Don't take offence now. But did you ever go farther with her?"

Hugh wasn't sure whether to lie or not but decided there was no point anymore.

"There was a lot of foreplay all right, but she capitulated in the end."

Rory smiled. "That's the way it was then. Maybe it'll be easier this time round." He let out a saucy laugh that ended in a rasping cough.

Hugh was almost shocked by Rory's overt suggestions and was unsure how to respond. "It won't go far," he muttered, though he knew that it already had, in a way.

"So, she's taking you to the theatre group, I hear."

"Apparently."

"Well, there's not much competition there. The men are all fags."

"And mostly under fifty. What do you know about this guy Jerry?"

"Oh, Jerry McCoy. They call him Jerry the Real McCoy. Fancies himself as a comedian, but like all of them stand-up guys, no one laughs at his jokes, except himself. He's been putting on the same show for the last thirty years."

"I've never been much of a fan of stand-up. It tends to lack subtlety."

Though after eight, Hugh felt an urge to feel the mellow heat of the soft orange sun that was filtering through the trees in the garden. "It's still light outside. Shall I take you for a canter round the garden?"

"If you're strong enough to carry me on your back?"

"You're after getting awful lazy in your old age. Come on now. Get up out of that. You need the exercise."

Rory seemed even lighter than the last time he held him. Even his ribs seemed sharper and more prominent. They shuffled slowly out the back door and on to what used to be the lawn but was now an expanse of rank overgrown grass and weeds.

"Tomorrow I'm going to cut the lawn and paint that gate below," said Hugh with resolve.

"Joan would like that."

"By the way, the bungalow looks empty. Is there no one living in it?"

"No, we just boarded it up."

"That's a pity. Surely you could get some rent out of it."

"It's more trouble than it's worth. When they leave, you spend as much on repairs as you got on rent money."

The light rain had given way to striated cloud, shattered by the fiery rays of the setting sun. *Ireland*, Hugh thought, *always changing. Drizzle one minute, bright sunshine the next.*

As they walked round the garden, Rory pointed to trees they had played under as children. Hugh remembered the tree house they had built in the crown of an old ash, how they had scoured the farm for old bits of wood and nails. They had had some good times in there, proud of their rough-and-ready castle in the sky.

Rory had made a rope ladder that was nearly impossible to climb and was used more as a swing than a ladder. The tree house had never been particularly sturdy and one windy night it ended up a heap of tangled boards on the ground. They never rebuilt it.

One part of the garden was cut off from the rest, a hollow surrounded by five ash trees arranged symmetrically in a circle. The old man had said they had been planted by their great-grandfather, but Hugh had always liked to believe it was a place where sacred rituals took place or an outdoor senate chamber where the Little People assembled on starry nights to discuss Little People affairs. There was something deeply spiritual about it, and the well shaft formed by the trees indicated a direct and unimpeded pathway to the heavens above. They sat there in silence for a while, on a roughly-hewn granite gatepost that had been placed there for the odd soul who wished to imbibe the serenity and tranquillity of the secluded spot.

After about twenty minutes, Hugh felt that Rory was beginning to sag, his legs no longer able to support his body. Hugh decided it was time to steer him back in the direction of the house.

Rory heaved a sigh of relief when he was once more by the fire in the kitchen.

They had a light supper of cold meat and salad. Rory nibbled at a piece of cheese and a slice of cucumber. The television was turned on, which put paid to any conversation. There was nothing on that was of any particular interest to anyone, but the sound and fitful movement emanating from the box were enough to lull them into a semisomnolent state, as they stared blankly at the flashing screen.

Hugh wondered whether it was ever going to be possible to talk to Rory about the nonexistent loan. Yet, he would have to at some point. He was the only one who could resolve the matter and prevent a permanent rift between himself and Joan.

■

The following day, after helping Rory with his ablutions and making him comfortable by the fire, Hugh decided to devote himself to jobs that needed doing around the yard. He started with the grass. After a great deal of cursing and swearing, his arm nearly pulled out of its socket by the starter rope, the mowing machine spluttered into life. However, mowing the rank grass was not easy. It took ages to whittle down the tangled mass of uncut silage. In the end, it only looked marginally better than before and, if it were not cut again soon, it would quickly revert to its primal state.

Painting the gate was easier but took a great deal longer. He had to sandpaper all the rust off and then bring the paint back to life with white spirit and elbow grease. As he settled down to the job, he found that he quite enjoyed it. It was something he would never have done back in Esperance. He would have got one of the lads to do it. Yet, he quite liked being immersed in such a simple and fulfilling task.

A number of cars passed but he didn't look up. He knew he would know none of the drivers now. Many were townies, who fancied a rural life but were not part of the old community. Some of the drivers clearly expected to see Rory and beeped their horn at him. When Hugh did look up, many waved, perhaps guessing he was Rory's brother home on holiday.

At one point, a tractor stopped and an elderly man got off. He had a red bloodshot face and a cap perched almost vertically on the crown of his head, his dazzling white pate in stark contrast to his blazing cheeks. Hugh thought there was something vaguely familiar about the round face and lively green eyes.

"Is it yourself, Hugh? Or are me eyes playing tricks on me?"

Hugh had no idea who this old man was, but he laid down his brush temporarily and got up to greet the stranger.

"Am I that changed, Hugh? Joe Brady. Do you not remember me?"

Joe Brady, my god! So this grey old man was a contemporary. "Joe, it's good to see you. How's the form?"

"Not too bad. Trying to save the bit of ould hay for the winter. You'd get a day of drying and then the rain'd come just as you were ready to bale it. Australia is treating you well by the looks of it."

"You haven't retired yet, I see, Joe."

"You must be joking. I have no sons to take over from me. Four girls and not a one of them married to a farmer. Unless I get shot of the place and head off to the Bahamas, I'll be working until the day I don't get up in the morning. Did one of your boys take over your place?"

"No, but I have a good lad looking after it."

"You're lucky then so. If I paid a man to look after my place, he'd take all I make. Farm workers get paid a whole heap of money these days. It's almost better than having a farm of your own. No risks. Protected by the state. Sure, there's no incentive these days to be a farmer."

Hugh looked at this old man and realised that he must look just as old. Yet, inside they were still young men.

"How's the brother?"

"Not so good, Joe, but he's hanging in there."

"We're all praying for him in the townland. He's a good lad, the best neighbour anyone could have. There was many a time he helped me out above and never asked for a shillin' piece in return."

"He has a good heart all right. One of the best."

"Well, I'd better be on me way. Will you be around for a bit?"

"It's hard to tell, but I'll be here for a while longer anyway."

"I understand. I understand. All the best then so."

Hugh had vague recollections of Joe Brady. He'd been a quiet boy, always bottom of the class, if he remembered correctly. They had never been best buddies, but he and Mat used to often pass through the Brady farm on their rounds of the townland. He remembered their dairy and the churning of the milk and the slabs of yellow butter lined up on the bench ready to be wrapped in grease-proof butter paper.

■

Slowly, Hugh was getting settled in to a routine on the farm. His presence there made it possible for Joan to do things she hadn't done for some time. She was able to devote herself more to the house, which had been neglected, so she said, and make cakes and buns, which had always been her favourite pastime. Joan also took advantage of Hugh's presence to go into town to one of the large supermarkets and do a "big shop."

However, Hugh could see they were becoming dependent on him. Rory and he made the trip to the bathroom down the corridor at least five times a day. Without his help, Joan would have had to manoeuvre the potty under him and clean up any mess or spillage afterwards. Although Joan was used to washing him, she was happy to hand this job over to Hugh.

Maggie had rung the previous night to confirm their outing to the theatre. Though he had had his doubts, he decided to go, as much to get some respite from the claustrophobia of the house as anything else. She had asked if he could pick her up in Joan's car, as she didn't like driving at night. Joan had no objection. So, it was agreed that that's what they would do.

It was a dull day outside. The sky was covered in a thick blanket of grey cloud. He had no desire to go out, and he had decided he wasn't going to force Rory to go for a walk either. Instead, he perused the cluttered library shelf and the motley collection of books that had accumulated over the years. He found books, now tattered and moth-eaten, that he had read as a teenager, Hardy, Thackeray, and Trollope, not to mention all the encyclopaedias that dated back to the early twentieth century, from which he learnt far more than he ever learnt at school. He assumed they must have been bought in a car boot sale, or its equivalent, to impress visitors who might marvel at the scholarliness of the Gormans.

Hugh had intended to take advantage of Joan's absence to ask Rory about the supposed loan he had received, but when Rory woke up after his nap, he was clearly in no state to discuss matters that might cause stress. He was in pain and was having difficulty breathing. Hugh offered to hook him up to the ventilator, but he pushed it away.

"Hugh, my time has come…The angels are beckoning to me… It's not that I mind…It's the waiting I can't stand." Rory spoke in gasping mini-bytes, pausing after each to get his breath back.

"There's always hope, Rory," said Hugh, knowing that in his case it was hardly true. He didn't believe in miracles any more than he believed in God and the angels.

"I'm a gonner…and I don't want you to pretend otherwise…I can take the truth…I just wish it would end…"

Rory's voice was so weak Hugh had to lean in to hear him. "Shall I get O'Malley to come out?"

"Only if he's going to finish me off…"

"He can't do that, Rory. Medical ethics."

"Fuck medical ethics…I'll sign a piece of paper…if that's what he wants."

"It can't be done, but he did promise to ease your pain. I'll give him a shout and get him to come out in the morning."

"Good lad, Hugh."

Hugh knew that Rory would like him to be by his side at all times. His presence was a comfort to him. Should he postpone the outing?

"I'm going out with Maggie tonight. Will you be all right without me?"

Rory etched a smile on his emaciated face. "I won't stand in your way."

"You never did, did you?"

"You have a good time, boy, and don't hurry home."

Hugh smiled. He would always be "boy" for Rory.

"Will you be all right alone with Joan?"

"I'll be grand, Hugh…She don't stand for no-nonsense…but she's a real trooper at heart."

"Oh, she is that. Can I get you something before I go?"

"A strong cup of tea…with oceans of milk and sugar…"

Though he didn't want to admit it to himself, he would be relieved when Rory was out of his misery. What was the point in dragging out life when death was inevitable? He thought of his grandfather Brendan, who died in his sleep at the age of eighty-four. What a perfect way to go?

■

Hugh was strangely apprehensive as he got into the car. It was almost like a first date. He had considered cancelling his outing with Maggie, but he didn't want to disappoint her. In the back of his mind, he wanted to make up for his heartlessness fifty years ago. It was the price he would have to pay that worried him. What would she demand of him? How was she going to get her money back, so to speak? Was she really interested in having sex with him? What if he were unable to carry out the deed? Her whole image of him would be shattered forever.

But why did he care? Yet, he did somehow. It was something that had been left undone, and he hated unfinished business. But would it be the end or just the beginning? He was too old to be the "boyfriend," even if it was just one of Maggie's little jokes. He also had the feeling that he was too old to start something new, albeit the resumption of something old and, for Maggie at least, something that had never ended.

She was waiting at the foot of the steps of her impressive modern bungalow. Its large bay windows looked out on to an immaculately kept garden with rose beds full of all colours and hues. Bluish-red hydrangeas in full bloom created a magnificent array of colour all around the spotlessly painted house. Tom Kehoe must have made a fair packet, he concluded. Well, he knew all about secondhand car dealers. They rip off both the seller and the buyer by buying cheap and selling dear.

For a woman of seventy, Maggie looked stunning, he had to admit. She was wearing a yellow chiffon dress and high-heeled light-green shoes with a beige cardigan draped over her elegantly angled shoulders. She was heavily made up, but it was hard to tell. At a distance, she could have passed for a woman at least twenty years her junior. She must have spent hours subtly applying the dark eye shadow to bring out the green of her mesmerising eyes. *Any man*, thought Hugh, *will be proud to have her on his arm.*

"Just like old times," she said, smiling through the open window of the car.

"I don't remember ever picking you up in a Toyota Yaris."

"No. You just picked me up," she said with a playful chuckle. She got into the car and began to scrutinise him. "Let me have a look at you." After a few seconds, she said, "You'll do, though that shirt is a little on the dowdy side. Did Sheila not tog you out more fashionably? I want you looking like one of the jet set. Otherwise, how am I going to impress the crowd at the theatre?"

Hugh wished she hadn't mentioned Sheila, especially in a way that implied criticism. He reserved memories of his wife for private moments, when he could feel her beside him and imagine her interacting with his thoughts. She may have been a tough Aussie, but she was a wise woman and could be tender and loving when the occasion called for it. She had also been a good mother, though what went wrong with Brendan's upbringing they were never quite sure. Hugh just put it down to genes. He had taken after the old man, even if they were half a world apart and almost total strangers to each other.

On the way into town, Hugh asked about her children. She too had all sons, all successful. He wouldn't have expected otherwise. Nothing less than a professional would have satisfied Maggie. And they were all professionals—a lawyer, a doctor, and a vet, all working down in Cork.

"How come you don't live near them, Maggie?"

"Ah, sure they're all too busy to be bothered with me. I go down every three weeks or so and stay for a few days. When I think they've had enough of me, I come back to Connick to be near Deirdre when she's over. To be honest with you, Hugh, I never liked Cork. I know Tom was from there, but I always felt an outsider. The Cork people are not like us. I'm sure you know what I mean."

"Oh, I do, all right. I had thought about coming home once, even put out a few feelers. I'd been out there for a few years and had a desperate yearning for home. I thought I'd never be able to get used to life in Australia, but I knew Sheila wouldn't have been happy in Ireland, knowing nobody, trying to adapt to a new country and a new life."

"But that's what you did."

"It was easier for me. I chose to leave Ireland. Anyway, it would have been foolish to return. It would have meant starting from scratch, getting a loan to buy a place, if such a thing were possible. So I decided I couldn't inflict that uncertainty on her. But there was something else too, I think." Hugh hesitated because he had never expressed this before.

Maggie looked keenly at him expecting a revelation. "What's that?"

"I was afraid of what I'd become if I came back."

"What do you mean?"

'That I might revert to old habits."

"You weren't any different from all the other young men of the time."

"Still, I didn't trust myself. In Australia, I was able to deny my past. I didn't have to live it down. I was able to be a new man, a much better man than I had been."

"That's not true, Hugh. You're being too hard on yourself."

"No, Maggie. I was heavily into the drink, and it was only a matter of time before I became like the old man."

"Your Da was a lovely man, Hugh. The ould drink got a hold of him. That's all."

"Exactly."

"But you were different people. You had your mother's strength, her self-restraint."

"The truth is, as much as one would like to deny a connection to one parent or the other, we inevitably have a bit of both."

"True enough."

Hugh looked out across the undulating landscape, animals grazing contentedly in miniature fields, the hedges and ditches thick with vegetation. The longer he stayed, the more familiar it became; and the more familiar it became, the more it tugged at his heartstrings. He knew very well that he could sink back into Ireland as easily as he had slunk out of it. And the beauty of it was he could be virtually anonymous, living the life he had always wanted, free of worries and responsibilities.

It would have been quite impossible when Sheila was alive, but now he couldn't help feeling there was something appealing about it. Yet, after a lifetime of short-lived whims that were never allowed to come to fruition, he knew he had to be careful, especially now that Sheila was not there to draw in the reins and stop him from galloping off into the sunset. And the Irish sunset was one you could easily gallop off into—on a winged horse that led to a fairy-tale future, to *Tír na Nóg*, the Land of Eternal Youth. He chuckled to himself. His unbridled hankering after the unfamiliar often took him off in dangerous directions.

"What are you so amused about?" she said, noticing the dimples erupting on his chin.

"Oh, I was just thinking how easy it is to be led astray by the fugitive lurking within us, telling us to go in search of a dream. We're never content with what we have, always on the run, looking for something new, in the false belief that it will somehow be better than what we already have."

"Now what made you think of that, Hugh?"

"The thought that I might be happier living in Ireland."

"By the time I'm finished with you, Australia will be purged forever from your heart and mind."

"I wish it were that easy. I have children, grandchildren, not to mention a sheep station to run."

"So you intend to work till you drop, is that it?"

"I can think of a lot worse things to do."

"Well, I can think of a lot better. More time for yourself, reading, gardening meeting people…"

"The reading and the gardening are fine. It's meeting people I could do without."

"I didn't realise you were such a recluse, Hugh Gorman."

He was not a total recluse. He liked being in select company, but he knew he didn't need people like others did. "I'm happy enough communicating with myself. Not that I'm totally antisocial. I'm as happy as the next man to have a convivial chat, but a whole evening exchanging stale news and mundanities is something I can do without."

"I know your type. The worst kind of husband for a woman who needs a companion she can open up her heart to. Poor Sheila!"

He laughed self-consciously. He knew there was a lot of truth in what she said. Had he been a bad husband? Would Sheila have wanted him to be more communicative? More attentive?

"You're too self-sufficient. That's the trouble with you, Gorman. You don't need people."

Hugh wondered whether this was true and realised that in part it was. Yet, he knew he would go mad in total isolation. Since Sheila passed, he had felt lonely, especially in the evening at the time when they would watch the news and an episode from some series or other. It was not so much because he had no one to talk to. Their conversations had never been particularly scintillating. It was her presence he missed; the sharing of common space, her rowdy existence in the bed next to him—she snored more loudly than she would ever admit—her energetic fussing around the house, the sure knowledge that she was working in the vegetable patch at the back of the house, her quiet concern for his needs; she never pampered him, but after so many years of marriage, they knew what each needed from the other.

The town hadn't changed all that much. Apparently, it was now full of migrant workers from Eastern Europe. According to Rory, you were as likely to hear Polish or Romanian spoken in the supermarkets as you were English. It was no longer the parochial market town it had been. Was this a good or a bad thing? Probably good. It was inevitable really. He believed in a multicultural, multiracial society, like Australia in many ways, as long as everyone was tolerant of each other's idiosyncrasies, religious habits, and dress codes.

He didn't like uniformity. Difference was good. Much better, at any rate, than pretending to be the same in public while remaining different behind closed doors. He had employed men from all parts of the world on his station, and he couldn't say that one nation or race was any better or worse than the other. On the whole, he believed that if you treated a man decently, then he'd probably respond in kind. There were exceptions of course, like

Nicky McGuire, who ran off without repaying a hefty loan he'd given him to open a garage on the outskirts of Esperance.

Maggie showed him her favourite place to park, on a side street just down from the theatre. It was only when he got out of the car and was walking towards the main street that he began to get cold feet. "I don't know whether this is such a good idea, Maggie. How about I go for a long walk around town and come and pick you up later?"

As expected, she gave him a tender belt on the arm. "There's no chickening out now, young man. You're not going to spoil my hour of glory. Look, they're not such a bad crowd. They're theatre people—open-minded and kindhearted, who adore a bit of hot gossip."

"So, that's what I am," said Hugh drily.

"As far as they're concerned, but not for me." She beamed enticingly at him; and for a moment, he thought he'd have no trouble diving in and basking in her translucent eyes.

"I just don't want to be a laughingstock, Maggie, pretending I'm something that I'm not."

She threaded her arm through the crook of his. "You're talking like an old man."

"Most people think I am."

"Let them think what they like. Sure, I knew an ould fella once that got married at eighty-five to a young one of thirty-six."

"Poor woman!"

"And they had a child together too."

"Poor child!"

"Well, she was devastated when he passed away at ninety-two."

"And the child?'

"No doubt he was too."

Had she deliberately misunderstood his question?

Hugh had forgotten what an elegant building the theatre was, a remnant of Victorian England or a nostalgic reminder of it, with its portalled entrance and faux Grecian columns. He wondered whether the quality of the performances merited its grandiose façade. But did it matter? It may not have been the Gate or the Abbey, but it no doubt drew the local crowds. He remembered as a child seeing some great "pantos" there, the rousing music, the slightly off-key singers, the extravagant costumes, the ham actors, and slapstick humour. They were amateur productions, but the energy and enthusiasm of the actors made up for their lack of professionalism.

He could hear raucous laughter from within. He wondered whether it was forced or genuine. He remembered from his brief sojourn at the college in Limerick that the theatre crowd were always the loudest, and phoniest, at least so he thought at the time.

They all turned when Maggie and Hugh entered side by side. There were kisses and hugs all round. Then, their attention turned to him, the highlight of the evening. He hated being under scrutiny, especially now that his physical flaws were all too obvious. But the ground was unlikely to swallow him up, and it was too late to beat a hasty retreat. So, he'd have to grin and bear it.

Hands darted out in front of him. He didn't know which one to take first. So, he took the one closest, not altogether sure which face it corresponded to, the bright unadorned girl in her twenties with the tousled mousy hair, the dark Italian type with a receding hairline, or the man with the whiskers and curly salt-and-pepper mop? They looked like a friendly crowd anyway.

While the hand-shaking was in progress, out of the corner of his eye, Hugh noticed an overdressed man in his midsixties kiss Maggie three times, twice on one cheek, once on the other, two over the odds, in true continental style, and rather too passionately, he thought, but actors were like that. It must have been the man himself, Jerry "The Real" McCoy. He still had one arm over her shoulder when he greeted Hugh with an overcrowded mouth of yellowing teeth, reminiscent of Lucky Luke's horse, Jolly Jumper, and his crooked grin.

"So you're the Danny Boy from down under we've been hearing so much about," he said with a surprisingly good imitation of an Aussie accent, something he himself had never acquired, despite a half-century in the land. "Over for a bit of a holiday, are we?"

"Well, I'd hardly call it that. My brother is dying."

The masquerade of a grin receded slightly. "Sorry to hear that, mate." He had forgotten to revert to his Irish accent.

Hugh immediately regretted mentioning his brother's condition, especially as he was still clinging to the hope that Rory might recover. Stating that he was on his deathbed was an inauspicious presumption, playing into the hands of fate.

"Well, that's life, I suppose, Hugh. We've got to make the most of it while we can."

Hugh didn't respond. Probably this Jerry character was not as outlandish as he looked, with his pink shirt, red-spotted bow tie, and rubicund cheeks. To crown it all, he was wearing a black-and-white striped jacket that made him look like an oversized golliwog. *Why do some people want to be stereotypes?* he wondered. *To be recognised for the buffoons they are?* He was obviously your typical actor who had failed to make it in the big city and was now inflicting himself on a less critical small-town audience.

Having had these thoughts about the man, Hugh reprimanded himself. He knew he had a tendency to prejudge people, though his gut instincts were more often than not correct. Was it possible that he saw Jerry as a rival? Surely he wasn't jealous. He certainly had no right to be.

"You're in for a great treat tonight, Hugh. In honour of your presence, Maggie is going to sing 'Danny Boy' for us. Aren't you, Maggie?"

Maggie gave Jerry a reproachful look. It was obviously something they had not fully agreed on. "Oh, I don't think Hugh would want that. He's probably fed up of hearing it."

"He hasn't heard it sung by you, our resident songbird, the Maria Callas of Connick. If that doesn't melt your heart, Hugh, nothing will."

"I'd love to hear Maggie sing but—"

"No buts. I'll tinkle along on the piano just to help her out. First, though, we have to rehearse our play. We have an audience to stun in a matter of weeks. So, chop, chop, everyone. Get into role, please. Act one, scene one. Maggie, how are we on lines?"

"I'll be fine with a little prompting."

"Tut, tut, I want you all to be word perfect by next week. Now, Maggie, tear yourself away from your beau from down under and embrace *The Beau Defeated*." That said, he rushed off in the direction of the auditorium in a flurry of flailing arms.

"What in God's name was he talking about?" said Hugh.

"That's the play we're doing. *The Beau Defeated* by Mary Pix."

"I've never heard of it."

"Neither had I till Jerry dug it up from somewhere. It's a massive cast, as you will see, but it's a great laugh. A Restoration comedy, written by a woman."

"Really?"

"Which is probably why it never became as well-known as those written by men."

Hugh smiled. This was the first time Maggie had revealed her feministic side, which he found at odds with the impression he had always had of her, the staunch spouse catering to her husband's needs.

She led Hugh into the murky theatre, which reeked of old wood and stale air, bringing to mind a cobwebbed attic, inhabited by bats and pigeons that slid in under the roof tiles. People were creeping around like ghosts in the shadows of the auditorium, which he found unnerving. The stage lights were on, but dimmed. Bits of furniture, in Louis XV style, were scattered around the stage in what was clearly a rudimentary set.

"Don't mind Jerry, Hugh. He can be a bit obnoxious at times, but he has a good heart."

"I'm sure," said Hugh, not altogether falsely.

"I'd better be going. I'm in the first scene."

Then, she did something he hadn't anticipated. She took his hands and drew them to her chest. He looked around, hoping this intimate act had not been observed. Yet, he had the distinct feeling that a multitude of prurient eyes were peering at them out of the darkness. He had never been a romantic man, and this act, which he considered not altogether appropriate for people of their age, embarrassed him. Fortunately, it was too dark for her to see the heightened colour of his cheeks or the uneasy contraction of his forehead.

"Now, don't expect too much. We're only amateurs, you know."

Looking into her timorous eyes, which flitted and fluttered like a bird unsure of the giant creature gazing at it, he forgot for a moment that she wasn't the Maggie he had loved fifty years ago. He felt the same urge to throw his arms about her and promise to always take care of her. Yet, he held back, as he had then, as if to surrender to her would be like parting with his very soul. "I have no doubt it'll be much better than anything I've seen done by the am dram group in Esperance," he said mechanically.

"I wouldn't count on it. If you find it too painful, I'll understand if you want to go for that walk." She let go of his hands, grudgingly, and took two steps towards the backstage door. Turning again, she gave him a timid rotating wave, as if wiping the dew off the side window of a car. It reminded him of how she used to say goodbye to him before she set off across the fields, how she would linger, blowing kisses at him—raspberries she called them—issuing from her lips like an endless stream of fluttering butterflies. "See you later, Alligator." "In a while, Crocodile."

How innocent and childish it all was, he thought. The lessons of life had still to be learnt. Nevertheless, it was not a part of his life that he would have wished to bypass, despite all the uncertainty and frustration that he had to go through before making his decision to emigrate.

He took a seat near the back of the theatre. He didn't want to be too conspicuous. He could slip out unnoticed, if the play turned out to be too dreadful. He knew all about sitting through abominable amateur productions. Although not much involved in the theatre herself, Sheila liked to support those of her friends who were and she never liked to go alone, which was why he had had to endure them with her. He would often fall asleep in the middle or just close his eyes to shut out the embarrassment he was sure the actors must be feeling. The worst part of it was having to go backstage afterwards and congratulate them on their "superb" performance. He hated being hypocritical. So, he just smiled and shook their hand wordlessly, though they probably guessed he didn't think much of their shoddy production.

Without Sheila, he swore he would never put himself through it again. He had never been much into theatre, though they would always go and see an Irish company perform whenever it came to town. That was different. They were professionals. Sheila and he had enjoyed plays by Brendan Behan, John B. Keane, Sean O'Casey, and many others. For Hugh, it was like a dip in a mountain lake, freezing at first but good when you got into it. Yet, it always left him with a feeling of estrangement. The sights and sounds of Australia seemed almost alien to him and for some time afterwards he felt as if he were in limbo, like a spirit wandering between two worlds, neither of which he felt totally at home in.

Maggie appeared on stage in what he assumed was a seventeenth-century costume made of ornate silky material, which boosted her bust and buoyed her behind. On her head, she was balancing a blond wig that resembled a small beehive, which gave her a haughty, conceited air. When she spoke, it didn't sound like Maggie McQuilty at all, more like Maggie Smith, with a high-pitched pseudo-upper-class English accent—a total transformation.

While Mrs. Rich (Maggie) was overdressed, Betty (the servant) was underdressed, with bare arms and an expansive cleavage. The dialogue was fast and witty and it soon became evident that Betty was the hero of the day with her incisive humour and apposite digs at the absurdity of the social mores of the time. Mrs. Rich, on the other hand, was the ambitious, conceited upstart, intent on acquiring social status by marrying a titled gentleman, despite her advanced years. Hugh found himself laughing out loud at the repartee between the witty Betty and the obsessed Mrs. Rich, rendered beautifully by both actors. He tried to commit some of the lines to memory.

> MRS. RICH: I quarrel daily with my destiny, that I was not at first a woman of quality.

> BETTY: Well, well, madam, you have no great reason to complain. You are at least very rich, and you know that with money, you may buy quality. But birth very often brings no estate.

> MRS. RICH: That's nothing. There is something
> very charming in quality and a great name.

As he listened to the dialogue, Hugh couldn't help thinking how little things had changed since the play was written over three centuries before. Money could still buy status. With enough of it, along with a healthy amount of diplomatic chicanery, you could even become president of the United States.

By about 9:30, everybody, particularly the older actors, was beginning to tire. Maggie, on the other hand, was in her element, drawing energy from the dramatic tension. She was a natural, Hugh concluded. How different he and she were. He couldn't help thinking that life with her would have been a nightmare—parties, social gatherings, golf even, God forbid. She wouldn't have been happy without people around her.

"All right, darlings. Let's call it a night," said Jerry, springing up from his seat near the stage. "Wonderful, wonderful! The presence of our Australian friend seems to have inspired you all. Maybe we can persuade him to be a regular at our rehearsals."

Maggie peered into the darkness looking for Hugh in the gloom at the back of the theatre.

Hugh waved back. "Great! Well done, everybody. Thoroughly entertaining."

"I hope you're not in a hurry, Hugh," said Jerry. "The highlight of the evening is still to come. All right, everyone, relinquish your costumes and let's gather in the auditorium for a glass of wine. Not Australian, I'm afraid, but the next best thing, French from the Loire valley."

Hugh emerged from the shadows and waited self-consciously near the front of the auditorium, while the actors appeared in dribs and drabs from backstage. Maggie was visibly rejuvenated, her face flushed with exhilaration.

"Well, what did you think?" she said. "Was it awful?"

He could tell she knew it wasn't. "It was brilliant. I had no idea you were such a good actress."

"You always underestimated me, Hugh Gorman," she said with a provocative smile. "Well, now you know I'm more than just a pretty face."

"I never thought that, Maggie," he retorted equivocally.

The lady who had played Betty, a buxom blonde wearing skintight jeans and a tight-fitting T-shirt in her early thirties, still the servant off stage, brought a tray of glasses and laid them on a table near the front. An older man, who had played Mrs. Rich's brother-in-law, opened the bottles of wine.

Jerry was first to be served. He took three glasses of wine and came over to where Hugh and Maggie were standing. "Isn't she wonderful?" said Jerry, beaming at his protagonist.

"She is indeed," said Hugh, wondering whether there was or had been anything between them. He lifted his glass in the air. "Well, here's to the success of the play."

"Have you ever trod the boards yourself, Hugh?"

"Oh god, no! I wouldn't be seen dead up there."

"It takes a bit of nerve all right. I lost mine a long time ago. I now just try and bring the best out in others."

"Don't mind him, Hugh. He's a brilliant actor. It's just that he's an even better director."

After a couple of glasses of wine, Jerry said, "Shall we, Maggie?"

Suddenly, she reverted to the bashful girl he had known, nervously chewing the inside of her lip. Was she having doubts about singing for him? Or was it the song itself?

"Ah, Jerry, I'm not sure Hugh wants to listen to me singing. He's already seen me make a fool of myself on stage," she added with a certain degree of false modesty.

False modesty was the order of the day, it appeared.

"Maggie, darling, I insist. You do a wonderful Danny Boy. Hugh will love it, won't you, Hugh?"

Hugh was stuck for words. "Of course…I'd…love to hear Maggie sing," he stuttered.

"Well, that's it then." He took her hand and drew her towards the stage.

Then, she halted, jerking herself free of Jerry's grip. "I'd prefer to just sing from here. I'd feel awful self-conscious up there on my own."

"You'll be with me, my dear."

"Still. I'd prefer to be down here," she said, literally and metaphorically putting her foot down.

"Suit yourself, love," he said with a sigh of resignation and, with surprising alacrity, hopped on to the stage and settled himself in front of the piano.

Maggie leant against the stage, her face eclipsed by the intensity of her concentration. Was she trying to recall the words? Or was she the actress getting into the mood of the song?

"Are you ready, love?" said Jerry, displaying his virtuosity by running his fingers skilfully over the keys.

"As ready as I'll ever be," said Maggie, taking a deep breath and turning her head slightly in Hugh's direction. She smiled wanly, as if to say, "Forgive me, but he insisted."

Jerry led her in to the first verse. "Oh, Danny boy, the pipes, the pipes are calling…" Her voice broke, and for a moment, Hugh wondered whether she would be able to carry on but he should have known Maggie better. She was not one to be easily beaten. She let out a few sharp puffs to expel the evil spirit from her lungs, paused for a moment to compose herself and then raised a hand to indicate that she ready to go from the top.

This time she dived into it with greater assurance. "The summer's gone, and all the roses falling. It's you, it's you must go and I must bide."

But he never came back when "the summer was in the meadow or when the valley was hushed and white with snow." He stayed away, perhaps afraid of the bewitching effect she might have on him.

"I'll be here in sunshine or in shadow, oh, Danny boy, oh Danny boy, I love you so!" Had she secretly been waiting for him? Despite marriage, children, and wealth?

No, don't flatter yourself, Hugh Gorman! You weren't worth it, and you know it, and no doubt she did too.

"But when ye come, and all the flowers are dying, if I am dead, as dead I well may be, you'll come and find the place where I am lying…"

He raised a hand to his face to hide his juddering lips. Fortunately, it was too dark for her or anyone else to see him wipe away the fugitive tear that ran helter-skelter down his cheek.

She was not dead. She was there standing in front of him singing with a clear, steady voice. Did she know or suspect the effect she was having on him? The guilt, the regret, neither of which he had been fully conscious of before, were welling up inside him, inundating his heart, nullifying the last fifty years of his life.

The audience burst into applause. She had put her heart and soul into, he knew. Yet, she had controlled her emotions far better than he had. Did the words mean the same to her as they did to him? Or was it just her way of getting back at him for his callous desertion all those years ago?

He didn't join the mill of people gathered around her. He would have plenty of time to congratulate her later. He needed time to recover his composure, to come to terms with how she had made him feel. He knew it was not Maggie alone that had triggered the eruption of sentiment. It was the thought that he had voluntarily sentenced himself to a life of exile without reprieve.

Yet, he knew at the back of his mind, like the lifer who has spent most of his life behind bars, what it feels like when you're finally let out on parole. Prison has become your home. Anything beyond its walls engenders feelings of alienation and insecurity.

After the crush of admirers had subsided, it was she who came to him. He was sitting with his chin resting on a bony fist, in a state of overstated composure. He was no longer reeling with emotion, but he was still feeling the aftermath of the tsunami that had washed over him. He had nearly drowned and was still grappling with the feeling of being alive.

"I'm sorry," she said, laying her hand on his shoulder. "Did it upset you?"

"Ah, no," he lied. "It's a very moving song. And you sang it beautifully."

"My voice isn't what it used to be, but I wanted to do my best for you."

"You did that all right," he said unable to hide a degree of tenderness. He felt a sudden impulse to take her hand and hold it. A discreet intimacy had insinuated itself between them, and he felt the need to express it. He stared at the thin sinewy hand dwarfed in his. It was the hand of an old person, indelibly tanned and covered in sunspots. Yet, it was still soft and very feminine.

Being attractive is important to her, he thought. She still wanted men to desire her. Or was it simply an unwillingness to give up on life?

She was so different from Sheila, who had sunk indifferently into old age. Then again, Sheila hadn't had to make an effort to keep him. She could count on his love. She knew that he would find her desirable no matter what, despite the ravages wrought by time. He had been faithful and would remain so until the end. What an easy relationship they had had. Too easy perhaps, mundane almost. They had not had to compete like other couples did, undermining each other's self-esteem in order to levy subservience. It had been an equal relationship. They had been a team, appreciating and applauding each other's merits, while at the same time tolerant of one another's weaknesses, which they had grown to accept in time.

"I think you're tired, Hugh. Shall we go?"

"You're the one who should be tired, Mrs. Rich. It seems that you have endless reserves of energy."

"The theatre does that for you. Still, it's getting late for us oldies."

Hugh looked up at her with an amused frown. She understood at once what he was implying.

"Okay. Even us young ones need sleep."

With some relief, Hugh said his goodbyes and wished them every success with the play. He needed space, to be able to breathe freely. He left Maggie still blushingly basking in praise. She was at home among these kind, openhearted people, who showered their affection on her with what seemed like wholehearted sincerity.

As he was waiting under the portals for Maggie to extricate herself, he was approached by Jerry "The Real" McCoy, who strode over to him with the confidence of a gunslinger in a '60s Western.

Oh god, Hugh thought. *There's going to be a showdown.* The conjectural rival lovers stood squarely facing one another, sizing each other up.

It was Hugh who backed off. He had never fought over a woman, and he wasn't about to start now. To come between Maggie and him was the last thing he wanted. If Jerry wanted exclusivity, he could have it. In many ways, it would release him from the status of hypothetical lover, and he could return without qualms or regret to his former state of solitary widower and erstwhile boyfriend.

"Thanks for coming tonight, Hugh," said Jerry in a surprisingly conciliatory manner.

Hugh was taken aback by the gentleness of his voice. He suddenly felt stupid for assuming that Jerry's intention was to duel with him.

"You made Maggie very happy."

Hugh smiled sheepishly.

"You were once a very important part of her life, I believe."

"When we were children, yes."

"I thought you were very close later too," he said bluntly, demanding confirmation or contradiction.

Hugh became wary again. He had prematurely let his guard down. Clearly, Jerry's concern went deeper than he let on. "I suppose you could say we were courting for a while."

"Could say?"

Hugh took exception to his interrogatory tone but decided for Maggie's sake not to overreact. "We were young. We messed around together for a while."

"That's one way of putting it, I suppose. Until you left for Australia?"

"Yes." Hugh had no idea where this conversation was leading, but it was making him feel very uncomfortable. He looked anxiously towards the door to hurry Maggie along.

"Maggie and I have become very close since her husband died. She's a lovely person and a born actress."

"Indeed," said Hugh, still unsure what this was all about.

"We have a very special relationship."

So that was it. "Look, Jerry, I have no intention of coming between you. In fact, I'll be going back to Australia shortly."

"Well, that's exactly the point, Hugh. She will be very upset if you allow your relationship with her to deepen and then you just shoot off back to Australia. Like the last time." The final phrase was uttered with poorly disguised censure.

So he knew everything. "Are you suggesting that I shouldn't see her again? I think that might upset her even more."

"All I'm saying is, be gentle. She may appear strong and resilient, but there is a fragile side to her that you may not be aware of."

Hugh resented the insinuation that he didn't know Maggie, especially by someone who was little better than a complete stranger. It was the implication that he didn't understand Maggie that riled him most. He had grown up with Maggie, for God's sake. He had watched her change from confident little girl who loved teasing boys into a sophisticated teenager who knew how to tease them too. What right had he to assume he knew her better than he did? "Look, if you two are having something, I'll keep my distance, but please spare the lecture. I know Maggie better than anyone."

"Are you sure?"

"Bloody sure!"

"Look, I'm sorry, Hugh. I know that you may consider this none of my business, and you'd be right to be angry, but I do love her, not as an '*amant*' but as a dear friend. I simply want to protect her. She is very easily led."

Hugh let out a wry guffaw. "I don't know who's being led here, Jerry. All I can say is, she's an adult and should know how to look after herself by now."

"Yeah, you're right. I'm sorry. Here let's shake on it." Jerry put out his hand, which Hugh regarded for some moments before finally taking.

Hugh didn't know what to say. So, Jerry's concern for her was selfless and his love too, it seemed. He felt he should apologise for his heated reaction to what turned out to be mere altruism, but his pride prevented him. Whatever his motives, Jerry should not have interfered.

Maggie appeared from between a huddle of actors. Neither of them had seen her coming. "So you two are having a natter. Has Hugh told you how much he liked the play, Jerry?"

"Absolutely!" he said with mock jollity. "And I was just about to tell him how we would appreciate his input at future rehearsals."

"I'll do my best to get him to come again, but he's a hard man to pin down and a bit of a hermit."

"Perhaps we'd better be going, Maggie," said Hugh. He'd had enough geniality for one night. "I don't want to be too late home."

"Okay, come on, so. Let's go." She took his arm, and they sauntered out into the dim-lit street. He had seldom seen the town at this hour. He was surprised by how lively it was, not just people standing outside pubs with a glass of beer and a cigarette. There were plenty just drinking coffee or sitting on benches chatting.

Hugh said nothing on the way to the car. He just let Maggie dispense the gossip she had gleaned backstage. It meant nothing to him, and he made no effort to understand who or what she was referring to.

"They seem like a nice crowd anyway," he said as they got into the car.

"You'd really like them, Hugh, if you got to know them. They've been like a family. I honestly think they'd do anything for me if I was in need."

Hugh manoeuvred out of the narrow streets and got on to the main road back to Connick.

"I don't know what to make of your man, though," he said, taking up the conversation from where they had left off some miles back.

She understood who he was referring to. "Oh, Jerry is a lovely man. A bit eccentric perhaps, but he has a heart of gold. He has been a great comfort to me."

"I got the feeling he was a bit overprotective. He was being awfully motherly, clucking around you as if you were a stray chicken. He said I should be careful not to hurt you. I more or less told him you were old enough to look after yourself."

Maggie stopped applying lipstick and flipped the mirror back into its socket behind the sun shield. "Did you really?" she said with a laugh. "What else did he say?"

"That you have a fragile side that I'm apparently not aware of."

"He did, did he? I daresay that set you off."

"Is there something that I should know, Maggie?" he said in a calmer tone.

She hesitated for a moment. "Ah, no. There are things I suppose I shouldn't have told him, things that may have affected my past but not my present."

"Like what?"

"It doesn't really matter, Hugh. Let's forget it."

"Well, if you can tell Jerry 'The Real' McCoy, surely you can tell me."

"I shouldn't have told him. I shouldn't have told anyone really. But sometimes you feel the need to unburden yourself and, well, he was there and willing to listen. That was some time ago now. The trouble is people form an opinion of you because of something that happened to you a long time ago, and they think that's how you still are. But we change, become stronger. We grow protective layers of skin."

Hugh thought of his own situation and realised that this was true, but he couldn't help being intrigued by the "past" that she didn't wish to share with him. He had assumed he knew everything there was to know about her. After all, they had met, albeit intermittently, in the fifty years of his life down under. He had imagined she lived a typical middle-class life, looking after a home, having children, being a good wife, and finally joining a theatre group to fill the void left by a dead husband. Yet, the truth was he had no idea about her life or what kind of relationship she'd had with Tom, whether she had been happy, frustrated, bored, or simply indifferent.

"Tell me, Maggie. Sure, you know me. I won't form a false opinion of you. I know you too well."

He winced even before the hand struck him. "You don't know me at all, Hugh Gorman. You've never understood me, and you never will. I'm still eight years old as far as you're concerned. The cheeky little one with the blond pigtails that pretended not to like boys. Whatever opinion you have of me, I'm sure it's miles from the truth."

"Maybe if you told me what this 'thing' is that you seem set on keeping a secret I may understand you better."

"No, I want you to see me as I am now, without any baggage from the past. What does the past matter anyway?"

He turned his head towards the current Maggie and wondered whether he could ever see her as she was now. The image of her as a twenty-year-old girl was etched in marble on his brain. As for the "baggage," he had no idea what she could be referring to and had no real desire to find out. What he did know was that you can never erase your past. It follows you around like a shadow, or more precisely a spectre, haunting your every attempt to renew yourself.

He turned left at the crossroads and took the narrow road that led to the hills and Connick village.

"I often wonder, Maggie, whether we change all that much. I sometimes think that what we acquire through life is nothing more than a veneer. I don't think I've changed a great deal. Matured maybe, but not changed. I'm still the layabout I was then, despite the trappings of success and the wisdom acquired through multiple mistakes. What about yourself?"

"Oh god, Hugh, I don't know. I gained some confidence with age, that's true, but there are times I find it hard to keep my spirits up, which is not helped by the relentless march of time over my poor ould declining body. Old age is a very cruel thing."

Hugh felt he was hearing the real Maggie for the first time. Her self-assured, almost arrogant air was, as he suspected, just a façade. He also understood the effort needed to keep it up—the personal trainer, the beautician, and the weekly visits to the hair salon, not to mention the constant endeavour to convince herself that life didn't end when she could no longer turn young men's heads. But far from despise her for it he admired her tenacity, her tireless clinging to the remnants of her splendour. This was what she believed defined her, her elegance, her stunning beauty. He would like to have told her that she was more than that, that she had a beautiful soul, which he had recognised from a very young age but had never got round to telling her, and probably never would.

They entered the village of Connick, which still consisted of no more than a dozen whitewashed cottages. The pub was exactly as it had always been, the same sooty yellow window frame that looked as if it had been painted with a spatula not a brush. A driver, lost in the hills, parched with the thirst, would never have suspected that behind that gloomy facade was a pub, unless he looked closely at the name above the glass front—O'Doherty's Public House—that had faded to near obscurity.

A supermarket and a petrol station had opened up to one side, with a fish and chip shop attached. *That is an improvement at least,* he thought. The grey church, where he had unwillingly attended mass on Sundays throughout his childhood, was unchanged. Still grey and uninviting. Why he had wanted to visit it again he was not sure. Perhaps for Rory's sake. His brother had always been a much more spiritual person than he had. Besides, he had reached that point in life when it's comforting to make believe there might be an afterlife, that he might actually be rejoined with Sheila in heaven.

Maggie's bungalow was about fifteen minutes beyond the village along narrow winding roads, the banks of which had been recently trimmed to allow two vehicles to squeeze past without damaging the paintwork. Her garden gate was open so he drove in, crunching over the white gravel as he swung round to the steps that led to her front door. He didn't switch off the engine.

Maggie didn't open the door to get out as he expected. "So, that's it then," she said with a sigh. "Our evening out ends here."

"I feel a bit guilty about leaving Joan alone with Rory," he said, more as an excuse than anything else. What was he afraid of? Hurting her again or being hurt himself?

"What could happen? They'll be fast asleep by now. Come on in. I've made us a light supper. I thought you'd be hungry. I promise I won't keep you long."

The truth was he was starving. They had left before tea, and he hadn't eaten anything since lunch. Another glass of wine wouldn't go astray either. It would help him sleep. He turned off the engine.

Inside, Maggie assumed the role of the polite hostess. She ushered him into the sitting room, and having made sure he was duly impressed by the interior, she turned to prepare dinner. "Be a darling and open the wine while I dress the salad."

Maggie's house was immaculate; heavy velvet curtains in a deep Bordeaux colour hung over the windows and a balcony door that most likely led into the garden at the back. The furniture, mostly mahogany, shone like polished gold. Framed photos of relations covered the top of every flat surface. He recognised some of the faces—her father and mother, Johnny and Jo, who had been like second parents to him as a child. Most of the younger people he didn't recognise but suspected they were her sons and Deirdre's daughter, Aisling, whom he had never met. It must have been an old photo. She couldn't have been more than twenty when it was taken. The resemblance to Maggie was quite astounding. He had to look twice to make sure it wasn't her. The eyes were exactly the same, those penetrating light-green eyes. The chin, though, was more prominent and the nose turning up slightly at the end. He wondered what age she was now and whether she had married and had children.

One-half of the table had been set for two. Maggie had rightly anticipated that he would accept her invitation to eat with her. The bottle of wine, wrapped in a Burgundy-coloured linen napkin, was sitting on an etched silver saucer. He extracted the cork and smelt the bouquet. Only the best for Maggie. He poured them both a glass and went into the kitchen to find her. Spotify was playing a '60s mix. Van Morrison was singing "Brown Eyed Girl." He smiled and began singing along.

Hey, where did we go?

Days when the rains came

Down in the hollow

Playin' a new game

Laughing and a running hey, hey

Skipping and a jumping

In the misty morning fog with

Our hearts a thumpin' and you

My brown-eyed girl

You, my brown-eyed girl.

Seeing that he was in a good mood, she joined in and it wasn't long before they were jiving around the kitchen floor. Hugh noted with awe how nifty she still was on her feet. Her personal trainer was doing a good job, no doubt about it.

Do you remember when we used to sing

Sha la la la la la la la la la la te da

Just like that

Sha la la la la la la la la la te da, la te da

So hard to find my way

Now that I'm all on my own

I saw you just the other day

My, how you have grown

Cast my memory back there, Lord

Sometimes I'm overcome thinking 'bout

Making love in the green grass

Behind the stadium with you

My brown-eyed girl

You, my brown-eyed girl

Do you remember when we used to sing

Sha la la la la la la la la la la la te da

By the end of it, they were both laughing their heads off and gasping for breath. "My god! That was good, Hugh Gorman. I haven't done that for fifty years. Tom had two left feet and as much rhythm as an ould sow. What about Sheila?'

"She tried doing a bit of *ceilidh* dancing, but she didn't stick at it."

"Here take these in." She handed him a quiche and a bowl of salad. "Put those on the table while I bring the bread and butter." He saw that it was a loaf of soda bread. He hadn't had it for years. Sheila complained that the soda gave the bread a bitter taste.

When they had put the food on the table, Hugh went to sit down but she stopped him. "Let's chill out first," she said, touching his arm with the tip of a finger. "I'm feeling all sparkly after that dance."

Hugh smiled at her use of the term "chill out." It seemed so juvenile but Maggie was like that, ageless, forever young at heart.

She took her glass and sat on the dark leather sofa. Hugh wondered whether she would think it too forward if he sat beside her, though he didn't want her to think he was being coy. After all, the dance had brought them close in every way.

"You don't have to sit half a mile away from me, Hugh. I won't bite. I might ravish you, but I think you're well capable of beating me off…if you want to, that is."

He laughed and edged closer to her along the slippery sofa.

"That's better. Tell me, Hugh. Were you ever unfaithful to Sheila?"

Hugh gave her a queer look. Trust Maggie not to mince her words. "What would you like me to say?"

"The truth, unless you don't want to spoil your saintly image."

"Is that how you see me? No, I never was. She was the only woman I ever went with, Maggie. I suppose in this day and age that would be considered something of an anomaly. I'm no saint, though, I assure you."

"Not the only woman, Hugh."

"Sorry?"

"There was one other woman."

He cast his mind back to remember an indiscretion but if there had been, how could she know about it? "Which other woman?"

"Me, Hugh!" she said, looking at him reproachfully.

"Well, I wasn't..."

"Oh god, Hugh, and I thought you had a good memory. Or were you so wrapped up in the idea of hightailing it out of Ireland that you didn't know what you were doing? Surely you remember the day we both lost our virginity. I did try to stop you. At least I made a show of trying to save my soul from eternal damnation. After all, I had been brought up a good Catholic girl. But I let you, because I thought, well, we were going to get married anyway."

Of course, he hadn't forgotten the first time they made love, had intercourse, that is. It seemed so natural, and despite her half-hearted protests, he knew she wanted him. Perhaps he never fully understood how much it meant to her. He was not indifferent himself, but other things took precedence. Those weeks and months before he left Ireland were such a turmoil of conflicting emotions. She was right. His mind was on other things, making all the preparations for his departure and hiding his real intentions from his family. The letter from Sheila's father confirming his job hadn't arrived, and he was worried that he was going to go halfway round the world only to find himself unemployed. He'd bought the ticket and there was no getting his money back. Besides, he had decided he couldn't live at home, or in Ireland for that matter, any longer. He needed to get away, as far away as possible. He cast his mind back and remembered the sharp shriek of pain and delight as he entered her and the traces of blood afterwards. Why had he forgotten that? Did it mean so little to him? Or did it mean so much that he needed to banish it from his mind?

"Of course, I remember, Maggie. I don't think either of us enjoyed it very much."

"That was the first time."

"What do you mean?"

"We enjoyed it plenty of times after." Hugh pursed his lips, in doubt or regret, she was not sure. She put her hand on his. "Don't worry. I've forgiven you, but I've never forgotten that it was you who deflowered me."

Hugh smiled at the word *deflower*. It seemed so Elizabethan. When was the last time anyone had used that word? "I'm sorry, Maggie. I let you down."

"If it were nowadays, I'd probably have to thank you for initiating me into the world of sex, but in those days, it was like crossing the Rubicon."

"It was inconsiderate of me. I was just thinking of myself," he said.

"I got over it a long time ago. Besides, you left me with beautiful memories."

Why did she make it sound as if that was all she had? Memories. Hadn't she had a long marriage with three lovely sons and, as far as he could tell, a decent husband? Surely they were enough to cancel out the pain of his brutal departure? At least, that was what he had always wanted to believe.

He wondered whether he too cherished memories of their youthful love. There had been something reckless about it, like riding a motorbike at top speed without a helmet, hair flying wild in the adrenaline rush. Like a summer flower, it was not made to last. It was not expected to live longer than a day. And lurking behind it all there had been that indomitable force pushing him away. He had always thought Maggie had been a victim of circumstances. He wanted to believe that he too had been a victim of sorts, the butt of some external dynamic; but perhaps for the first time, he realised that that force came from within. It was a part of him, a part of the negativity that had dominated him and perhaps still did. He was his own victim, and Maggie was not a victim of circumstance but a casualty of his destructive self.

"I wish things had been different," he said wearily. "I wish I had been different."

"Well, they weren't and you weren't," she said with an exonerating smile, laying her hand on his.

"I wish I could make up for it, but I think it's too late now."

"It's never too late."

He looked at her, wondering if she had lost touch with reality. They were both in their seventies, and however much they tried to deceive themselves, there was no getting away from it.

"Well, you can make up for it tonight."

Hugh felt his heart miss a beat. Was she really proposing what he thought she was? "Are you sure that's what you want, Maggie?"

"What do I want?" she asked teasingly.

"You tell me."

"Now that would be telling. And take all the fun out of it. It's up to you to decide what I want, Hugh Gorman."

"And what about Jerry? He said—"

"Feck Jerry. He's just an old mother hen. Unless..." She looked at him sternly. "Unless you're not up for it."

"Well, to be honest with you, Maggie. If you're referring to what I think you are, it's been some time."

"That goes for both of us then so. It's been far too long, but the truth is men don't usually do one-night stands with women of my age." She turned squarely and fixed him with her hypnotic eyes, demanding a straight answer to the question she was about to ask. "Am I too old for you, Hugh?"

"As far as I'm concerned, you're still twenty, Maggie. I'm the old one."

"Not a bit of it. I saw the young women at the group ogling you. There was lust in their eyes."

"In your imagination, Maggie. Look, are you sure you want to start over with me? It could be a terrible letdown. Neither of us is all that young anymore."

"I'm prepared to take that risk, if you are. Besides, what do we have to lose?"

All he could see was those bright green eyes when he leant in to kiss her. She responded immediately, squashing his lips against hers, a hand pressing the back of his head.

They were too old and experienced to spend too much time in foreplay. There was no point in putting off something that might never happen again.

"Come on," he said, lifting her up in his strong arms. Did he sense some hesitation, a slight retraction? Maybe, but it had nothing to do with prudery or decorum he was soon to discover.

"Don't be too shocked now. I'm not as firm as I used to be. My personal trainer does his best, but there is a limit to what any human being can do, barring plastic surgery."

Next to the bed, he was unsure how to proceed. Sex with Sheila had followed a pattern. He didn't have to think. He fumbled for a while rather like a teenager having his first sexual experience. But Maggie was so at ease with whatever he did he realised he didn't have to think anymore. Just take things as they came.

He started undressing her, and she began to undress him. It was a slow and somewhat agonising process, neither knowing quite what would be revealed. It wasn't long before they were both naked and under the sheets. She was thin, but her breasts were still full and the nipples long and pointed, as he remembered them. It was as if nothing had changed. They were back in 1971. This time, however, he was determined to enjoy it and damn the consequences.

As it happened, they both did. Nearly fifty years of marriage had at least taught them something about love, how to arouse, and be aroused.

When it was over, Maggie lay back in bed, raised her arms in the air, and screamed, "Hallelujah, baby!"

It was fortunate, Hugh thought, they were not in a hotel room. All the other residents would have been woken by the cataclysmic event of Maggie's orgasm and its boisterous aftermath. He wondered if her screams could be heard by Deirdre in the house next door. He assumed not, as there was no sound of the *gardaí* patrol car screaming to her rescue.

Hugh too stretched out with an intense feeling of satisfaction. He had proved that he wasn't past it yet, something that had crossed his mind on many occasions in recent years.

"Now that was worth waiting for, young man," she said, looking sideways at him, her eyes glittering.

"I'm afraid I kept you waiting a bit."

"Only fifty years, but as long as you're not planning to skedaddle off to Australia tomorrow, we can make up for lost time."

"I can't promise anything, Maggie. I'd love to stay on, but I do have a business to run. And when the boss is away, things start going downhill."

She turned away with a sigh. "You must do what you have to do, Hugh."

She tried to affect indifference, but he could tell that he had disappointed her.

"I'll just have to make the most of you while you're here." She rolled in on him and smothered him in kisses. She hadn't changed.

He would willingly have stayed the night, but he couldn't get rid of the nagging feeling that he might be needed at home. Reluctantly, he said, "I ought to be getting back. I don't want to give free rein to Joan's bawdy imagination. She doesn't have all that high opinion of me as it is, but if she thinks I took you to bed the first night we went out together, I would sink to rock bottom in her esteem."

"Don't underestimate her, Hugh. She's probably more broad-minded than you think."

"I doubt it."

"You will have a bite to eat before you leave."

"That quiche did look delicious."

As she was slipping on a silky negligée, she paused and looked across at him. "Do you think the guys at the theatre guessed we were going to make love tonight?"

Hugh smiled at her mischievous chuckle. "I didn't even know it myself, so I can't imagine they did."

"I'm sure they could tell something was up."

Hugh realised that that was what she wanted them to think. "I very much doubt it. As far as they're concerned, anyone over sixty is past it. Sure, didn't we think the same when we were their age?"

"Did we?"

"Well, maybe not you, Maggie."

It was going on 2:00 a.m. when Hugh crept into the house. Fortunately, Joan hadn't locked the back door as she usually did. He wondered whether she was still awake, waiting to hear his footsteps on the stairs. He could imagine her turning on the light, putting on her glasses and tut-tutting at the hour. Once a reprobate, always a reprobate.

He was stepping as lightly as his substantial body would allow. Then, his foot landed on the step that creaked. As a teenager, he swore his father had put it there deliberately to catch him slinking into the house after hours. In those days, he would count his way up and avoid the telltale step but that was a long time ago. In the silence of the night, it seemed to make a terrible racket, setting off clamorous alarm bells. He saw the light under the door of Joan's bedroom come on. She was still awake, waiting for him, just as his mother used to do.

"Is that you, Hugh?" she said irritably.

"Sorry, Joan. Maggie kept me."

"Come in, will you, and shut the door behind you. We don't want to disturb Rory."

He realised there was no getting out of it. She would always be his big sister, though he had no appetite for a mouthful at this hour. He was still on cloud nine, feeling absurdly youthful and brimming with unfounded optimism.

Joan was sitting up in bed, looking pale and long-faced. "What time is this to be coming home? Have you no respect at all in you?"

She sounded just like his mother. "I'm sorry if I disturbed you, Joan."

"It's not that, Hugh. It's your brother. He's in a bad way."

"I know that, Joan, and it was he who told me to go out and have a bit of fun. I was hoping to get home in time to get him ready for bed, but Maggie had prepared supper and I didn't want to let her down."

"You could have told her you had a brother on his deathbed."

"You managed all right without me anyway."

"We did not. He was screaming with the pain. I was at my wit's end. Finally, I called O'Malley out."

"Why didn't you give me a shout? I'd have come at once."

"Rory wouldn't hear of it. He said you were probably in the bed with your one."

"Whether I was or not, I still would have come. So, what did O'Malley do?"

"Morphine. It's the only thing that'll do any good now."

"Poor ould Rory! He's a gonner then so? Did he say how long he's got?"

"No, he wouldn't say."

"I'll talk to him tomorrow."

"You're never in the right place at the right time, are you, Hugh? I really needed you here tonight, and you were off gallivanting with that woman. I thought you'd have a bit more sense at your age."

"I had the impression you liked Maggie. You seemed keen enough to get us back together."

"She's a very vain woman, Hugh. All she thinks about is her looks. And she got awful uppity when Tom's brother bought out her share of the business. She must have got a fortune for it."

"You're being hard on her, Joan. She's not all she makes herself out to be."

"Don't I know?"

"I mean there's a soft side to her."

"So, you did go to bed with her."

"That's neither here nor there. Don't blame Maggie. It's my fault. I should have said no when she invited me in for supper."

"But you couldn't say no, could you?"

Hugh wondered whether she was just jealous that he had had a good time, or did she genuinely believe he should have been at home with them? She had always resented the fact that he had been the one to have a good time while she stayed at home being dutiful, looking after their mother, then their father, and finally tending to a man she never loved. And now Rory. But he wasn't like her. He didn't believe in sacrificing himself for others. He would do what he could but within limits. He was no Mother Theresa, and there was no point in pretending that he was. And if Joan fancied herself as a saint, she should do it uncomplainingly and not act the martyr all the time. "I'm going to bed now, Joan. I'll sort things out in the morning. Try and get some sleep now."

"I don't understand you, Hugh. How can you shag a woman that should have hung up her panties a decade ago and then sleep like a baby when your brother is choking to death?"

Though angry that she should chastise him, he had difficulty holding back a smile. He hadn't realised the words *shag* and *panties* were part of his sister's vocabulary. Nonetheless, she made him feel guilty just as his mother had. Was he so selfish? Wasn't it enough to feel concern? Did he also have to show it by abstaining from pleasure? "You've had a hard night, Joan. You're angry. With me? With life? I don't know. I've said I'm sorry. What more do you want?"

"You're always sorry, Hugh," she said bitterly.

"Good night, Joan." He turned and left the room.

He had difficulty getting to sleep. Joan had spoilt the lovely evening he'd had with Maggie. He felt guilty that he couldn't do more for Rory, who was the only person apart from his immediate family that he would have willingly died for.

He dropped off to sleep just before dawn. When he woke up a few hours later, the first thing he remembered from the night before was not Joan telling him off but Maggie, their sexual escapade, and the intimate tête-á-tête afterwards. It made him feel warm inside, a kind of subdued excitement that promised good times ahead.

For the first time since Sheila died, he realised how empty he had felt. He had been living a time-honoured routine, but with the vital part missing—Sheila. It was ironical that it should be Maggie who made him realise how much he had loved his wife. Maggie was fun. Maggie was lovely. Maggie was sexy even at seventy. But she could never replace Sheila. Was it right even to let her try?

He looked at his watch. It was gone nine thirty. He should have been up ages ago to help Rory with his morning ablutions. Joan would have further reason to rebuke him. He jumped out of bed, threw on his clothes, and tried in vain to plaster down his unruly hair.

He went straight to the sitting room, bypassing the kitchen. Rory was half-sitting up in bed, his eyes drooping drunkenly. He didn't seem to be in pain. Surely the morphine could not be still having an effect. Rory opened his eyes with difficulty when he saw Hugh approach, a faint smile appearing on his blotched lips.

"Sure, it's the man himself. Did you have a good evening with your one?"

"Not bad. I heard you had a bad turn. It was lucky O'Malley was able to come out."

"Oh, he cursed Joan to high heaven, so he did, but he came anyway."

"Are you not in pain, lad?"

"It's manageable. O'Malley came out early and gave me a shot. I said you wanted to see him, but Joan didn't want to wake you. She said you came home late. I said more power to you, but for some reason, she has it in for you."

"She's just worried about you, mate. Don't put any pass on her." He knew he was saying that to himself as much as to Rory. "Did you have any breakfast?"

"I was waiting for you, boy. Joan thinks I should only eat healthy. But I want you to fry me up a bit of ould bacon, be damned, as crisp as you can make it without carbonising it and bring me a cup of sweet tay with oceans of milk. I'll down that all right."

Joan was in the kitchen, but she didn't turn when he entered.

"Rory wants me to fry him up some bacon. He says he'll eat that."

"It's not good for him, Hugh, but I suppose you'll give it to him anyhow."

"It's not the bacon that's going to kill him, Joan, so why make all the fuss? And he wants a cup of strong sugary tea."

"Well, you know where everything is. You can do it yourself."

"I'm sorry about last night, Joan. If I'd known—"

"You should have known. Sure, can't you see—"

Hugh turned and saw that Joan had erupted into shuddering sobs. *Even dormant volcanoes can't hold it in forever*, he thought. He went over to her and put his hands on her shoulder, but he didn't know what to say or do that would give her any comfort. Rory was her last companion. Without him, the house would be no more than a mausoleum, inhabited by uncommunicative and ungrateful ghosts. That was her reward for years of devotion and administration. He decided he would call the girls in the morning to see what their plans were for her mother when Rory passed.

She pushed him away because he was no use to her at that moment or at any time perhaps. He tried his best, she knew, but his best was never good enough.

"I hate to say this, Joan, but we've got to think what's going to become of you when Rory goes. You can't go on living here all alone. You'll go mad."

"And why shouldn't I? Don't Maggie and Deirdre live alone most of the time?"

"They may have their own house, but they live next door to each other. The nearest house to here is half a mile away."

"I've been alone all me life. It won't be any different."

What did she mean by that? "How can you say that, Joan? Rory and you were always close."

"You're alone when you have no one you can really talk to. You were the only one who'd ever listen and show understanding."

"Do you mind if I call Margaret and Soibhán to let them know of the situation?"

"You will not. I don't want you interfering in my business. Margaret has enough to think about."

"We're all family, Joan. You're too overwrought at the moment to know what's good for you. The girls have a right to know what's happening."

"You can ring Margaret if you like but not Soibháin."

"Why not? The truth is you haven't said a word about her since I got back."

"We don't speak any more."

"Why not? Did you have a row?"

"I won't have her in my house."

"Why on earth not?"

"She wanted to visit me with her partner."

"What's wrong with that? I didn't even know she had a partner."

"Her partner's a woman."

Hugh had to laugh, which he knew was not the right thing to do.

"They even got married, if you ever heard of such a thing."

"When was that?"

"Last year."

"It's the first I heard of it."

"She kept it very quiet."

"Only close family. I don't blame her. What was it like?"

"I have no idea. I didn't go."

"You didn't go? To your own daughter's wedding?"

"It wasn't a wedding, Hugh. It was a parody. Sure, it's totally against nature and the teachings of the church."

"Who gives a feck about the church? Aren't they still living in the Middle Ages?"

"I do, Hugh. We have to believe in something."

"We can always believe in humanity. And like it or not, homosexuality is a part of nature. Otherwise, there wouldn't be such a thing."

"I wouldn't expect any other opinion from you. Sure, they're all heathens out there in Australia."

"Homosexuality is no longer considered a perversion, Joan. Some people are born like that, and it's about time we accepted it as normal."

"Well, I don't have to accept it and I won't."

"That's a terrible pity, Joan. Siobháin is your daughter and, whether she's a lesbian or not, I'm sure you still love her. And I've no doubt she still loves you."

Joan said nothing. Though doubting his own powers of persuasion, he was hoping that maybe he had managed to implant some doubt in her mind.

"Okay, I won't ring Siobháin so, but let me at least have a chat with Margaret. I know with the kids and all it may not be easy for her to come down, but at least the choice should be hers."

"I'll give you her number later. Go on now and give your brother the junk he wants. At least it's food of sorts. He didn't eat anything at all yesterday."

Frying up the bacon reminded him of his childhood, that mouthwatering smell that brought on a mammoth appetite. They used to eat porridge back then too with real cream and salt. He hadn't had a breakfast like that for over fifty years.

In the end, Rory didn't eat much. He ground each mouthful like a goat chewing the cud but then had difficulty swallowing it. The tea at least helped to wash some of it down.

Rory was silent most of the time. The nonstop chatter had completely gone out of him. Hugh wondered what it was like to be staring into the face of death, for he knew Rory was under no illusion that these were his last days on earth.

"Is there anything else I can do for you, lad?" said Hugh, removing the plate of bacon that was mostly left uneaten.

"I'm not much company for ye, boy, but you sitting there is a great comfort to me. I'd love it if you held me hand at the last. It's a terrible thing to say, Hugh, but you were the only person in our family I really loved."

Hugh was unable to respond. A lump that threatened to set off a flood of tears had formed in the crook of his throat. With difficulty, he managed to squeeze out the words. "Did you not love Mam, Rory? She had a good heart."

"She was a hard woman, boy, whatever you say. She wasn't able to show love. Maybe it wasn't her fault. I don't know. But I think she drove the old man away and instead of taking up with another woman, he took up with the drink instead. It was the frustration that drove him to fits of violence."

Hugh understood what Rory was saying. He knew what frustration can do to a person. "There was no justification for it, though. He had no right to lay a hand on her."

"Oh, you're right there, boy. I don't condone it. But I don't remember our mother holding us or hugging us when we needed it. She'd sooner give us a clout around the earhole if we fell and hurt ourselves. 'That'll teach you to be careful,' she used to say. Don't you remember?"

Hugh did remember, but somehow, he never held it against her. He assumed all mothers were like that, and it was the job of siblings not parents to offer solace. It was Rory who would put iodine and Elastoplast on a grazed knee or commiserate after a hard knock. As a consequence, Hugh did the same for Rory, though Rory was the one who never cried, however badly he was hurt. "Sure 'tis nothin', Hugh, on'y a bit of ould blood. I'll be as right as rain in no time."

"It was that generation, Rory. They didn't believe in molly-coddling. And maybe they were right. I often think the younger generation have it too easy."

"A bit of ould love and affection now and again don't do no one a bit of harm, Hugh. I know you were closer to her than I was but—"

"I always thought you were the one closer to her."

They both smiled and said, "You see," almost simultaneously.

Hugh sat with Rory until the bacon on the plate had coagulated into a grey corpus of fat. Rory dozed erratically. Hugh could tell he was in pain despite the morphine. There would come a time when even that would do little good to mitigate his suffering. In the hospital, they could regulate it; but at home, it depended on O'Malley. And as a busy country doctor, he couldn't be permanently on hand to provide relief.

Hugh decided to give O'Malley a call and went to the phone in the kitchen. Fortunately, Joan had gone out to feed the hens or get vegetables from the garden.

O'Malley was not in the best of moods. "Look, Gorman, I made it patently clear to Joan that Rory should be hospitalised. Otherwise, he is going to suffer inordinately. For some reason, she has got it into her head that he'll be better off at home. But this is not the case. Now, I'm only the doctor. I simply advise. I cannot impose my wishes. So, there's nothing I can do but visit morning and evening and hope that in between times he is not in too much pain."

"But he is going to die, isn't he?"

"There is no point in lying to you. It's a matter of days."

"In that case, why can't we hasten the process?"

"I think we've been through this before. The only thing we can hope for is that his body gives out before the pain becomes unbearable."

"And the morphine?"

"It can only do a certain amount. Barring total sedation, there is nothing that can contain pain in its entirety."

"I see. So we'll just have to let nature takes its course."

"We'll see when the time comes, Mr. Gorman. Now, I have a busy schedule. I will call round about seven tonight."

"Thank you, Doctor."

What did O'Malley mean when he said we'll see "when the time comes"? What time? Was it possible that the doctor would do the humane thing in the end? In the meantime, he would have to spend as much time as he could with Rory, as his presence seemed to give him more comfort than anything else. He knew that Maggie would want to see him now that the embers of their old passion had been stirred, but Rory would have to take precedence. He decided to call her to explain the situation.

"Hi, lover boy!" she exclaimed perkily. "I was wondering when you'd call."

He realised at once that they were on a totally different emotional wavelength. All the excitement of the previous night had drained out of him. It was almost as if it hadn't happened. He should have been with Rory not her. And he had no idea how he would feel towards her once it was all over and had returned to Australia. "Rory is in bad shape, Maggie."

"Oh god! I'm sorry to hear that."

"It's going to be hard to get away. He needs me 24-7. I'm sorry. You can come round if you like, but it's not going to be much fun."

"I'm a bit squeamish when it comes to sickness and pain. I found it hard visiting Tom in hospital. I'm not very good around the dying."

"I understand. Well, perhaps it's better that way. Rory might find it hard having visitors at this point. Thanks for last night, by the way. The quiche was superb."

"Just the quiche?"

"Everything was. I hope we can do it again sometime. But for now, I have to be with Rory. I also have some family matters I need to sort out. We'll be in touch though. Very soon, I hope."

"Sure, Hugh. I hope last night was not just a one-night stand."

"I hope not." He didn't know what else to say. He could lie and make promises but that was not his way. "Keep well, Maggie. See you around so."

There was a long silence. He wondered whether she had hung up, but her voice eventually reemerged from the black hole on the other end of the line.

"That's what you said to me the night before you left for Australia."

"What was that?"

"'Keep well, Maggie. See you around so.' I knew then that it was all over between us."

"Maybe this time it'll be different. Time will tell."

"Aye, time will tell. Keep well, Hugh." With that, she hung up.

He was not sure whether she was angry or upset or simply wished to bring the conversation to a close. He could not worry about that now. He had other things to think about. Apart from his concern for Rory, he was worried about Joan and what would happen to her when Rory was gone.

Rory was in a bad way for most of the day. He would sometimes writhe and yelp like a sick puppy that knows nothing can be done to ease its pain. His lungs seemed to be caving in, and his breathing was terrifying to watch. At moments when it seemed the end had come, he would reach out for Hugh's hand and grip it with shocking force. Hugh hoped that some of Rory's pain was being transferred to him, but he knew that however much he wished it he could not share in his agony. Though he willed his beloved brother to hang on to life, there were times when he found himself wishing that the end would come sooner than later.

O'Malley arrived at the time he had said. He was glum and taciturn, hardly bothering to greet Joan and Hugh. He just nodded and walked straight through to Rory. He made no attempt to hide his concern when he saw the state Rory was in.

"How are you feeling, Rory?" he asked, sweeping the palm of his hand over his mouth as if to wipe off any signs of alarm. His question was clearly rhetorical. How could he be feeling? He must have known that any respite from the pain was agonisingly short-lived.

Rory, however, put on a brave face and managed to rasp, "Could be worse, Doctor. Could be worse."

Hugh wondered how worse it could be. He dared not think.

The doctor's bedside manner was a great deal better than his gruff acknowledgement of the other siblings. He held Rory's hand for some time, talking to him soothingly, before taking out the needle and giving him the morphine injection. Hugh supposed even doctors do not become inured to suffering and death.

The injection took effect almost immediately. Rory's features visibly relaxed. Soon his eyes were drooping. Hopefully, sleep would follow.

On his way out, O'Malley took Hugh apart. "He should sleep for a while now, but if he wakes up in the night, give him one of these." He handed Hugh some pills in a brown bottle. Hugh noticed it had no label. "Only increase the dose if things get very bad. And remember. An overdose could be lethal." He looked around as if to make sure they were alone and in a hushed voice said, "I'll leave it to your discretion. You understand? Good night now, Mr. Gorman."

Hugh watched O'Malley get into his car and drive off. Was the doctor trying to say that if he gave Rory an overdose no one would blame him for it or even suspect him of having done so? After all, O'Malley was the one who'd be signing the death certificate. Suddenly, the full magnitude of what he had been asking of O'Malley came home to him. The doctor, however, had turned the tables on him, and it was now he who would have to carry out the deed. Yet, the idea of signing the death warrant on his brother, even for reasons of compassion, was unthinkable. It was a terrible responsibility that the doctor had fobbed off on to him. No, no, he couldn't do it. He quickly dismissed the thought from his mind. He would use the pills at his discretion to reduce the pain, but that was all.

With Rory asleep, he was in two minds whether to go for a walk or call Margaret. He would like to have wandered the fields, maybe drop in on Maggie, but the thought of getting detained made him have second thoughts. As he crossed the kitchen, he saw that Joan was not there. It was an opportunity to start dealing with family matters.

Margaret picked up almost at once. In the background, he could hear the screaming of children playing boisterous games.

"It's your uncle Hugh," he said, trying to top the din.

"Uncle Hugh! What a surprise! Are you calling from Australia?"

"No. I'm at home…in Connick. Uncle Rory is in a bad way. I think the cancer has him beat."

"Oh, no! I'm so sorry. Poor Uncle Rory. How long do they give him?"

"A day or two." He'd said it, pronounced his death sentence.

"Should I come down?"

"That's up to you, Margaret."

"Oh god, things are crazy here right now. Enda is away on business, and I'm stuck with the kids. I honestly don't think I can. Has he asked to see me?"

"No. I doubt he wants to see anyone in the state he's in."

"Tell him that I love him, Uncle Hugh. But three rowdy kids…"

"No worries, Margaret. I was really calling you about your mother. We have to think what's going to become of her when Rory's gone. She's going on seventy-eight. I don't know whether she can go on living here alone. As far as I can gather, she doesn't have all that many friends either and—"

"What are you suggesting, Uncle Hugh? Mam and I have never got on well. I was always much closer to Da and Uncle Rory. She's so interfering. We'd be fighting like cat and dog."

"And Siobháin?"

"Well, ever since she came out, Mam won't have anything to do with her. She wouldn't even go to her wedding."

"Do you have her number?"

"Yes. But she's virtually written Mam off. So, I doubt you'll get much joy there."

"At least, if you could visit every now and then, just to make sure she's taking care of herself."

"You know what it's like, Uncle Hugh. Both Enda and I work very hard. We're trying to pay off a mortgage. And whenever we are free, the kids have parties and God knows what else and need to be ferried here and there. And there's ructions when they miss anything their friends are going to."

"I understand. I just thought I ought to let you know the situation. Your mother likes to make out she's very tough, but when it comes down to it, I'm not sure she'll do all that great here on her own."

"Might she go and live with you in Australia?"

"I suggested it, but she rejected it out of hand. Besides, I'm not in her good books either at the moment. Something about a loan I'm supposed not to have paid back."

"Oh, yeah, I vaguely remember her talking about it. So it's some sort of a misunderstanding?"

"Absolutely."

"And Mam won't accept it."

"You know your Mam better than I do."

"What does Uncle Rory say?"

"I've been avoiding the issue. I don't want to upset him."

"I think you may have to, Uncle Hugh. Otherwise, it's going to come between you and Mam for the rest of your lives."

"You're right. But it's not your problem…Anyway, if you can't make the journey down, why don't you give your Mam a call? I think she might appreciate it. Don't tell her I spoke to you."

"I should call her. It's been ages. Thanks, Uncle Hugh. We always envied you out there in sunny Australia. We were sorry we never got to know Brendan and Niall better. How are they doing, by the way?"

"Okay. I don't see much of them. Australia's a big place."

"A bit bigger than Ireland, eh?"

"About a hundred times."

They both laughed.

"Give Uncle Rory a hug for me."

"I will."

Hugh remembered Margaret as a child, bright-eyed and quick-witted. She was the academic one, destined for university and a career in medicine or law. Siobháin was prettier but more introspective, always creating something—writing stories, painting, making things. She could concentrate for hours when it came to completing a piece of handicraft but lessons she regarded as a bore.

Joan was still not back. He assumed she had gone for a walk. It was a beautiful early autumn evening. He was tempted to head off himself, but he needed to call Siobháin and get it over with.

Siobháin picked up at once.

"It's your uncle Hugh. The Aussie."

For a moment she didn't seem to know who he was and then said, "Oh, Uncle Hugh. I'm sorry. You've been out of the picture for so long. I was really sorry to hear about Sheila, by the way. How are you coping?"

"One carries on. But when you lose your partner, you lose the better half of yourself."

"No doubt my mother told you that I am married."

He could tell from the coolness in her voice that she expected a cool response. "Yes. Congratulations!" he said overenthusiastically. He didn't want to sound in any way critical.

"It wasn't a big do. Just a few friends and relations. We didn't bother inviting people living on the other side of the world."

"No worries. What does your partner do?"

"She works in films."

"I'd love to meet her. God knows when, though. It's hard enough getting back home, let alone taking trips to England. We should have a big family reunion. I'll try and get the boys to come over."

"It's a nice idea, Uncle Hugh, but I won't be invited. Mam won't have anything to do with me."

Hugh thought he heard a sob or a sniff on the other end. She was clearly not indifferent to her alienation from her mother. "I'm sorry about that. Put it down to the narrow-minded of the older generation."

"Yeah. I wish it was as simple as that."

"Look, I'm calling about two things. Firstly, Uncle Rory. I'm afraid there's very little hope."

"Oh, no! I had no idea he was so bad. I only get news indirectly now, and Margaret said nothing the last time we spoke. I knew he wasn't well but…"

"Your mother has been in denial, I think. It's only now coming home to her that he can't beat the cancer this time."

"I'd so love to see him. Should I come over, Uncle Hugh?"

"It's best to remember him as he was, Siobháin. I'll tell him that you're thinking of him. That's all he wants. He is very fond of you both. You are the daughters he never had."

"I spent so much time with Uncle Rory as a child. He was always telling me yarns and stories. He told me plenty about you too."

"Oh god, the pair of us were fair ould boyos in our time."

"You broke many hearts, so I'm told."

"Don't believe a word of it. It was all just good fun."

"What was the other thing you wanted to tell me?"

"I don't want to interfere, Siobháin. It's up to you to sort things out with your mother, but I'm worried about her living here alone when Rory is gone."

"I don't think there's anything I can do to help. I've tried to bridge the divide, believe me. I even tried writing, but I never got a reply."

"I gathered as much. You see, she was brought up in another age, an age of intolerance."

"I still love her, Uncle Hugh, and I would be very upset to see her pine away in Connick, but if she is not prepared to accept who I am, then there's nothing I can do about it."

"I'll try and knock some sense into her. But the Gormans are a stubborn breed. Thank God you took a lot from your father's side."

"Thank you, Uncle Hugh. Being cut off from my home has been very hard."

"She still loves you, Siobháin. It's just her conscience getting the better of her. I can't promise anything, but I'll do my best to get her to see sense."

"I wrote a book called *On the Other Side of Wisdom*. It's a novel about a woman's struggle to come to terms with her sexuality. It hasn't sold many copies, but it has had good reviews. If she were to read it, she might see that it was not easy for me either to accept who I am."

"Why don't you send a copy to Connick care of me? I'll leave it lying around, and maybe she might be tempted to pick it up. Who knows?"

"Thank you, Uncle Hugh. It might work. Please give Uncle Rory kisses for me and tell him my thoughts are with him."

Hugh put down the phone and suddenly became aware of someone standing behind him. He turned and saw Joan staring wild-eyed at him.

"Who were you talking to?" she said challengingly.

"Siobháin."

"And who told you to interfere in family business?"

"I think she has the right to know that her uncle is about to die."

"She's no longer part of this family."

"Don't be ridiculous, Joan. Anybody'd think she committed some heinous crime. Did you know that studies have shown that homosexuality may have to do with the desires of the mother during pregnancy? Now don't tell me you didn't want a boy? Didn't Tom want a boy to take over the farm when he got too old? And I'm sure you didn't want to let him down, right?"

"That's all nonsense. Sure, how can a mother make her child into a homo?"

"It can't be proved categorically, but there are strong indications that it is possible. So, you shouldn't blame her. Maybe you had a hand in it too. Besides, what difference does it make? It's only sex. She's neither a pederast nor a mass murderer. The important thing is that she discovered herself and is now happy with the partner of her choice."

"And what is it she's going to send you?" she said, one eye cocked in a suspicious leer.

"One of her books. It's a novel about a woman coming to terms with her sexuality. It sounds very interesting."

"For you maybe."

"Don't you want to understand your daughter, Joan? I wasn't going to tell you, but she was crying on the phone. She loves you and feels you've banned her from her home. And there's nothing worse than being cut off from your roots." As soon as he said it, he realized he was also talking about himself.

Joan said nothing, but he realised he had touched a chord.

"I'd better go in and see how Rory is doing," he said and left Joan in silent contemplation.

Rory was still sleeping, but not peacefully. His face would convulse in what Hugh assumed were jabs of violent pain. When the drug wore off, he'd wake up and the agony would begin again. Hugh decided to make himself a makeshift bed in the parlour next to Rory so he was at hand if needed.

Sleep got the better of him around eleven, and he fell into a surprisingly deep slumber. It was around three when he heard Rory calling him in a weak grating voice.

He jumped to his feet. He was fully clothed except for his shoes. "I'm here, lad. What can I do for you?"

"I'm choking, Hugh. For God's sake, do something!" It was as if he was trying to suck air through a straw but the end kept closing. His chest was heaving frantically. Hugh applied the ventilator to his mouth and slowly his breathing became more regular.

When he had recovered a little, he lifted the mouthpiece to speak. "Jes', the pain is something terrible, Hugh."

For Rory to complain, Hugh knew that the pain must be excruciating. Rory always had great tolerance for pain. He went into the kitchen, got a glass of water, and located the pills O'Malley had given him. When he brought them back, he held one up, "Do you think you can swallow this? O'Malley said it'll dull the pain."

"I'd swallow a fuckin' brick if it gave me some relief. Break it in two, though, so it don't choke me. Though it might be a better way to go than the way I'm going now."

Hugh administered the pill, but it took some time to take effect. Eventually, Rory removed the ventilator and wheezed, "That's some pill O'Malley gave you, Hugh boy. You could pull all me teeth out, and I wouldn't let out a squeak."

"Well, I won't be pulling your teeth out, lad. If I could pull the fuckin' cancer out of you, I would, though."

"I know you would, boy. Sure, I'd do the same for you if I had the chance."

There was no point in saying that he would never have the chance, not now, not ever. "That's good to know. That cancer is a right oul' fucker if ever there was one."

Hugh sat with Rory for some time, watching him drift in and out of sleep. He wondered how long this could go on. If only his heart would give out, but he knew that that was unlikely to happen. Rory had a strong heart that would hang on till every other part of his body had failed.

Rory was thirsty, so Hugh gave him some water. Then, he had a go at eating a slice of apple Hugh peeled for him.

When Rory finally went back to sleep, Hugh found that he was no longer tired and just tossed about on the lumpy sofa, thinking about everything, but unable to come to any conclusions about anything. Nothing is clear-cut in this world, he thought. There is never just one right direction in which to go.

He couldn't get over how disconnected Joan and her daughters were. Yet, he supposed all families have their troubles. Brendan had been an enormous headache for them. He began wondering whether he had been as intolerant as Joan was to Siobháin. Should he have been more understanding? As parents, were they in some way to blame for his weaknesses? Maybe he had been too hasty to condemn when he should have offered help. Did Brendan feel abandoned like Siobhán felt now? Was it too late to patch things up? He had no idea how Brendan felt about him. He couldn't tell how much love was left between them. Though Brendan had been a disappointment to them, he had never stopped loving him. You could never stop loving your child, whatever they did. A son might give up on a parent, though, like he did on his father.

The situation with Joan and Siobhán is not beyond repair, he thought. He just didn't know how to jolt Joan out of her antiquated mode of thinking. They say love can conquer all, but in this case, he wasn't sure.

At some point, he must have nodded off because he was woken by Joan clattering around in the kitchen. He wondered whether she was doing it deliberately to get him up and about. He looked at his watch. O'Malley was due any minute.

Rory smiled at him when he approached the bed. He was now too weak even to speak. Hugh pulled back the sheets and extricated the dirty nappy and replaced it with a clean one. *The human cycle*, he thought, *from baby nappy to adult nappy*. Why did the end have to be so demeaning? Was it God's wish to humble us before we present ourselves before the pearly gates of heaven?

O'Malley came and went without more than a word or two. There was nothing much he could say. It was no longer a question of treatment but pain management, which Hugh thought must be frustrating for a doctor whose primary aim is to prolong life.

Hugh tried to tempt Rory with a bit of crispy bacon, but even that was no good and he ended up eating it himself.

After Rory fell into a Morphean slumber, Joan invited Hugh to have a cup of tea with her in the kitchen. He hoped that this might be some sort of peace offering, as they had said little in the past few days that had not contained some degree of animosity.

It was Joan who broke the silence. "I'm glad you're here, Hugh. I wouldn't be able to cope without you."

"I know I haven't always been here for you, Joan. I had my own troubles, but I couldn't be absent this time. Rory and I were more than just brothers. We were best buddies. Any bit of decency I have in me, I owe to him. I didn't get much of it from Ma and a lot less from Da."

"Was I so horrible to you, Hugh?"

"No, Joan, I didn't mean to imply that, but you were distant. I saw you more as a nanny than a sister."

"It's been a quare ould life, hasn't it, Hugh? I often wonder what the sense of it is. The only satisfaction I got out of it was the two girls, and then one of them goes off and becomes a lesbian."

"You should be very proud of your girls, Joan. They're both very accomplished, each in their own way. A successful lawyer and a published author. And that was all your doing. You instilled ambition into them and made sure they got a good schooling. I can't say I had all that much success with my boys, with Brendan at any rate."

"The trouble is, Hugh, we don't learn how to bring up our children until it's too late."

"It's not too late with Siobháin, Joan. Your two daughters are the only real family you have. When all is said and done, uncles, aunts, cousins, nephews, and the like couldn't give a damn about you. You're very lucky to have two girls who love you. I have two sons who couldn't care if I lived or died."

"That's not true, Hugh. Why do you say that?"

"Because it's a fact. Do they ever ring to find out how I am?"

"Do you ever contact them?"

"You have a point, I suppose, but their mother was the one that kept us together. I'm a bit like yourself, I suppose. I expect too much of them, and then when I do see them, I don't seem to be able to find a connection."

"I suppose we were never taught how to show love."

"Maybe it's time we both thought about rallying the troops before it's too late. I was thinking I should see more of my grandchildren. Sure, they hardly know me."

"You're right, Hugh, but it's hard to reject what you were brought up to believe."

"Prejudice, that's all it is. When I went out to Australia, I had to question a lot of my beliefs, and let me tell you, it wasn't easy. But slowly my mind opened up a bit, and I began to see things different. And now I don't take anything for granted. I keep an open mind about everything."

"I wish it was so easy."

"I never said it was easy. What I did say was that Margaret and Siobháin are the most precious things you'll ever have, and you don't want to lose them to the world. Because, let me tell you, the world will swallow them up no trouble, and they'll be lost to you forever. When Rory is gone, and there's no point in pretending he's not on the way out, you need to get into that Yaris of yours and drive up to Dublin of a weekend or take a trip over to London, see Siobháin, meet her partner, and take in the sights while you're about it."

Hugh could see by the strained look on her face that what he was suggesting was like asking her to take a trip to the moon. *Maybe if I stay on a little longer*, he thought, *we can do it together so that she will see it was not beyond her capabilities.*

A light drizzle had descended on the land, which in normal circumstances would have had a dismal effect on him, but somehow it fitted his mood and he felt the need to immerse himself in it. He borrowed Rory's oilskins and boots and headed for the fields.

"Where in God's name are you going in this weather?" said Joan to his back as he exited the kitchen door.

"To prepare for the inevitable."

Joan looked at him incomprehensibly.

It was like swimming in a cold sea, the water running down his face like a river of tears. Soon he was warm inside his protective clothing and the rhythmic swishing across the wet grass had a soporific effect on him. He stopped thinking. All he did was listen to the whistling of the wind and the cawing of the gulls as they engaged in their perpetual battle with the elements. For as long as he was on the move, the world and its tribulations hardly existed.

Despite having had very little sleep, he felt revived after the walk. The heat of the house would no doubt make him feel drowsy, but he could sit in the chair next to Rory and they could doze together. He spent some time just staring at the human wreck that was now his brother.

It's probably a good thing, he thought, *that we don't know how our life will end or when.*

He remembered when they were young how proud they were of their strength. They were constantly engaging in some contest or other to see who could lift the heaviest bag of barley, who could run the fastest, or who could throw a bale of straw the furthest. Back then, other people were destined to die, not them. They were immortal. Old age was so far in the future it had no meaning for them. Old people had always been old. They had always been cranky and eccentric, with their crooked legs and hunched backs, their distorted, comic faces, drooping jowls, and wispy hair. Old people were objects of ridicule to be mimicked and made fun of. And now here they were old themselves, objects of pity and derision. He remembered his father saying once that people shouldn't be allowed to live beyond seventy and maybe he was right.

That afternoon, Hugh was woken from a disturbed sleep by the sound of his mobile phone ringing. It was a call from Australia. Trouble at the station?

He was surprised to hear Brendan's voice. They hadn't spoken for over a year. He had no idea where he was even, whether he was working or living in the street, whether he was married or single. He could have been dead for all he knew.

"Hi, Dad." He sounded sheepish.

"Brendan. How's the form, son? It's been a long time."

"Not so good. I need your help."

When didn't he? He wondered how much he needed this time.

"I'm in a bit of a bind, Dad. I need some cash badly."

Hugh sighed. "What is it this time? Another gambling debt?"

"No. I had a bit of an accident, ran into a fellow's Corolla. Did some damage."

"How bad?"

"Pretty bad."

"Anybody hurt?"

"No."

"That's a blessing at least. Won't your insurance cover it? You were insured, I hope?" Not that it would have surprised him if he hadn't been.

"That's not it, Dad. You see, I'd had a few drinks. I was catching up with some of the mates from work, you know how it is, and—"

"Jesus, Brendan, you're forty-two years of age. Isn't it time you fucking well grew up?"

"It could happen to anyone, Dad. You know what it's like. Everybody's buying rounds. You can't say no."

"It's a two-letter word. It's as easy to say no as it is to say yes. I can forgive the youth for their follies, Brendan, but you're damned near middle-aged."

"You're right, Dad. I need to be stronger."

How many times had he heard that? "So how much is the fine?"

"Well, it's not exactly a fine, Dad. You see, I'm being held in custody, unless someone bails me out."

"Oh, for Christ's sake, man. Do you know where I am?"

"In Esperance?"

"I'm in Ireland, Brendan. Your uncle Rory is dying."

"I'm sorry to hear that, Dad. I didn't know."

"Well, how could you, I suppose? We haven't spoken for a while. So, how much is the bail?"

"Twenty thousand dollars," he muttered, rattling it off under his breath.

"Did I hear right? Twenty thousand dollars? Are you fucking codding me? How much over the limit were you? You must have been fucking blotto!"

"Well, that's not all, Dad. I had a few lines of coke on me and a fair amount of grass."

"Christ all fucking mighty! I have a good mind to leave you there."

"I know. You'd be perfectly within your rights, Dad. But—"

"All right. I'll arrange for the money to be sent. Do you have a decent lawyer? You're going to need one. Where are you, anyway?"

"Melbourne."

"Melbourne. Okay. Send me an account number and all the rest, and I'll make the transfer. In the meantime, look for a lawyer. If you can't, ask Niall. He might know of one there."

"Thanks, Dad. I'll find a way of repaying you. I swear."

"How did you get involved in drugs, for God's sake?"

"Well, life is expensive. I couldn't make ends meet. I was just doing a bit of dealing on the side, you know, part-time."

"Oh, Christ! What's your day job then?"

"I'm the manager of a supermarket."

"Well, at least you're the manager."

"More like assistant manager."

"Are you sure you're not the assistant to the assistant manager?"

"Well, the manager leaves me in charge when he skives off to spend an hour or two with his cuddlemuffin."

"Is that what you want to do in life? Be the assistant to the assistant manager?"

"No, Dad. And I want to talk to you about that, but I can't right now. They're telling me my time's up. When can you get me the moolah? It's bloody awful in this place."

"I'll do it as soon as I can. Look, son, we've got to talk. Call me when you get things sorted."

"Yes, Dad, I promise. And thanks."

After hanging up, Hugh sat stewing in anger for at least five minutes. He couldn't believe it was possible for a son of his to be so stupid. He was so pissed off he was in two minds about sending him the money at once. It would teach him a lesson if he sweated it out in jail for a few days, but he decided he couldn't do that. Sheila would have been horrified that he could even contemplate such a thing. Besides, he had made a promise, and despite everything, Brendan was his son.

Rory was still asleep. So, he went upstairs and transferred the money to Brendan's account from his smartphone. He just hoped it wasn't a made-up story in order to pay off a poker debt.

He went into the kitchen to make himself a cup of coffee. Joan was there and noticed his dark looks. "You can't do any more for him than you already have."

For a moment, Hugh thought she was talking about Brendan but then realised she was referring to Rory. He didn't want to tell her about the phone call. He was ashamed of his son, ashamed of himself for having a son that dealt in drugs, drove drunk, and worked as an assistant to the assistant manager of a supermarket.

"Why don't you pop up to Maggie's? It'll cheer you up."

He glared at her. "Jes', Joan, will you make up your mind? One minute you're vexed because I'm seeing her. Then next you're urging me to go and spend the afternoon with her."

"You had a bad night. You need to get out of the house for a bit."

"Thanks for your concern, Joan, but I have no urge to see Maggie at this time. I need to be with Rory. He's likely to be in great pain when he wakes up."

"But sure, didn't O'Malley give him a shot?"

"That won't last more than a couple of hours."

'So, what can *you* do about it?"

"Be with him." He thought it best not to mention the nameless pills O'Malley had slipped into his hand the evening before.

No sooner had he spoken than they could just make out the sound of Rory's voice from the next room. It was so weak it was little more than a moan. They both rushed in to see what he wanted.

Rory had a hand half-raised in the air. He was trying to say something, but neither of them could decipher what it was. Hugh put his ear to Rory's mouth. He was asking for one of the mystery pills. Hugh looked at Joan. She would have to know he was in possession of a strong painkiller. However, she didn't need to know its ultimate, nefarious purpose. For the moment, the pills were able to dull the pain.

But for how long? he wondered. There would come a time when even they would lose their sedative powers.

As the day wore on, it became clear to Hugh that he was never going to be able to ask Rory about the loan. There was no longer any way of proving that he had never received the money, as Rory alone possessed the answer to the riddle. So, it seemed the rift between him and Joan would remain forever.

Rory didn't eat any lunch. He had virtually given up eating. Apart from an occasional sip of water, he received no sustenance at all. It was as if he had decided to starve himself to death.

How long can the human body go without food? Hugh wondered. *A long time*, he supposed, *when there is a dogged attachment to life.* Bobby Sands lasted sixty-six days.

That afternoon, before receiving another pill, Rory grabbed Hugh by the arm and whispered into his ear, "I want to die, Hugh boy. Can you arrange that for me? I want it to be over."

This cry for help nearly broke Hugh's heart. He was in possession of the means to end his pain, but he lacked the courage to do it. This both angered and shamed him. He thought about almost nothing else all day as he sat staring at Rory. His only hope was that his brother would die before the need for the pills became imperative.

The trouble was, if he left it too long, Rory would not be able to swallow them. Even now, it would not be easy. Only a narrow window of time remained before it was too late. With the pills, Rory would slip painlessly into an eternal sleep. Yet, even that reassuring thought did not allay his misgivings. If only it were just sleep, but he knew it was no more than a euphemism for death.

O'Malley came at his usual time and was as taciturn as ever. As he was leaving, he called Hugh over. "I hate to see him like that, Hugh. I think the time has come. Things are going to get a lot worse." He got into his car and was about to drive off when he stopped and wound down the window. "Call me in the morning if there are any developments. I'll be out at once."

It seemed very clear that O'Malley was giving him the thumbs-up. But could he do it? His logic told him that there was no point in prolonging Rory's torment. Yet, his conscience invariably prevailed in the unequal contest that was playing out in his head.

That evening, the morphine wore off very quickly. By ten o'clock, Rory was crying out for a pill, but the effect lasted no more than an hour or two.

They both slept in fits and starts. It was around four in the morning when Hugh realised this couldn't go on any longer and decided to take the bull by the horns. Rory was awake but unable to speak. Hugh could read the pain and pleading in his eyes, the longing to be finished with life. It was now or never.

A drop of whiskey might make it easier for us both, he thought. He found a half-empty bottle of Jameson's in the cupboard and poured them a glass. When Rory saw the whiskey and the pile of fragmented pills scattered around it on the tray, he managed to etch a smile. He knew what was on offer. Deliverance.

Hugh took a long sip of whiskey before holding the glass to Rory's lips. "Here's to us, Rory me ould son. I'm sorry I wasn't around to share more of our lives." He had to fight back the tears that were welling up inside him.

"Sure, you're here now," Rory whispered. "When I need you the most."

Hugh's hand shook as he slid one piece of pill after the other into Rory's mouth, washing each down with a slug of whiskey. By the end of it, Hugh expected Rory to be quite drunk, but his eyes were as clear and lucid as ever.

When he had swallowed the last pill, Rory's face brightened for a brief moment in an effort to bid farewell to life. Then he grabbed Hugh's hand in a vicelike grip, as if determined to take him with him, or at least part of the way.

It seemed to take ages for the grip to slacken. Slowly, Rory subsided into a deep sleep. His breathing became shallower and more fitful by the minute. Yet, his hold on his hand remained as tight as ever. It wasn't until he felt the hand go cold that Hugh knew that it was over. He looked at his watch. It was 7:35 a.m. He unclasped Rory's hand from his, hoping there would be no postmortal sensation of separation, for he didn't want to be parted from his brother until he had well and truly passed through the gates that delineate this life from the next.

Joan got up at her usual time, around 8:00. When she entered the room, she knew from the look on Hugh's face and the bluish pallor of Rory's that he was gone. She burst into violent sobs, grabbing Rory's cold hand and holding it to her cheek. Hugh put a hand on her shoulder, but she was unaware of his attempt to partake of her pain.

Before O'Malley arrived, Hugh disposed of the little brown bottle so that no questions would be asked, by Joan or anyone else who might be curious about its contents. There was no need for anyone but he and the doctor to know, or even suspect, the ultimate cause of Rory's death. O'Malley seemed relieved and was more sympathetic than he had been in previous days. As he was leaving, Hugh took him aside.

"I want to thank you, Doctor, for all you've done."

"I did no more than my duty, Mr. Gorman."

Hugh could see the doctor wished to bypass any reference to the pills. So, he decided to leave it at that. "And if you don't mind sending the bill to me personally."

"I'll tell my secretary. Thank you, Mr. Gorman. I suppose you'll be going back to Australia soon."

"I don't know. I want to see Joan settled first."

"Yes, of course. I'm very glad you were able to come over. It would have been very hard for her to handle Rory's death alone."

"Certainly."

"Well, good luck then. I'd be grateful if you could let me know when and where the funeral will take place."

"Definitely, Doctor."

As he reentered the house, Hugh found it hard to believe that he would not see Rory sitting in the armchair by the fire, smoking a cigarette and drinking tea, a cocky smile on his face, eager to engage in juvenile banter. Instead, he saw Joan, sunk in a stony silence of grief. Rory had been the last of her charges. There was no one left for her to take care of now. But who would look after her in her final days? Hugh realised that it was imperative that he bring about some sort of reconciliation between Joan and her daughters.

He made some tea and put a cup on the table beside her, but there was no indication that she noticed it. She just carried on staring at the empty armchair by the cold fire, possibly trying to conjure up the remnants of Rory's fading image. Hugh decided not to try and force her out of her catatonic state. He would let her come to terms with her sorrow in her own time.

Meanwhile, he had to make the funeral arrangements. He remembered the name of the local undertakers, Jeremiah Finnegan and Sons, high-class undertakers, and looked them up in the telephone directory. The "high-class" had always amused him, as if anyone really cared if the undertaker was high, low, or middle class, as they lay tucked you up in their wooden box.

He found the phone number and called them. One of the sons rattled off "Jeremiah Finnegan and Sons, high-class undertakers. Herbert Finnegan speaking. How can I help you?" in what was an oddly melodious voice for an undertaker. "Of course, Mr. Gorman, we'll be with you within the hour." It was clear from the enthusiasm in his voice that Hugh had made Herbie's day.

Then, he remembered there'd have to be a wake. Was Joan up to it? They'd need to provide food and drink for the mourners. Couldn't Finnegan and his sons do that? He didn't want to take too many initiatives without consulting Joan, but when would she emerge from her private vigil?

Finnegan himself came with one of his sons, a younger version of the old man. Finnegan must have been eighty if he was a day. He was tall and gaunt with an elongated dour face, pronounced cheekbones, and long locks of yellowing white hair. He was aptly mournful and obsequious, in true Dickensian style, the habits acquired through years of disposing of the dead. Needless to say, he was very willing to cater for all of Hugh's needs and wishes and would make sure to send him a detailed estimate of all expenses before the day was out.

Hugh wondered whether Joan actually knew what was happening, as she didn't seem to recognise Finnegan, though she must have known him. After all, he had buried both their parents. And Jeremiah Finnegan's was not a physiognomy you could easily forget. Joan said little, apparently happy to let Hugh take control. Thankfully, the Finnegans, father and son, were very willing to take charge of everything. They would take Rory away in the hearse and return him, shaved and groomed, dressed in his best bib and tucker for the wake.

The rest of the day Hugh spent calling friends and relations in various parts of the country and abroad.

Siobháin was the most distraught of all and wept uncontrollably for some time until she finally managed to speak. "I can't believe Uncle Rory is dead. It's the end of an era."

"Not completely," said Hugh. "Your mother and I are still alive."

"Yes, sorry, Uncle Hugh. You know what I mean."

"Of course," he said.

"I want to come to the funeral, but it's going to be very unpleasant if Mam won't speak to me."

"You must come. You never know. Miracles do happen."

"Should I bring Leonora?"

"Perhaps not. One step at a time."

Enda still hadn't got back from his business trip in the Middle East, and Margaret was doubtful she could make it. "The drive down from Dublin with three kids would be an absolute nightmare!"

"Just call your mother when you get the chance. She's taken it very badly. Worse than I expected. They were joined at the hip those two."

"I doubt Uncle Rory would agree. Mam certainly felt very close to him, but Uncle Rory liked to keep his distance."

"Could you do me a favour, Margaret? Call Siobháin and tell her she must come to the funeral. I know she wants to, and it might be an opportunity for the pair of them to sort out their differences."

"I'll do my best, Uncle Hugh, but the rift goes very deep. And Mam is a very stubborn woman."

"Don't I know it? I'll keep chipping away at her shell to see if I can't get through."

■

Jeremiah Finnegan himself called that afternoon. He was pleased to inform Hugh that by utilising all his available staff and facilities, the wake could take place on the Tuesday, two days hence, and the funeral the day after.

Hugh didn't know where to start informing the neighbours of the wake and funeral. So, he chose two or three at random in the hope that word would get round. It soon became abundantly clear that Rory had been greatly loved in the townland. They all had a good word to say about him. He had been a quiet, unobtrusive man with a kind, generous heart. Other than that, he had not been in any way remarkable, Hugh concluded. He would not remain for long in people's memories, but for a brief time at least, he would be remembered as a good man. What more could anyone ask for?

All Hugh's efforts to communicate with Joan had failed. She spent most of the time in her bedroom. So, on the morning of the wake, he brought her up a cup of tea and a piece of toast and marmalade. She made no sign of having heard the door open as he entered the bedroom. He wondered whether she was still asleep. Then, he saw her stir.

"It'll take time, Joan. But you've got to eat something."

Surprisingly, she spoke. "What's the point? There's nothing left worth living for," she said with her back still to him.

"That's not true, Joan. You have your daughters."

"My daughter."

"If you insist."

"And she can't even come to her own uncle's funeral. Do you think she'll even bother coming to mine?"

"It's hard with three children and her husband away."

"Stop making excuses. I might as well have no children at all."

"Well, I can tell you, you have one daughter who loves you and is very keen to come to the funeral, but she's afraid of the reception she'll get."

"Have you been interfering again, Hugh?"

"Someone had to inform people. And I've told Siobháin that she has to come, and I'm going to make up the bed in Rory's room for her."

To his surprise, Joan didn't respond at once. He couldn't tell whether she was angry with him or not. "She wanted to stay with a friend, but I told her that was stupid. There's no point in avoiding the issue. You two have got to have it out, one way or another."

At this she turned and faced him. "For God's sake, Hugh, not in Rory's room!"

"And why not? She has no fear of ghosts."

"Will you stop it, Hugh! I'm in no mood for your infantile humour."

"Well, she's coming whether you like it or not. If you want to talk to her, you can. If not, we can pledge a vow of silence and have a very quiet few days."

"Is she bringing…whatchamacallher…your one…with her?"

"You mean Leonora. No. I thought it best not, for the time being at least."

"*You* thought it best not. That's great. You're back in the house a couple a weeks and you're already taking over. I suppose you'll want to take the farm too when I'm gone."

"Don't be so ridiculous! For two days, you have been incommunicado. We have the wake tonight and the funeral tomorrow. Someone had to do something. As for the farm, I gave up any claim to that a long time ago. It was yours by right, and I never questioned it. So, stop talking nonsense."

"I'll have to sell the place to pay the doctor's bills and the funeral expenses. And what am I going to live on?"

"You don't have to worry about O'Malley or Finnegan. I'll take care of them. As for what you're going to live on, I have some ideas, but maybe this is not the time to discuss them. We have other things to think about."

Joan's face softened slightly so that she looked more like the sister he loved as a child. His heart went out to her because he knew that below that hard exterior was a woman bursting with love she wouldn't allow herself to express. "You mean, you're going to pay for all that?"

"I said I would, didn't I? Besides, I owe you."

"I don't want to be indebted to you, Hugh."

"There are no such things as debts between brother and sister."

She looked at him curiously. She must have been thinking of the loan he was supposed to have received and not paid back.

"So, sit up there now and eat your breakfast. Finnegan and his crew will be out soon to set things up for the wake."

"But sure, who's going to come? No one's been told."

"It's a small community. Word gets round. And I've made a few phone calls."

"Oh god, I haven't been to the hairdresser's for months. I must look a sight."

"You look grand, but if you want me to drive you into town, I will. Finnegan's lads won't be out till the afternoon. Here, sit up now and let me put the tray on your lap."

She sat up and pulled a dressing gown around her shoulders. He helped wedge a pillow behind her back. "Well, this is a treat, Hugh. I haven't been so cosseted since I had the chicken pox seventy years ago."

"It's well overdue, Joan. Things are going to change around here."

"And how do you think that's going to happen with you at the other side of the world?"

"Eat your breakfast now. We can talk about it later. You need your strength for tonight and tomorrow."

"It's going to be as bad as that then?"

"It's not bad at all as long as you don't kick against the pricks."

"I'd forgotten how bossy you were, Hugh Gorman."

"It's a family trait."

"Rory wasn't like that at all."

"You're right. But he had his stubborn side too. Now do you want me to take you into town or not?"

"Ah, no, Hugh, sure it's not right to be beautifying myself so soon after Rory's passing."

"Well, it's not a beauty contest, so I wouldn't worry about it. You look grand as you are. By the way, I saw some lamb in the freezer. I thought I'd make an Irish stew for lunch."

"You will not. The kitchen is my department. You've done enough already. Why don't you go for a walk? The next day or two are going to be very trying."

"I didn't tell you. I'm picking Siobháin up from town this afternoon at half past seven. She's taking the bus down."

Joan looked suddenly anxious. "Jesus, Hugh, I don't know if I can face her."

"Well, first of all, you need to think how you're going to make it up to her for not going to her wedding."

He thought he had possibly overstepped the mark, but he detected a look of contrition on her face.

Yet, she was still unable to accept the error of her ways. "And why should I?" she said with an obdurate pouting of the lips.

"Whatever your principles regarding homosexuality, you were wrong not to go to her wedding, the most important event in anyone's lives. She was deeply hurt and still is. Somehow, you're going to have to ask for forgiveness, but you need to know something, she's not about to apologise for being what God made her."

"I feel ashamed, Hugh. It was cruel of me. I should have talked it over with you. But where were you, only thousands of miles away?"

"Don't blame me now, Joan. Besides, the telephone was invented over a hundred years ago. All you had to do was pick it up and dial the number."

"I hate talking on the phone. Oh god, Hugh, how am I going to look her in the eye?"

"As long as you don't think about it too much, everything will go swimmingly."

"Oh lord, I wish it were that simple." She sighed and covered her face with both hands as if on the point of tears. "Leave me in peace now to eat me breakfast, will you? And don't go near the stove. No man is going to cook in my kitchen. But you can make up the bed for Siobháin. And then you can clear out and go for a walk. And don't be late for dinner."

■

Hugh had not intended to go and see Maggie, but halfway along his walk, he realised he was only a few hundred yards from her house. But he wasn't sure whether he should pay her a visit unannounced. Her hair may not be styled to her satisfaction, and she may not have her makeup on. It would be very embarrassing for her if she opened the door in a dressing gown and slippers and saw him standing there. He dithered for a while, wondering whether it was wise to raise her hopes and expectations when he was in no position to live up to them. Yet, if they were to enter into a more permanent relationship, he would be seeing her all the time unkempt and in her dressing gown and slippers. He had seen her naked, after all, and that had not been too bad at all.

He continued along the road, still uncertain what to do, until he was outside Deirdre's house. He heard what sounded like English voices. Then, he remembered that Deirdre had married an Englishman called Leonard, a heart surgeon from Oxford. He wondered whether they were over on holiday, or had they retired back to Ireland? Deirdre was trimming the hedge by the road and noticed Hugh standing there.

"Hello there," she said in a jolly English-sounding voice. "It's a lovely day for a walk."

"Deirdre, is that you?"

She looked myopically through the leaves and branches of the hedge. "Do I know you?" she said cautiously.

"You used to. I'm Hugh Gorman. It's been a long time."

"My goodness, Hugh, forgive me. Come in and meet my husband, Leonard."

She trotted down to the garden gate and opened it for him. Like Maggie, she was still a handsome woman but clearly less obsessed with her looks than her sister. "Leonard, come and meet Hugh Gorman. We saw a lot of each other as children. Before we all went our separate ways."

Leonard was a handsome man in his midseventies. He had an intelligent, bright face. "Very pleased to meet you, Hugh."

"Maggie told us you were around," said Deirdre. "We were very sorry to hear about Rory. He was my first love, you know, when I was six, I think. Shall I give Maggie a shout? We can have coffee in the garden. Leonard has put out the garden furniture.

We're going to be spending much more time here now that Leonard has retired."

"I love Ireland," he said. "It's my second home. We'll miss Aisling and the children, of course, but they're old enough to travel on their own now. So, we hope to have many visitors."

"Aisling," said Hugh ponderously. "We've never met."

"Well, I hope you'll get the chance, unless of course you're rushing off back to Australia. She's arriving tomorrow afternoon. By the way, we will be coming to Rory's funeral, but we may have to leave early to collect her from the airport."

"I'm picking up Siobháin this afternoon. She's coming down on the bus. Do they know each other?"

"No. Aisling was brought up in England. It's her fiftieth birthday this Saturday. We're having a little party for her. I hope you and Joan will be able to come. You'll still be around, I hope?"

"Oh, yes, I've got a few things to sort out before I go back."

"Wonderful."

Leonard had already served the coffee by the time Maggie arrived. As always, she was looking splendid. He was glad he hadn't surprised her in her dressing gown.

On seeing Hugh, she came over and put her arms around him. "I'm so sorry about Rory. I know how close you two were."

Somehow, Hugh didn't feel sorrowful any longer. He had resigned himself to Rory's death long before it actually happened. Even the guilt he thought he would feel did not last long. The acts of living and dying are painful, but death itself can be a deliverance. At least that thought helped to ease his conscience. "It's Joan I have to worry about now. She's going to be very lonely down there on her own."

"Don't worry, Hugh," said Deirdre. "Leonard and I will look after her. We'll become best friends again, I promise."

After coffee, Maggie asked Hugh if he could pop over to her place and change a light bulb. "You're so tall you can reach it. And my ladder is a bit wobbly."

"Don't bother Hugh, Maggie," interjected Deirdre. "Sure, Leonard can do that."

"Leonard has enough to do. Come on, young man. It won't take a second."

She took Hugh by the hand and led him through the gap in the fence between the two gardens. Hugh was aware that Deirdre and Leonard's eyes were on them and wished Maggie were not so overt about their having become lovers again.

As soon as they were out of sight and earshot, she grabbed his head and, raising herself on tiptoes, attacked his mouth with hers. He responded in kind but couldn't help thinking that it was not entirely appropriate for someone of his age. When she finally removed her mouth from his, she said, "I've missed you these last few days. Tell me you missed me."

It sounded so adolescent, but he had to admit that he had missed her, at least in the moments when he wasn't occupied with Rory and the arrangements for the wake and funeral.

She put her two arms around his waist and held him to her. "I hope you don't regret the other night."

"No, not in the least. As I said before, the quiche was delicious," he said, raising his arms to fend off the slap he knew he was about to receive.

"Oh, you!" she squealed.

"No, it was great, Maggie. There's still a bit of ould juice left in us, I think."

"I want to make the most of you while you're here."

"I'm not rushing off unless Brendan needs me." He didn't want to go into detail about his problems with Brendan, though he knew he would have to go back to Australia soon unless Brendan found himself a good lawyer.

"I really want you to meet Aisling. She's a lovely girl. I also want you to help me choose a present for her. She's going to be fifty. I want it to be something special."

"Why me? I'm the last person you need to help choose a present. Sheila said I never got her anything she liked."

"Well, if we do it together, there's a much better chance it'll be the right thing. Will you stay for lunch?"

"I wish I could. Joan's expecting me. She's just coming out of a deep depression, so I need to be by her side. Besides, Finnegan and co will be arriving to arrange things for the wake. Will I see you tonight?"

"I want to see Joan, but I'd faint if I saw Rory lying in the coffin."

"You don't have to come. I'll pass on your condolences."

"So when can we go into town? I know a shop that has lovely clothes."

"Do you know her size?"

"Oh, yes, we could wear each other's clothes. We have exactly the same build."

"What if she's put on weight?"

"Aisling, no! She's very health conscious like me. Shall we say Thursday? That'll give you some time to recover after the funeral."

Hugh gave it some thought. "Yeah, I think that'd be fine."

■

Joan seemed to be more or less back to normal when he returned for lunch. She had regained her place in the kitchen and was happy to be providing again, especially for Hugh, who "always ate like a horse" and thus rewarded her culinary efforts. He realised that her whole reason for living was to be able to look after others and that she had no real interest in looking after herself. He dreaded the thought of her living alone in that dark, dreary old house.

She was less talkative than usual, and without Rory to keep the conversation stoked, there were long periods of silence. No mention was made of Siobháin's arrival, though she must have been thinking how she was going to overcome the rift she had created between them.

Then, as they were sitting having a cup of tea, she said, "Is it true what you said?"

"What's that now, Joan?"

"That they can't help it?"

He had to do a double take before he realised she was refer-ring to Siobháin. "Well, if you think about it, Joan, who would choose to be gay with all the prejudice there is against them? I can't imagine anyone willingly choosing to be part of a minority group that is frowned upon by the church and a sizable proportion of the population."

"So, I should feel sorry for her, by rights?"

"I very much doubt she'd want that. All she wants is your acceptance. Look at it this way, Joan. If you didn't know that she was gay, would it make any difference to the way you feel about her? No. So, if you can't accept it, just ignore the fact that she pre-fers women to men in the bed department."

"It's hard for someone like me, Hugh."

"I know, Joan. Don't think it was easy for me?"

"Is Brendan gay?"

"As far as I know, he's not."

"Well, that's good, I suppose. It's hard when it's your own child."

"It requires a leap, Joan."

"What do you mean?"

"A leap out of the mental rut we're in. You know, thinking that that's the way things are and they can't be otherwise."

"Maybe I'm too old to leap, Hugh."

"I'm not asking you to leap a fence twice your height."

"This seems much higher than any fence."

"All you need is the will to do it and you can."

"I'll try, Hugh. I really will."

■

With everything that had been happening, he had almost forgot-ten about Brendan. He assumed that with the money he'd sent he'd make bail and find a lawyer who would help to get him out of the mess he was in. Nevertheless, he decided to ring and find out if things were on track.

Brendan sounded a lot perkier than he had done the last time they spoke.

"Well, you made bail anyway. Have you found a decent lawyer? Now don't take the first one you find in the phone book. Shop around a bit. I have a lawyer friend in Esperance, he might know—"

"I won't need one, Dad."

"Don't be a fool now, Brendan. You can't defend yourself. Lawyers may be—"

"They've dropped the charges."

"What? Impossible! No one caught drunk driving and in possession of drugs could get off without a sentence of some kind."

"Well, it seems we got lucky, Dad. The arresting officer was a man by the name of Nicky McGuire. He says he knows you. Tried to make a go of some business or other in Esperance after working on the station, but things didn't turn out as he planned so he joined the police force in Melbourne."

"Nicky McGuire, by the holies! How much did he want for his trouble?"

"Nothing. He says he owes you. He didn't tell me why."

"I gave him a loan, which he never paid back."

"That figures. He seemed like a nice guy. Spoke very highly of you. How much was the loan?"

"Ten thousand, something like that."

"Well, Dad, it seems he's paid us back twofold."

"I can't believe it. You mean the slate has been wiped clean."

"He says the papers miraculously disappeared. Don't ask me how. He must be sleeping with the magistrate or something. But as far as the cops are concerned, my little accident never happened, and the insurance covered the damage to the Corolla."

"Are you absolutely sure now?"

"I'm out of jail, Dad, and back in my apartment. I even got my job back at the super."

"Amazing!"

"Yeah, I feel it was a kind of sign, Dad. I've got to clear up my shit."

"Right. There's no harm in having a drink, lad, but make sure someone else does the driving."

"Don't worry. I've learnt my lesson. By the way, last time we talked, you mentioned something about me coming back and working on the station. Were you serious?"

"Did I say that? Well, maybe I did. I can't remember. I certainly want you to have a share in it, but you'll need some time to learn the business side of things."

"I'd really like that, Dad. I love the station and Esperance too. It's just I never thought you'd trust me with the place, and then we had a few blues, so I thought it best just to get out."

Had he driven his son away, just like his father had driven him away? "I'm sure we can work things out. By the way, you're not gay, are you?"

"Gay? What the fuck, Dad?"

"It's just your auntie Joan asked me and I said that as far as I know you're not, but then I started thinking and I realised I didn't know for sure. I've never seen you with a girl. And, well, most lads of your age are married."

"Just because I'm not married doesn't mean I'm gay. I just don't seem to be able to stay in a relationship for long, that's all."

"It's not the end of the world. Besides, there's still plenty of time for you to meet someone."

"When I get back home, I might find myself a nice girl."

"I hope so."

"How's Uncle Rory?"

"God, I forgot to tell you. He passed three days ago. The funeral is tomorrow."

"I'm sorry, Dad. I know you were close."

"Life goes on."

"When are you coming home?"

"Soon, I hope. I have things to sort out here. By the way, I've been thinking. Why don't you quit that Mickey Mouse job you have at the supermarket and fly back to Esperance as soon as possible? Don't wait for me to get back. I'll tell Ron to expect you. Just do as he tells you for the time being, all right? He's a good lad."

"You don't know how happy that makes me, Dad."

"I'll call again in a few days to make sure you've settled in."

"Thanks, Dad, and we'll sort out the money you sent me when you get back."

As soon as he put down the phone, Hugh wondered whether he had done the right thing encouraging Brendan to return to the station. What if he continued to drink and sell drugs? *Still, enjoy the moment*, he thought. He still couldn't believe Nicky McGuire had come up trumps. Mind you, it didn't cost him anything, except a rap over the knuckles if he was caught fiddling with the books. Still, it saved them a fortune on lawyer's fees and Brendan spending time in jail, ruining his chances of a making a decent career for himself.

The next hurdle he had to face was Siobhán and Joan.

■

At about five, Finnegan the Younger came with his crew to set up for the wake. Fortunately, Rory would arrive later, so he would not have to lie in state for too long. The sight of him was sure to drive Joan back into a state of melancholy. Until then, however, she took charge of the crew, reprimanding them if they moved a piece of furniture without asking her first or leaving a cigarette butt in an ashtray. "Be careful with that now, or I'll crucify yez." "Put a scratch on that and there'll be hell to pay." Finnegan's men were soon cowed into submission.

With any luck, he thought, *the whole proceedings might take her mind of the fateful meeting with Siobhán and the ordeal of the wake.*

The bus arrived at the stop outside O'Byrne's pub exactly on time. He hadn't seen Siobhán for years. He didn't know what to expect. Would she have half her head shorn and tattoos down both arms? Would she wear men's clothes and walk with an androgynous lope? When she stepped down from the bus, however, he was surprised to see that she was more or less as he remembered her, except for her hair, which was shorter and had streaks of grey in it.

He didn't know whether to kiss her or not, but as it turned out, he didn't have to decide. She took the initiative and kissed him on both cheeks. "Uncle Hugh, I'm so glad to see you. Mam didn't come with you then?"

"She's at home terrorising Finnegan's men."

"Finnegan?"

"The undertaker."

She laughed.

When they were in the car, Hugh turned and gazed at her for some moments. "You're looking great, Siobháin. Just as I remember you."

"A little older perhaps."

"Age is in the mind."

"I'm so glad to hear you say that. I get the feeling that so many old people think their life is over when they reach a certain age. They end up just sitting around waiting to die."

"Yes," he said thoughtfully. "I'm a little worried about your Mam. It won't be easy living alone at Connick."

"Yes, looking after Da and us gave her a purpose. The house was her domain. Without Uncle Rory, she'll have no subjects to rule over."

"It's not just that, but I think she's getting a bit too old to be living alone. I wouldn't mind if there was someone close by to look in on her every so often."

"There are plenty of neighbours and relations scattered around the place."

"True, but from what I can gather, she hasn't exactly cultivated relationships with either over the years."

Hugh started the car and pulled out into the road. They were soon on the road back to Connick. Hugh felt inexplicably happy to have Siobháin in the seat beside him. She gave off a distinct scent of stale perfume, enclosed spaces, and youth. Though she was not young by young people's standards—she was over forty—but for him, she was in the prime of life.

"Tell me about Leonora," he said suddenly. He wanted to establish from the outset that he harboured no prejudice against their marriage.

"Well, she's a film producer, which is a crazy job, by the way. I sometimes don't see her for weeks on end. Other times we're never out of each other's sight. But it's very fulfilling work and pays well. So, I wouldn't ask her to give it up."

"How did you meet?"

"About five years ago, she approached me to design some costumes for a futuristic film they were making, and it was love at first sight. It's not an easy relationship by any means. She can become edgy when she gets tired, but as long as she's happy, I'm prepared to put up with it."

"Would you ever consider coming back to live in Ireland?"

"I've never really thought about it. I feel I'm not welcome here. At the moment, at least. But the truth is if things were different, I'd be quite happy to spend at least some of my time here. I never know where Leonora will be working, America today, Scotland tomorrow, China the day after. I do get a bit lonely sometimes. I have mates in the city of course, but I feel much closer to my friends and relations here. We have so much in common."

"I can't be sure, but I have the feeling your mother may be coming around. I've been doing a bit of gentle, and sometimes not so gentle, brainwashing. I can't guarantee anything, but I'm keeping my fingers crossed. Are you nervous about confronting her?"

"Mam always scares me a little, but the truth is any contact with her and my home would be better than none at all."

"I know what you mean."

As they passed through the village of Connick, Siobháin saw an old school friend and asked Hugh to stop the car.

As she got back in, she said, "Mary was one of my best friends at school. She runs the supermarket now."

It was dusk when they drove into the yard. Hugh could see that Siobháin was looking anxious. Rather than going straight in, she waited beside him while he took her bags from the boot of the car.

Finnegan's crew had taken over the kitchen and were ready to serve drinks and titbits to the mourners. Hugh wondered where Joan was and realised that Rory was most likely already on display in the parlour, and Joan would have taken up her place beside him.

Hugh thought it best to get it over with and led Siobháin straight through to the parlour. Joan was not immediately visible, sitting as she was on the other side of the coffin, a huddled, hunched figure in black. Over her head, she was wearing a black shawl, which made her look more like a mourning widow than a bereaved sister. Hugh wondered whether that was how she felt.

There was a strong smell of incense and some candles flickered in the dark corners of the room. Otherwise, there was no light. He heard Siobhán break into sobs when she caught sight of Rory, who lay stiff yet lifelike in the ornate coffin, reminding Hugh of a waxwork figure in Madame Tussaud's. Finnegan had done a good job. The wrinkles and furrows of Rory's face had been smoothed out, and the rouge on his cheeks made him look as if he was just having forty winks before the party began. Only the hands, placed symmetrically over his chest, suggested that it was an artificial pose, arranged by someone else. Soibháin bent over and kissed his forehead. Hugh saw tears fall on Rory's face and wondered whether they would mar the makeup or, as often happens in children's fairy tales, bring him back to life. He didn't believe in either miracles or fairy tales—he had regretfully shed his childish innocence a long time ago—but in this case he would willingly have suspended disbelief, if only for a minute or two.

Siobháin finally looked up and saw her mother sitting crouched on one of the hard wooden chairs that were usually tucked in under the dining table. "Hello, Mam," she said, peering over the top of the coffin. "I'm sorry," she added ambiguously.

Hugh was glad she said sorry, not because she had any reason to ask for forgiveness. He felt she was not just saying sorry for Rory's death but for everything, sorry for not being the daughter her mother would have liked, sorry that her mother could not accept her for what she was.

Joan didn't respond at once. She just stared at her daughter with a wistful yearning Hugh could not quite define.

Each was trying to gauge what the other was thinking and feeling, deciding whether it was possible to break through the thick concrete wall that separated them.

"Hello, love," said Joan eventually. "I'm glad you came. I'm sorry too."

Sorry for what? Hugh wondered. Sorry that she had behaved so cruelly towards her daughter or sorry that Siobháin had not turned out to be the daughter she would have wished for?

"I'm glad, Mam."

At least Siobháin wanted to believe the former.

"It's a bad time, child, but we'll get through it, with the help of God."

"Yes, Mother, we will."

"You'll have to forgive me now. I need to be with your uncle Rory. We'll have time after the funeral to talk. Finnegan's people have taken over. I'm no longer mistress of me own house, thanks to your uncle Hugh. But I suppose it's nice not to have to worry about things. Someone out there will make you a cup of tea, I daresay."

Hugh took Siobháin's bags up to Rory's room. "You don't mind sleeping in his bed, do you?"

"No, of course not, Uncle. This used to be my room once. Besides, I can feel his presence, smell it too. It's as if he were here, in the room."

Hugh had not noticed it before but, yes, there was a definite smell of his brother, which was not wholly unpleasant. It reminded him of both himself and his father. He had not been aware before that families give off a distinct scent. He scanned the space to find the marks of his brother stamped on the room but it was practically bare, not a picture, not a photo. It was almost as if he had wished to depart without leaving a trace. His smell too would eventually fade, as others invaded and slowly took over.

When Hugh had laid her bag on the bed, he said, "Why don't you rest for a while? It'll be a long night."

"No. I need to be with Mam."

"All right so. It went well, I think, your first contact. I think your mother will come round in the end."

"I hope so but I'm not counting on it. And to be honest with you, Uncle Hugh, I'm not sure I can forgive her for what she did."

"I know, but you must understand that we were brought up in the dark ages. It's not easy for us oldies to adapt to the modern way of thinking."

"Well, you have, Uncle Hugh."

"Australia did that for me."

As they entered the parlour, Hugh whispered, "You don't have to stay up all night. You can leave that to your mam, though I'll try and get her to bed as soon as possible after midnight."

"I'll sit with her for a while, if she doesn't mind."

"Why should she? She'll appreciate it, I'm sure."

People started coming in about 9:00. Most of the younger people Hugh didn't know. The older ones had to introduce themselves, as in most cases they had changed beyond recognition. Some had got stout. Others had lost their hair. Often the faces of people he knew in his childhood had become so misshapen they bore no resemblance to the image he had of them in his mind.

It was tiring meeting so many people, but he also found it interesting finding out how their lives had panned out. Some had done well for themselves. Others less well. And some had remained stationary. It was hard to say if they had had a happy life, though there was something about the Irish he realised that allowed them to make the most of a bad situation. As a nation, he felt, they were a positive, go-ahead people, which probably explained why Ireland had prospered in the intervening years.

There was a good turnout for the wake. There were some tears and a lot of sorrow for the loss of a good man. At around one in the morning, it seemed as if no one else was coming, so Hugh told Finnegan's men to clear up and go home. If anyone else came, he'd serve them himself.

Joan had shaken many hands and received a lot of well-wishing. She looked all in when Hugh went to persuade her to go to bed.

Siobháin was still valiantly sitting beside her, silently sharing in the vigil. He realised what a godsend she had been. Joan needed the female touch, the gentle affection and quiet compassion he felt he was unable to give.

"Siobháin, why don't you go off to bed now? You must be exhausted."

"I'm grand, Uncle Hugh."

"You go on to bed, child," said Joan. "And thanks. Your presence made it a lot easier."

Siobháin smiled and got to her feet. "I'll see you in the morning then so," she said, laying a hand on her mother's shoulder.

Joan didn't take it but looked up at her daughter with a wan smile.

When Siobháin had left, Hugh said, "It's time you went to bed too, Joan. You need your strength for tomorrow."

"I need to stay with Rory."

"Rory'll be grand without you. Sure, he's not going anywhere. And if he does, good luck to him."

She gave him one of her reproachful looks but followed it with a jaded half-smile.

"You go off to bed now," said Hugh. "I'll stick around for an hour or two in case some latecomer turns up."

He saw her try to rise to her feet, pushing with both hands on the seat of the chair. *She is getting old*, he thought. He helped her up and led her to the kitchen.

"Oh god, look at the state of it. I should never have let anyone take over my kitchen."

"Don't worry, Joan. The lads here'll have it spick and span by the morning. Isn't that right, lads?"

"Oh, it is, Mr. Gorman. There won't be a cup or a plate out of place by the morning."

"There'd better not be," said Joan as she turned and headed for bed.

Hugh couldn't help smiling at her indefatigable need to keep her domain intact.

■

To make absolutely sure Joan's kitchen was shipshape, Hugh got up early. As it happened, Finnegan's men had left it in a far better state than it had ever been, though Joan would no doubt be loath to admit it. Siobháin was up early too and joined Hugh in the kitchen.

They were drinking a cup of tea when Joan appeared dressed and ready for the funeral. Hugh poured her a cup. "Will you have something to eat with that, Joan?"

"No, I don't feel like it."

"You should eat something. It's going to be a long day."

"I have no appetite for food. I wanted to go and say a last farewell to Rory, but when I saw the coffin fornent me, I couldn't bring myself to look. Isn't that an awful thing, Hugh?"

"Not a bit of it. It's best to remember him as he was, not lying there like a fallen statue."

She sat down and drank her tea dolefully. After some time, she looked up and cast a waxen smile at her daughter. "Thanks for sitting with me last night, Siobháin love. I felt terrible alone with Rory gone and your uncle itching to get back to Australia."

"I'll stay as long as you need me," said Siobháin flatly. "I'm in no hurry to get back."

"Well, I hope you'll be able to stay a few days longer anyway."

"Siobháin'll stay as long as you need her," interjected Hugh. "Did you not hear what she said?"

"I'd like that."

"No bother, Mam. Sure, I can write and paint here just as well as I can in London."

"Is that what you do then, Siobháin, to make a living?" asked Joan ingenuously.

Hugh was surprised she didn't know. The rift between mother and daughter was indeed wide.

"If you can call it that. I basically design film and theatre costumes, but the work is spasmodic. I can't say it doesn't have it benefits, though. It gives me time to write and paint."

Hugh couldn't help thinking she sounded like someone her mother had met for the first time.

"And you have to pay rent too?"

"Oh, I do. And rents in London are through the roof."

"I suppose they are. Sure, they're almost as bad in Dublin, so they say." She hesitated for a moment, pursing her lips as if trying to squeeze out some utterance or other. "What does…em… Leonora do then?"

"She's a film producer."

"So, she must be off and about all the time."

"Yeah, she's in Norway at the moment making some series or other…for Norwegian television, I think. I lose touch."

"It must be a bit lonely then on your own."

"A bit."

There was a heavy silence, during which he felt Joan was poring over something in her mind. Then suddenly, as if on an impulse she was unable to hold back, she said, "You could always come and stay here when she's away."

Siobháin looked severely at her mother, as if questioning her sincerity. "Are you sure about that now, Mam? You didn't even come to my wedding. Or have you forgotten? You wouldn't want to spend too much time with a lesbian now, would you?"

Hugh was taken aback by the intense bitterness in her voice, which she had given no sign of before. It must have been festering under the surface waiting to break through the epidermis at the first chance. He snatched a breath. So, it was out. The battle was on. Maybe better to get it over with. No point in dragging it out. He looked at Joan to see how she was taking Siobháin's sudden outburst of repressed anger. She was struggling with herself, he could tell, not sure what to say or which way to go.

"I had my reasons, child," she uttered at last, still unable to accept any blame.

"Well, you could have come out with them then, instead of refusing to meet the person I was going to spend the rest of my life with. You could at least have done that, but you didn't even send me a card to wish me well. Have you any idea how much that hurt, Mother? I was devastated. I swore I'd never speak to you again."

Joan raised her head in cowed defence. This was a first for her. She was the one who usually did the scolding. "Have you any idea what it was like to find out your daughter was marrying a woman?" she retorted, but in a lame voice. Only Hugh could tell she was quietly admitting she had been wrong. He only hoped Siobháin too could read her mother.

"I understand it was not easy for you to accept, but you didn't have to cut me off without a word. You disowned me, Mam. Do you know what it feels like to no longer have a home or a family?"

Siobháin turned her head to hide the tears that had begun to glisten in her eyes.

"I'm sorry, child. It was hard of me, all right. Though I never stopped loving you, not for one minute. I just couldn't condone something that was against what I was brought up to believe."

By now Siobháin was in floods of tears. Hugh could see that Joan too was on the brink.

"Come here, child," Joan whispered, rising unsteadily to her feet and putting out her arms. "Sure, I'm just an ould-fashioned one that is stuck in her antiquated ways. Uncle Hugh here has put me right on many things. And when all is said and done, does it really matter whether you're married to a man or a woman? As long as you're happy and you love each other. My only hope is that you'll be a lot happier than I ever was."

Siobháin looked up at her mother, trying to focus through the diaphanous membrane of tears, visibly shocked at what she was hearing.

"I shouldn't have let that out. It's just I didn't want you to make the same mistake I did. But I see I was wrong. The mistake would have been if you'd married a man, just to please me." Joan took Siobháin in her arms, and they both cried tears of relief. The Berlin wall had been toppled, and love could finally cross borders.

Hugh sat there, feeling slightly embarrassed to be witnessing such an intimate reconciliation, but pleased, nevertheless, that he had played a part in helping to bring it about.

When he thought that the tears had subsided, he said tentatively, "I've been toying with an idea these last couple of days that I thought might—"

"No more interfering please, Hugh," said Joan firmly. "You've done enough already."

"Well, it hasn't been all that bad so far, has it?"

She gave it some thought, and judging by her silence, he understood that the answer was in his favour.

"Go ahead then," she said grumpily.

"There's a beautiful house down the lane that is all boarded up and no use to anyone. If it's left like that any longer, it'll only start falling to pieces. I thought it might be a good idea to do it up for Siobháin, either as a permanent residence or when she's over. Then, the two of you wouldn't be on top of each other."

"And how do you think I could afford to do that?" exclaimed Joan. "And by the sound of it, Siobháin couldn't either."

"I'll pay for it. I've got a bit put aside."

"No, Mr. Moneybags. I'd sooner get a loan from the bank."

"Suit yourself, but my offer still stands. Personally, I think it's something that would benefit everyone."

"It's all too sudden. I need to think about it," said Joan dubiously.

"Yes," said Siobháin, sounding much like her mother. "It's too early to make such a drastic decision."

Joan looked up with fear in her eyes, afraid that her daughter might change her mind. "But we should give it some thought, nonetheless, shouldn't we?" she blurted.

With all the talk, Hugh almost forgot about the funeral and Finnegan's imminent arrival. "Did you talk to Father Joseph about the proceedings, Joan?"

"He called me himself. He wanted to know if there were going to be any speeches and I said no."

Hugh looked at Joan irately. "You should have asked me first, Joan. I might have wanted to say a few words. He's my brother too, you know."

"I don't like speeches at funerals. They're always very maudlin and insincere."

"You should have asked me anyway."

"If it's so important to you, I'm sure he can fit you in."

"Yes, don't worry, Uncle Hugh. I'm sure Father Joseph won't mind. I'd like to read something, if that's all right. It's a short poem I wrote on the plane coming over."

"That'd be lovely, Siobháin," said Hugh encouragingly.

"I still don't like speeches and poems at funerals," insisted Joan.

"It's become the custom, Joan. Apart from the fact that people expect it, a funeral without a few words from the bereaved is very impersonal."

"There are things I'd like to say too," said Siobhán. "And I can't think of a better place to say them. It will be my last chance to speak to Uncle Rory, and I'd like him and everyone else to know how much he meant to me."

"Suit yourselves. I see I have no say in the matter," said Joan tetchily.

"I think you should say a few words too, Mother."

"I've said all I want to say in private. There's no need for the whole world to hear it."

"That's fine," said Hugh placatingly. "We all have our own way of saying goodbye."

For some reason, the words "Break, break, break" began to echo in his head, along with the sound of crashing waves, those giant Atlantic rollers that he and Rory loved so much.

◾

Finnegan's men arrived at around nine, and at half past on the dot, the funeral procession began. Joan and Siobhán sat in the back, while Hugh sat in front. When they reached the lane gate, there were cars already lined up waiting to join the cavalcade. By the time they reached St Mary's, there was a column a mile long.

If Rory had any consciousness at all, he'd have been a proud man, thought Hugh. It was good to know that he had been so well liked in the townland.

Hugh doubted the church had seen so many people in decades. It was chockablock, with just as many outside as in. Hugh was suddenly overcome by stage fright. He had written nothing down. He knew what he wanted to say, but how would it come out in front of all these people? Then again, what did it matter? He would speak from the heart, and if it was no more than a sentence or two, so much the better.

At the end of the service, Father Joseph said Rory's brother Hugh and his niece Siobhán would like to say a few words.

Hugh stood up first and faced the crowd. "I'd like to thank you all for coming to honour my brother, Rory. I have no doubt he's a very proud man to see so many of the people he knew and loved gathered here today.

"Sometimes brothers and sisters don't always see eye to eye, but Rory was no ordinary brother. He bore none of the petty jealousies that can sometimes tear a family apart. He had no demands on life and no demands on others. He'd sooner give than take, deprive himself than deprive others. He was one of those rare, selfless, souls.

"Rory was not just a brother to me, but my closest and dearest friend. Growing up, he put up with me, his younger brother, following him around all over the place. He called me his shadow, I think. Then, at some point, we grew to be equals. But although I didn't know it at the time, I could never become his equal. He was my idol, my demigod, who taught me decency, kindness, and charity. Above all, we were connected. We understood each other in a way that only two brothers can. We came from the same place and grew up in the same place. That place kept us together all our lives, even though for the most of it we were thousands of miles apart.

"Rory was a good man. Not a great man. He had his weaknesses like all of us, but he was a decent man. He had a heart big enough to care for everyone. No sacrifice was too big, no gift too large. He will leave a vacuum not only in the hearts of his family but, from what I can see from your presence here today, in the hearts of everyone in the townland of Connick and beyond. Rory, my dearest brother and closest friend, we will meet again in the next life. In the meantime, may the journey be short and the road smooth. Goodbye, old son."

Hugh had not expected his speech would trigger tears. He thought he had got over that but he couldn't stem the flow when he said the final goodbye. Yet, he wasn't ashamed of them, and in a way, he felt they had a cleansing effect, like the Irish rain that washed over his face on his many walks over the land. As he sat down, Siobháin put her hand on his shoulder and whispered, "That was lovely, Uncle Hugh." Hugh wasn't sure how lovely it was. He only hoped that it conveyed what he felt.

"Thank you, Hugh. And now Siobháin would like to read a poem she wrote in her uncle's honour. Siobháin, please."

Father Joseph beckoned her to the altar where she stood beside Rory's coffin.

Siobháin seemed to shrink slightly as she stood in front of the massed congregation, her hand resting on the coffin. Had she memorised the poem? She seemed to hesitate, as if having second thoughts, until Hugh realised that she was simply composing herself.

"Uncle Rory was more than just an uncle to me. As a child, we were inseparable. He would take me everywhere in his van, on the tractor, on his walks around the farm. I learnt more about life from Rory than from any teacher. On my way over from England yesterday, I wrote a short poem. It is not a very good one, but it expresses my feelings for that kind, good-hearted man and the profound influence he had on me and my life. I have called it simply 'A Tribute to Uncle Rory.'

> *A beacon that glows in the darkness,*
> *a torch that lights the path ahead,*
> *a brightness that inspires,*
> *a spark that ignites*
> *has lost its fire and lustre.*
> *Yet, like an ancient star that*
> *shines in the night sky,*
> *long after it disappears into a black hole,*
> *he will continue*
> *to lighten*
> *and enlighten my heart,*
> *forever.*

"Goodbye, Uncle Rory."

Hugh could sense that the congregation wanted to clap, but it was not appropriate in this place of worship. Hugh put his hand on her arm and smiled. "Beautiful!" Hugh would like to have turned to see how many people had been moved to tears but he restrained himself. Joan, however, was quietly weeping beside him, her white handkerchief dabbing at her eyes and nose. He put his arm over her shoulder.

The rest of the funeral took place without anything untoward happening. They cried during the burial. They were duly mournful during the shaking of hands. At the gathering back at the farm, Joan said little, just listened, and thanked people for their condolences. Hugh was forced to repeat a hundred or more times a summary of what he had been doing during the last fifty, which became shorter and shorter as the afternoon wore on, bringing home to him that when all is said and done a life can be summed up in a few words.

Hugh was happy to see Mat and Bridie. They talked about Rory and the wild times they had as children, "terrorising" the townland, as Mat put it. Maggie came with Deirdre and Leonard. He liked them and thought that if Joan could bring herself to be a bit more sociable, they could become good friends. They apologised and left early to go and pick Aisling up from the airport. Hugh tried to persuade Maggie to stay, but she wanted to go with them. She hadn't seen Aisling for some time and was longing to see her. He supposed, having had three sons, Aisling represented the daughter she had never had.

That evening they were too exhausted to do anything but watch television. Siobháin said she was in the middle of a good book and would read for a bit in bed. Hugh sat with Joan, and they began watching a mediocre film. When it ended, they both awoke realising they had only seen the first few minutes of it.

◼

The next day, Hugh opened his eyes feeling relaxed but aware that he had many things to do before he could return to Australia. Apart from the bills that had to be paid, which he could do from a distance, he needed to see lawyers and sort out Rory's will.

Over breakfast, Hugh broached the subject. "Do you want me with you when you see Rory's lawyer about the inheritance?"

"What inheritance?"

"Well, didn't he have a half share in the farm?"

"No, he gave up his share years ago when the parents died."

"So, he died with nothing?"

"That's the way he wanted it."

"I had no idea."

Joan poured them both another cup of tea. "Rory wanted me to give you something," she said, grudgingly handing over an envelope.

"Why didn't he give it to me himself?"

"He didn't want you to read it till he was gone."

"Have you any idea what it's about?"

"He probably wanted to impart some secret to you that he wouldn't share with me," she said sullenly.

"You had the misfortune of being a girl, I'm afraid, Joan. When we got older, it was always about boys' things."

Hugh looked curiously at the sealed envelope.

"When did he write this?"

"He started it some time ago, before you arrived, and finished it the day you went for a long walk with Maggie."

"And he didn't tell you what was in it?"

"No, and I didn't ask. And to be honest with you, I don't really care, not now."

"I'll read it so, when I get the chance. Did I tell you Maggie wants me to go with her to choose a birthday present for Aisling? God knows why she wants me along. I haven't a clue what she'd like."

"She wants your company, I suppose. You know she never got on with Tom."

"No, I didn't."

"Perhaps I shouldn't be telling you, but they spent a lot of time apart, especially after the boys grew up. She was either up here or over in England with Deirdre. She's terrible fond of Deirdre's daughter, Aisling."

"So I gathered. Do you know why she and Tom didn't get on?"

"They had little in common. He was a townie and didn't understand her attachment to the country. She implied one day that he was jealous of something that happened in her past, before she met him. I met Tom once. I didn't like him. I thought he was a typical spoilt brat, and arrogant with it. He didn't want to let Maggie out of his sight, but she wouldn't have it. So, he started running after other women, to make her jealous probably. God knows. I gave up trying to understand people eons ago. Then, when he got older, he developed a partiality for the drink and spent more time in the pub than at home. I think she had a hard time with him."

"I'm sorry to hear that. She didn't mention anything to me about it."

"And why would she?"

"By the way, I forgot to tell you. Deirdre and Leonard have invited us to Aisling's birthday party on Saturday. Apparently, she's going to be fifty."

"Yes, Deirdre had a very difficult pregnancy, so they say. Maggie had to go over and spend the whole time with her. She virtually delivered the child for what I can gather and then stayed with Deirdre for quite some time after the birth."

'Is that right? I had no idea. When did she meet Tom then?"

"Oh, that was a good while after that. A year or two, at least. I think she was still hoping you'd come back. We all thought you two would get married one day. Mam would say a prayer every night that Maggie'd be able to lure you back home."

"I had no idea."

"It seems there's a lot you don't know, Hugh," she said with a crooked smile.

"Maggie wrote to me a couple of times after I got to Australia, but she certainly never pleaded with me to come home."

"I suppose you just weren't reading between the lines. A woman has her dignity, you know."

■

After breakfast, Hugh asked Joan for the keys to the lodge. She didn't put up any resistance, just said, "It's in a terrible state. I hope there's not too much damp."

"If there is, we can fix it."

"But if she sees it like that, she may not want to live there," she said anxiously.

"She will, whatever state it's in."

Despite his conviction that everything was fixable, he was worried about the house. It hadn't been lived in for nearly two years. A bad sign was when he couldn't open the front door. The wood had swollen, and it required a lot of shoving and banging to get it open. However, once inside it was evident that the house was in surprisingly good condition. It was fully furnished too. All it needed was a few new washers in the bathroom and kitchen and some redecoration. He was very relieved, as he had been overgenerous with his offer to fix the place up.

"Well, what do you think?" said Hugh turning to Siobháin.

"I love it, Uncle Hugh. It's enormous. There's even an extra room I can make into a studio."

"How do you think Leonora will take to the idea?"

"Oh, she'll love it. She adores gardening. I can see a lawn at the front and a vegetable garden at the back."

"I got the impression your mother is fairly reconciled to the idea."

"I wouldn't count on it."

The area around the house was nearly an acre and had enormous potential. There was a small stream flowing along a ditch at the far end of what would become the garden. "Mat, Rory, and I used to fish in that stream. We caught some lovely trout there at that very spot. The house didn't exist then, of course."

"I just like watching fish, Uncle Hugh. I'm vegan. But the stream is lovely. There's nothing more soothing than the sound of running water."

As they walked back up the lane to the house, Siobháin entwined her arm in his. He felt immensely happy that she felt close enough to do something so intimate. He had seen little of his Irish relatives except on holidays, which had become fewer and fewer as the years passed. He was glad they did not feel he was a stranger to them.

"I wouldn't tell Mam or anyone else, but it was Uncle Rory who urged me to go ahead and marry Leonora. It was just after same-sex marriage became legal in Ireland in 2015. I knew how Mother would react, but it meant so much to both of us that we should become an officially recognized couple. We didn't want to be an item just for a close circle of gay friends. It was Uncle Rory who finally persuaded me to go ahead. I can hear him saying it, 'To hell with it, girl, you only live once. You love each other and want to spend the rest of your lives together so why hide it under a bushel. Enjoy it. Shout it out from the rooftops.' He said that Mam would come round in the end and, well, God willing, it seems he was right, though it is only thanks to you."

"Rory was always a freethinker. He used to say, 'Never take anything for granted. Question everything, even if it's something you've believed in all your life.' And I've always done that, well, most of the time. Who was it who said, 'Only a fool is unwilling to change'?"

They both laughed.

"Rory was such a wise man, Uncle Hugh. What a pity he never married!"

"I always thought he'd marry Josie. You probably never knew her. He never told me exactly what happened between them. He implied she went off with someone else."

"He would have been a wonderful father. Da was okay as far as fathers go, but he couldn't be bothered much with children."

"It's funny how our lives turn out."

"Do you think it all boils down to chance?"

"Chance plays a part, no doubt, but we can foster chance, nurture it, so that it works in our favour. Of course, there are certain things we can do nothing about. But I do believe it depends very much on how positive we are about things. If we really want something, we can usually find a way of achieving it."

Hugh put his hand in his pocket to make sure he had remembered to take the key to the lodge. As he did so, he felt Rory's letter. He took it out and held it up to the light, as if it was a five hundred euro note and he was trying to see if the watermark was genuine. "Your mother gave it to me. It's from Rory."

"And you haven't read it yet?"

"I'm sort of putting it off."

"But why, Uncle Hugh?"

"I suppose I'm afraid of what I might find there. Rory always liked to surprise me."

"You're not thinking of leaving it unopened, are you?"

"It had crossed my mind. I don't know what skeletons might come tumbling out. In my experience, it's best to leave them fellows locked comfortably away in a cupboard."

"I wouldn't be able to do that. I would have to know. For better or for worse."

"I may read it tonight. Let him get well and truly through the gates of heaven before I start firing curses at him."

Siobháin laughed and tugged at his arm. "Let's see if we can help Mam with lunch."

"You can try. She won't let me within a mile of the stove. By the way, you will come to Aisling's birthday party, won't you?"

"Am I invited?"

"Of course, Maggie thinks you two would get on like a house on fire."

"I'll come then."

Maggie came soon after lunch to pick Hugh up to go into town. She seemed in great form, looking incredibly young and sprightly. It wasn't long before she started on her favourite subject, Aisling.

"How is she?" said Hugh.

"Adorable, as usual."

"Does she work?"

"Didn't I tell you? She's a microbiologist at Oxford University."

"My god, well, I suppose with parents like Deirdre and Leonard it's not surprising. If my father had been a heart surgeon and my mother a historian, I might have had a few brains too."

For the rest of the journey into town Maggie talked about nothing else but Aisling. He couldn't help thinking that she must be exaggerating a little. No human being could be so perfect. Still, he was intrigued and curious to meet her.

They parked on the quay, walked along the riverbank, and cut up to the main street. Maggie was exceedingly happy. She seemed to have a spring in her step that he could only put down to

Aisling's arrival. He tried to work out why she was so important to her. He could only attribute it to the fact that she had played such an important role in bringing her into the world and then taking care of her in those early months when Deirdre was recovering from the birth.

The clothes shop was very elegant, stocked with all the latest Italian and French designs. It was certainly not cheap, but it seemed Maggie spared no expense when it came to Aisling.

"What do you think of this, Hugh?" she said, holding a dress up that she had selected from the rack.

"It certainly looks pretty. But is it her taste? And will it fit her?"

"We have exactly the same taste and are the same size. We're like two peas in a pod."

The shop assistant came over with a broad smile on her face. "It's lovely, isn't it? Is it for you, Madam?"

"No, it's for my…my sister's daughter."

"Oh, your niece? Lovely. What's her size?"

"We wear the same size. If it fits me, it'll fit her."

"Would you like to try it on then?"

Maggie came out of the fitting room parading and pirouetting like a top model. Then, she did a quick twirl on the shop floor, causing the hem of the dress to splay out like the seats on a merry-go-round.

Hugh smiled but made no comment.

"So, what do you think?" asked Maggie expectantly.

"How about I buy it for *you*, Maggie? You look splendid in it."

"Don't be silly. This is for Aisling. So?"

Hugh looked it up and down and then viewed it from different angles as if it was a top-of-the-range sports car he was about to invest in. If it had doors, he would definitely have wanted to look inside and test the leather upholstery. Even still he was unable to make a pronouncement on whether he thought it a good buy or not. "I'm not sure. Maybe."

"Oh, men," exclaimed Maggie. "They can't make up their minds."

"Judging by his reaction, I'd say your husband likes it, Madam," said the young shop assistant, eying both of them reassuringly.

Both Maggie and Hugh froze for a second, a look of unease fleeting across their faces.

The assistant immediately realised she had made a booboo. "Oh, I'm so sorry. The gentleman isn't your husband. You are such a lovely couple, I assumed—"

"Don't worry," said Maggie, quickly trying to salvage the situation. "He's my boyfriend, which is the same thing these days, isn't it?"

The shop assistant tried to conceal her surprise with a strained smile. "Oh, well, then. Even better."

"I think we'll have it," said Hugh decisively. "If her niece doesn't like it, my…girlfriend can wear it. And I insist on paying for it."

"No, you won't, Hugh Gorman, but I will let you pay half. In that way, it can be a present from both of us."

"I've never met your niece, but anyway."

"You will love her, Hugh. I'm sure you will." She said it with such overstated vehemence it was almost as if she was afraid he might not.

"I'm sure I will, Maggie, though I am expecting no less than a goddess."

"She is one," she said emphatically.

Maggie insisted they write a note to put in with the present. She wanted it to be simple, something like 'From Maggie and Hugh, with all our love'.

"But she doesn't know me from Adam, Maggie."

"Well, she will know you on Saturday, and I know it's going to be love at first sight."

"If you say so."

"I've told her about you. She knows exactly what to expect."

"An old man way past his prime? No?" he said, noticing her saucy smile. "Don't tell me you've gone overboard about me too. Now she's going to be disappointed, if she even cares."

"Oh, she'll care all right. I've told her you were my first lover."

"Oh god, Maggie, you're incorrigible. This will be most embarrassing."

"I've even told her you were the man I should have married but foolishly let you get away."

"It seems to me you tell your niece things that someone wouldn't even tell their own daughter."

"That's the kind of relationship we have. She's both my niece and my daughter."

Hugh thought it might be nice to sit at a café by the river and have tea and cakes. Maggie loved the idea.

When the tea came, she said, "I wish you could meet her before Saturday. But I suppose I shouldn't push you too hard so soon after Rory's death."

"I think it would be much better if I met her along with everyone else. I wouldn't want her to feel under interrogation."

"She wouldn't feel that, but you're right. I can wait another day."

Maggie seemed overexcited, like a child about to have her first sleepover. Why was she in such a hurry for them to meet? Had she jumped the gun and told her they were about to get married?

After tea, they went for a leisurely walk along a shady path by the river. They watched a boat with noisy tourists go by and young people in canoes and kayaks, slapping rhythmically through the water. They held hands and said hello to the other elderly people out for their constitutional. Australia seemed so far away, but it was there nonetheless in the alcoves of his mind, telling him he was neglecting his duties, neglecting his son, neglecting what he had achieved in life.

On the way back, Maggie persuaded Hugh to stay for supper. He called Joan to make sure they hadn't prepared anything special, but apparently, they were just going to have leftovers from the funeral reception. Maggie opened a bottle of wine and prepared something simple. This time it was so much easier to lead Maggie into the bedroom. It was clearly something they had both been thinking about.

After they had made love, she said, "Would you mind staying the night, Hugh?"

"You mean, so that we can pretend to be husband and wife?"

"I know you're just codding me but, yes, why not?"

"Is that what you want, Maggie?"

"It's what I've always wanted."

"You know I'm going to have to go back to Australia, don't you?"

She turned her head away from him, and he was aware of her weeping silently.

"My life is in Australia."

She said nothing.

"Do you know what Esperance means, Maggie?"

"No," she said offhandedly, as if she didn't really care.

"It means hope. That's what I owe Australia. Hope."

She didn't respond. She just lay there. He understood her sorrow but felt incapable of doing anything that would help to alleviate it. He realized now it had been a mistake to go along with her need to resume where they had left off. Jerry had been right.

He didn't stay the night. He didn't want to shock Joan or Siobháin. He was meant to be in mourning, and he was in mourning, but as he had said to Siobháin, life goes on. Rory, more than anyone else, would understand that.

Joan and Siobháin were about to have an early night when he got back. Joan asked if they had found a nice present for Aisling. He said they did but didn't go into detail.

He turned on the TV, but there was nothing of any interest, just an Irish series that meant nothing to him and a talk show about matters Irish that he knew nothing about. So, he decided to have an early night himself.

He was about to turn off the light when he remembered Rory's letter. He was curious to find out what it contained but frightened too of what he might find there. He was about to throw it into the wastepaper basket when he suddenly changed his mind. It might hold something of vital importance, something that might affect Joan's life, money perhaps. He sat up in bed and with some trepidation tore open the envelope.

Rory's writing had never been good, but with some guesswork and a lot of imagination, he was able to untangle the scrawl.

Dear Hugh.

I have left instructions with Joan to give you this letter only when I'm gone. I suppose it was cowardice on my part that I couldn't tell you all this to your face. But now I am no longer, you can think what you like of me. I did you a great injustice, and I should have told you and begged your forgiveness.

You asked me about Josie in the past and you're right. I should have married her but the parents thought she was beneath me and she was only after my money, not that I ever had much of that, but the house down the lane would have been mine one day and half the farm. Well, you know me, Hugh boy, I never wanted to hurt Mam, though she might have got used to it if I had married her.

So, I kept on putting off the day when I'd pop the question. And I suppose Josie knew as well as I did that that day would never come. So, she hooked up with another lad from up the way, and she put it plain to me. She liked me but it was clear I'd never be able to cast the die, and she was getting on herself. So, she married your man instead.

I went through a rough time for a while. I kept in touch with her on the sly until one day she came to me and told me that for some reason his parents had kicked them out of the family home and they were homeless. Well, at about that time Uncle Patty died and left a fair amount to Joan. At first, she thought she'd buy another farm adjacent to ours, but we decided we were all right as we were. It would just mean another headache. So, the money was just sitting in the bank. Joan suggested we lend it to you because we knew that you were trying to buy out Sheila's brother's half of the sheep farm over in Australia. And that's what we agreed to do, and she asked me to arrange it all. But then Josie came and explained the whole situation with her man's family and I felt sorry for her. You see, Hugh, I still loved her. So, I gave her the money so that they could buy a place of their own.

It was only a loan, mind. She promised to have it back to me within five years, as soon as they started making something out of the farm. Well, the upshot is, Hugh boy, that I never got the money back. It seems that Josie's man was not much of a farmer, and in the end, he got a job in the fertiliser factory.

Now, I'm telling you this, Hugh, because of the terrible guilt that has been racking me all these years. I wasn't able to tell Joan the truth because I know she'd never forgive me. So, I'm leaving it up to you, boy, because I don't want you and Joan to be estranged forever. You see, she thinks you did her wrong. So, tell her, be damned. I won't mind what she thinks of me now. I'll be safely buried under six foot of earth.

I know it'll be hard for you to forgive me, and I don't expect you to, but you know I was always a bit lightheaded. The truth is I thought that if I couldn't make her happy by being her husband, I could at least make her happy by lending her the money. I think I done wrong, though. What did Polonius say, "Neither a borrower nor a lender be"? Sure, I only saw her once more after that. I don't doubt she wanted to pay me back, but she couldn't and so she just stopped communicating with me.

Well, boy, that's the story. The story of a weak man, who wanted to do what was right and ended up doing a terrible wrong to his brother and sister. When all is said and done, Hugh, the family is all that matters in the end. I won't go on. It's up to you to forgive me or not, to tell Joan or not. Just know this. You were the only person in the whole world I truly loved. Even my love for Josie and Joan fades in comparison. I hope I was able to say goodbye to you in a proper manner, but if not, I'm saying goodbye now. And, God willing, we'll meet again in the next life and you can give me a real ould bollocking.

Your loving brother, Rory.

Hugh knew he should be angry with Rory, but somehow his foolish act of generosity was just another side of his goodness. The letter had moved him to tears, not so much because of its content but because he could hear Rory talking to him once more, and he realised that it would be for the last time.

Despite being exhausted, he had difficulty sleeping. He was now faced with the dilemma of whether to tell Joan or not. On the one hand, he didn't want her to hold a grudge against him for the rest of her life. On the other, he didn't want to spoil the image she had of her beloved Rory, the loyal, honest brother, who had sacrificed everything for his family.

Sleep finally overtook him in the early hours, but it was a disturbed sleep, in which Rory and Joan were fighting and he was standing by unable or unwilling to intervene.

He came down for breakfast and found Joan and Siobháin chatting away like a mother and daughter should. Siobháin in particular was in great form. It appeared she was catching up on all the local gossip. When she saw Hugh, she yelled with delight and kissed him on both cheeks. "Uncle Hugh, come and have breakfast. Mam and I were just talking about old times. I was also telling her about Leonora and how we met."

He threw a glance at Joan to see how she was taking it. Though still reserved, he could tell that she too was happy. He sat down at the kitchen table but had very little appetite. He just smiled and nodded as mother and daughter gabbled on about people and things that were irrelevant to him.

Siobháin noticed that he had left some of his bacon and eggs on his plate. "What's wrong, Uncle Hugh? Mam says you love bacon and eggs."

"Oh, I do, I do. It's just I have a few things on my mind."

"Is it Maggie?" said Joan.

"Among other things."

"She's a handsome woman, Hugh, but she's very attached to Ireland. I doubt you'll get her to go back to Australia with you."

"There's been no talk of it."

"Is it just a fling you're having then?"

"I don't know what it is, to be honest with you. Life with Maggie would be like trying to turn the world upside down. I just don't think it could work out."

"How does *she* feel, Uncle Hugh?"

"We haven't talked about it, but I think she'd just like us to continue where we left off fifty years ago, but I don't think that's possible. So much has happened since then."

"Where is home for you now, Uncle? That's what you have to consider."

He didn't answer at once. The truth was he didn't know. In Australia, Ireland was home. In Ireland, Australia was home. He knew he had to make up his mind and face the loss of one or the other. "I suppose Australia is home for me now. I have the boys there, and my grandchildren and the station still means a lot to me. It's my life's work."

"But your heart is still in Ireland."

Hugh smiled. He had always admired his niece's perspicacity. Yes, his heart was still in Ireland, but everything else was in Australia. So, what was he? A dismembered being, never to become whole again. "You're right. My heart is in Ireland but my soul is in Australia. So, whatever I decide I will have to give one up."

"Can't you at least spend more time in Ireland?"

"It all depends on Brendan. He hasn't been all that reliable in the past. He seems determined to make a go of the station, but he's not one for sticking at things."

Siobháin put her hand on Hugh's arm in gentle reassurance. "Things will work out, I'm sure Uncle Hugh. Two days ago, I thought I'd never come back to Ireland and now thanks to Uncle Rory I'm about to take up permanent residence, if Mam agrees, that is."

"Oh, I do. I'd love to have you living down in the lodge. We could keep an eye on each other."

"I'm so happy, Mam, that you said that."

"It wasn't easy for me to accept Leonora, love. I belong to another generation. We had other ideas but they're outdated, I know, and I have to accept it."

Siobháin looked at her mother with deep affection and appreciation, aware of how difficult it was for her to say what she did. "Thanks, Mam. I'm sure you'll love Leonora. She doesn't have purple hair and hairy legs, I assure you. She's vegan, like me, has short brown hair, with blond streaks, but other than that she's very normal."

The atmosphere in the house seemed so conciliatory that Hugh thought that maybe it was the right time to tell Joan about Rory's letter, but he couldn't bring himself to do it. Just when the family was coming back together, Rory's letter might tear it apart again. On the other hand, wouldn't the unpaid loan just continue to fester like an unhealed wound between them? She could never forget it or completely forgive him for what he was supposed to have done or not done.

He decided to change the subject. "So, what are your plans for today, Siobháin?"

"I was thinking of going down to the lodge and seeing what needs doing. I can't wait for Leonora to see it."

"When you've decided, just let me know and we'll set things in motion. I promised Maggie I'd see her for lunch. Apparently, she's making a birthday cake for Aisling and wants me to put my mark on it, which is about all it'll be. My artistic talents don't go beyond squiggly lines and stick figures."

"For some reason, she really wants Aisling to see you two as an item."

"From what I can gather, she's told her all about us. To be honest, I don't really mind, if it gives Maggie pleasure."

They both looked at him intently possibly waiting for him to elaborate but he was not forthcoming.

"So, Siobháin, shall we go down to the lodge before I walk over to Maggie's?"

"I'd love that, Uncle Hugh! Mam, do you want to come too?"

"No, you two go on. The sight of the place makes me sad. It used to remind me of your Gran and now it makes me think of Rory. But once you've put your stamp on it, I'm sure it will take on a whole new life."

"It will, Mother, I'm sure."

■

It was a blustery late summer's day. Already the sun had begun to dip in the sky. Hugh tried to remember what winter was like in Ireland. It was nothing like Australia where winter could hardly be called winter. He remembered as a child waking up to frosted windows and having to scratch a peephole in the ice to see what the day was like. The house was cold too, but somehow it didn't bother them. The kitchen was always toasty, and by evening, the parlour had warmed up from the fire his mother lit early in the afternoon.

The wind was blowing from the south, and he could smell the salt on the air. It was that taste and smell that he associated so much with Ireland. He raised his head to the wind and allowed it to blow the grey locks off his forehead. He breathed in deeply hoping it would somehow embed itself on his DNA.

He could never get over how green Ireland was. That was something he never got tired of. Ireland was indeed the Emerald Isle, not only because of its myriad shades of green, constantly changing with the seasons, but for him it was also a jewel, a priceless dark green jewel that had no equivalent anywhere else in the world.

Instead of going through the gate on to the road, he went over the stile, as he used to as a child. It was a little overgrown through lack of use. but the stones were as he remembered them, the same dappled grey, in roughly hewn granite. He idled along the boreen, taking his time, helping himself to blackberries whenever he saw rich pickings. For some reason, he was far more observant than he had been in previous days. He noticed the birds scratching around in the undergrowth and the multitude of insects that inhabited the ditches by the road. Once again, after Rory's death, the countryside was coming back to life.

As he approached Maggie's house, he heard Deirdre and Leonard talking in the garden. He was about to say hello when he heard a third, younger, voice. He assumed it was Aisling. So, he decided to slip by unseen. For some reason, he was apprehensive about meeting her. He had a feeling that she was going to play a key role in his future relationship with Maggie. What he didn't know was whether it was going to be for the better or the worse.

Maggie opened the door before he even had a chance to ring the bell. She was looking as attractive as ever, but he was glad to see she was more casually dressed. She was wearing beige slacks and a loose orange blouse and flat slip-on shoes. Of course, everything was in perfect harmony with her hair and complexion. She put her arms round his neck and lifted herself up to kiss him.

"Dinner is ready," she said, taking him by the hand. "But I thought we'd have a drink in the sunroom first."

The sunroom was attached to the southwest corner of the house and was beautifully laid out with comfortable garden furniture and a table. It was full of orchids and other tropical plants that seemed to be thriving, giving off an exotic scent that permeated the whole area.

As she brought them both a drink, she said, "I hope I didn't keep you too late last night."

"I don't think I was missed."

"I've made the cake, but I thought we'd decorate it after lunch."

"You need Siobháin to help you with that. She's the artistic one."

"It doesn't have to be very artistic. I just wanted her to know it's from both of us." She laid the glasses on two mats on the table. "I thought you'd never come."

"Was I late?"

"No. I just wanted you here as quickly as possible. Every second counts. But I'm not counting down. That would be too depressing. I'm thinking up all sorts of ways of keeping you here as long as possible."

"I'm going to be doing up the lodge at the end of the lane."

"Really? It must be in an awful state."

"No, surprisingly, but as I'm going to be paying for it, I'd like to oversee the work. It may mean staying on for a week or two or coming back later in the year."

"How about both?" she said enticingly.

"We shall see," he said with an empathetic smile. He lifted his glass of wine. "Here's to us."

She raised her glass hesitantly. "Do you mean that, Hugh?"

"Of course, I do."

"Here's to us then," she uttered wistfully.

"Maggie, did I tell you about the letter Rory wrote to me before he died? Did you know anything about him giving money to Josie Flynn?"

"I know they were going steady for a long while but that's all. Didn't she marry a man from over Carlow way?"

"Yes. Joan inherited some money from her uncle Patty, and they had decided to lend it to me. Rory was going to arrange it all. In the meantime, Josie came along and pleaded poverty, and Rory agreed to lend it to her so that she and the new husband could buy a place. It was meant to be a five-year loan but, as so often happens, the money was never paid back. Rory never told Joan and there's been bad blood between us for years. I was aware of something wrong, but I never knew what. It all came out about a week before Rory died. My dilemma is whether I should tell Joan or not about Rory's letter."

"Of course you should, Hugh! You can't let this come between you."

"But it will destroy her memory of Rory."

"I'm sorry, Hugh, but Rory is dead. You are alive. My feeling is that Joan will forgive Rory in time. You must think of your relationship with Joan. You have to tell her."

Despite her vehemence, Hugh was not convinced. Joan and Rory had lived their whole lives together. They had formed a solid bond of trust. It would be a devastating blow for her to know that Rory had deceived her and had allowed her to blame him. He, on the other hand, would be going back to Australia. Nothing would change greatly. That resentment would remain, but he had put up with it for thirty years. He could tolerate it for another ten or however many years they still had to live.

He didn't want to argue about it with Maggie. From an objective point of view, she was right but it would be hard for her to understand his subjective feelings on the matter. "Yes," he said. "Perhaps I will."

Maggie once again proved herself to be an excellent cook. She admitted to having done a cordon bleu course in London during Deirdre's pregnancy, which had kept her in good stead ever since. After lunch, they sat on the sofa in the sunroom and dozed in each other's arms. When they had recovered from the wine and the meal, Maggie got out the birthday cake. It was a giant three-tiered sponge cake with fresh strawberries and cream between each layer. Maggie's plan was to use Smarties to write "Happy Birthday Aisling from Maggie and Hugh."

"Do you think Smarties are really appropriate for a fifty-year-old, Maggie?"

"You think not?" she said. "I hadn't thought of that."

"And, besides, how are you going to fit all those words on the cake?"

"You see, that's why I wanted your help."

"How about just 'Happy Birthday' or 'Best Wishes Aisling.'"

"No. It must have our names on it. How about 'Love from Maggie and Hugh'?"

"It'd fit, just about."

"Well, that's it then. I'll write Maggie and you write Hugh."

"I can just about manage that."

Maggie seemed immensely pleased with the result. "You can't imagine how delighted she'll be. I can't wait to see her face. Don't be surprised if she gets a bit emotional. She's very excited about meeting you."

"The boyfriend, eh?"

She punched him gently in the chest, took some leftover cream, and planted a dollop on the end of his nose, which he tried unsuccessfully to lick off with the tip of his tongue.

Maggie wanted to go for a walk, so she went with him a part of the way back to the farm. Hugh would have felt utterly content, if it weren't for his imminent departure. Though they were both trying to put it out of their minds, it was there nonetheless lurking in the background, casting a shadow over every moment of their happiness. She left him by the stream where he had to look for a way across without ruining his shoes. In the end, he found a spot where the river narrowed, and he was able to leap across.

When he entered the kitchen, Siobháin and Joan were in the middle of supper. "We weren't expecting you, Hugh. We thought you might stay the night with Maggie."

Hugh looked at Joan, about to refute her insinuation, but what was the point in denying what was in plain sight?

Joan got up and poured Hugh a cup of tea. "Will you have something to eat, Hugh?"

"Thanks, Joan. I've already eaten too much today. Maggie is determined to ruin my silhouette."

"Did you have a good day?"

"Very pleasant. She's easy company."

"It'll be nice to meet Leonard and Aisling again. It's been ages."

"By the way, Joan. I've been wanting to talk to you about something and now is as good a time as any. That loan you gave me. I'm going to pay it back, with interest. How much was it again? And fixing up the lodge is separate. It's a wedding gift from Sheila and me to Siobháin."

Joan stopped eating and dropped her knife on the plate with a clatter. She gave Hugh a piercing look that he was unable to interpret. Was it anger or grievance?

"You will not, Hughie Gorman. I won't take a penny off of you."

"But I have it, Joan. At least, I'll find it somehow. It'll be no bother."

"I won't take what you don't owe. I went into your room to make your bed. I saw Rory's letter there on the table by the bed. I was going to leave it alone, but God forgive me, I wanted so much to hear his voice again. I couldn't resist the temptation. I read it, and thank God I did, for I learnt the truth. I have been accusing you all these years of a misdemeanour you never committed. I found you guilty without trial or jury. I did you wrong, Hugh."

There was a long silence. His attempt at fabrication had failed. The letter had forever ruined Rory's chances of sanctification, not that it was something he ever sought.

"Sure, I never suspected Rory of such a thing," she continued. "Well, that's not true. If it had crossed my mind, I wouldn't have put it past him. The truth is he never lied. He just never told me the truth, which amounts to the same thing, I suppose."

"It was his chance to do a charitable act, Joan. Don't be too hard on him."

"Oh, Jes', Hugh, will you stop trying to find excuses for everyone? The man did you wrong, and may God forgive him. He damn near ruined our relationship. He was a weak man, Hugh. He should have married Josie and made the most of it. If he had, eventually we would have bought another place with Uncle Patty's money and all would have been grand. Everyone would have been happy."

"Well, it didn't work out like that," said Hugh with a sigh. "It's all out now, anyway."

"And a good thing too! It's just a pity it had to wait till after his death."

Hugh was glad it was in the open, but he was also sad that his sleight of hand had not worked. He had so wanted to keep Rory's image intact. *But then again*, he thought, *a true image is much better than a false one*. And who knows? He would have resented Joan's acrimony in the end.

He slept well that night, though he was anxious about his meeting with Aisling. What if he didn't like her? What if she was nothing like the picture Maggie had painted of her? How could he hide his feelings? He was too old for pretence. He wanted to spend the remaining years of his life at peace with the world, even if it seemed it did not want to be at peace with him.

■

Maggie insisted that they take the birthday cake across together. So, Joan and Siobháin went on to the party separately. Fortunately, the day was fine. So, it looked as if it would take place in the garden. Apparently, Leonard was a past master at handling the barbecue.

Maggie was hopelessly flustered as they prepared to set off next door. "Perhaps I should carry the cake, Hugh. I'm afraid you'll drop it."

"If anyone's going to drop it, you are, the state you're in. I won't let you down, I promise. I'll be on my best behaviour."

"This is no joke, Hugh Gorman. I've been dreading this moment for the last fifty years."

Hugh laughed. "Her fiftieth birthday? Imagine how I felt on my seventieth."

"You carry the cake, Hugh. I'll surely drop it and ruin every-thing. My hands are shaking as if I had the palsy."

"It's only a cake, Maggie."

"It's more than just a cake, Hugh. It's us…you, me, and Aisling."

Hugh could see that Maggie was in a terrible state of nerves. "How about having a quick one before going over? Nothing that a bit of Dutch courage won't cure."

"No, I want to do it with a clear head. I must think positive." She took a deep breath and handed Hugh the cake. "Our fate is in your hands now."

Hugh thought Maggie was being very melodramatic but refrained from making light of it. She must have had her reasons, he supposed, though he couldn't imagine what they were.

They walked solemnly along the garden path and through the gap in the fence. Hugh noticed that she had gone pale and was breathing heavily. "Are you all right, Maggie?"

"No, but there's no going back now."

A number of people had already arrived by the time they reached the house. Joan and Siobháin were there, talking to Deirdre.

Maggie led him into the dining room where he placed the cake gingerly on a sideboard. Maggie was looking around nervously. "I wonder where she is."

It was Hugh who noticed her first. For a moment, he thought he was looking at a younger version of Maggie. The only difference was her height. She was about a foot taller. She too was looking distractedly around her as if searching for someone in the gathering crowd. When their eyes met, there was instant recognition. Maggie must have shown her photos of him.

"It's Aisling! She's the spitting image of you," he said with delight. The intensity with which she stared at him almost hurt. There was something about her that he had not discerned in the photo, something so familiar that he was sure they must have met before. But he would have remembered and Maggie would certainly not have forgotten.

Still at a distance of some yards, they stood facing each other for some moments, appraising, weighing up, comparing the anticipated with the unexpected. Neither seemed disappointed. Maggie just stood there with bated breath. It was Hugh who spoke first. "Aisling. You are everything and more than Maggie made you out to be. I thought she must be exaggerating, but if anything, she didn't do you justice."

"She has a very inflated opinion of me, Hugh. I can call you Hugh?"

"I wouldn't want otherwise."

She stood their immobile, momentarily unsure what to do. Then, moved by some hidden impulse, she went towards him her arms out. "Would you mind if I gave you a hug, Hugh?"

Hugh was slightly taken aback, but Maggie had warned him of her tendency to get emotional. "I'd love nothing better."

Unlike Maggie, she didn't have to stand on tiptoes to reach him. In fact, she was only a few inches shorter than he was. He was surprised by how tightly she held him, as if satisfying an unrequited urge she had contained for a long time. He became aware of tears falling on his neck, followed by stifled sniffles. He held her from him and saw that she was crying.

"I don't think I deserve that," he said. "I'm only the boyfriend." His attempt at humour did not seem to lighten the mood. Now, Maggie was crying, and he found himself with an arm around each of the two blubbering ladies. Fortunately, everyone else was too engaged in conversation to notice.

"Now that I've got you two together," said Aisling, "I'm not going to let you out of my sight till the day is out."

"You may get very tired of me by then," he said. "I'm just an old man from Australia."

"You're far more than that to me. I want to find out all about Australia and your sons. Niall has three children, I believe."

Maggie had told her everything it seemed.

She asked question after question, confirming facts that she was already privy to. When he answered, she seemed to be assimilating everything, hanging on his every word. Other people came by but were given short shrift. No one else existed but he. Eventually her thirst was partially quenched, and she allowed him to ask her some questions. He found out that she had three children, two boys and a girl. Her eldest, Leonard, was about to start an internship at St. Mary's Hospital. He was going to be a surgeon like his grandfather. The middle one was a girl, Una, who was in her last year at Oxford, where she was studying computer engineering. The youngest, Hugh, was about to go up to Imperial College to study pharmacology. When he heard the name, he couldn't help wondering if Maggie hadn't had a hand in naming their third child.

The more he got to know Aisling, the more impressed he was by her intelligence and warmth. *If Sheila and I had been fortunate enough to have a daughter*, he thought, *I would have liked her to be just like Aisling.*

At some point in the afternoon, Maggie said, "I'm going to have to drag him away from you, love. We're going to bring out the cake."

Hugh shrugged his shoulders resignedly, making a sad clown's face, and followed Maggie into the dining room.

"Yes, of course, but make sure to bring him back to me quickly."

Maggie didn't try to fit fifty candles on the cake but made do with five. Hugh was assigned the task of bringing it outside and placing it on the table set up for the purpose. After singing "Happy Birthday," everyone clapped and her parents kissed her. Then, she came over to Maggie and Hugh.

"Maggie, I don't know how to thank you. You've given me the best birthday present anyone could have." Hugh wanted to say it was just a dress but didn't, which was fortunate, as he soon realised she was referring to him. "And he's much nicer than I could possibly have anticipated."

After everyone had eaten a slice of cake and watched Aisling open some presents, Siobháin took her by the arm to meet some of her friends from school.

■

Hugh took advantage of Aisling's absence to have a few words with Leonard, who had been sweating over the barbecue all day. "You did a great job, Leonard. Those sausages were delicious."

"Nothing like Irish pork sausages."

"You have a wonderful daughter. You must be very proud of her."

"Oh, we are, Hugh. She's turned out very well and her children too. Their father is also in the medical profession, you know. They met at medical college."

"I'm sorry he couldn't be here."

"He had a couple of operations to carry out that couldn't be postponed. Hopefully, you'll get to meet him some other time."

"I sincerely hope so. But Australia is so damned far away."

"Maybe we'll be seeing more of you now."

Hugh understood the insinuation but didn't want to commit to an unequivocal affirmation. "I certainly would like that."

"What is it? A twenty-four-hour flight?"

"Give or take. The idea is not to disturb your natural bio-rhythms, so they say, but as a doctor you'd know all about that."

"She seems to have taken a shine to you, Hugh. Deirdre and I are so happy. We had no idea how she would take it. Fortunately, she's a very sensible girl, always has been. A few years ago, it might have been more difficult. Everything seems to have turned out remarkably well considering. I'm just sorry it didn't happen sooner. None of us could really understand why Maggie wanted to keep it a secret from you. Aisling had heard so much about you, it was very frustrating for her not to be able to meet you."

Hugh had difficulty following what Leonard was saying but politely agreed with him anyway.

"I've never seen Maggie so happy. Her marriage to Tom was not great, you know, but no doubt she's told you the difficulties they had."

"No, but Joan mentioned something."

"She doesn't like talking about it. She never really loved him and I think that was the problem. It might have worked if she had been more tolerant of his peccadillos. He turned into a bitter old man in the end, especially when his philandering days were over. Her children have given her great support though, especially Aisling."

Though it struck him as odd, Hugh assumed that Leonard's referring to Aisling as her child was just a slip of the tongue. "She certainly seems very attached to her."

"They get on so well. They're like sisters. It was very hard for her, keeping everything from the family, but that's what it was like in Ireland back then. She would have been disowned and probably shunned by the community. It would have caused a great scandal. Deirdre and I couldn't have children, so we were very happy to bring her up as ours."

Suddenly it dawned on Hugh what he should have guessed long before. Aisling was Maggie's daughter. It explained so much.

Why she lived in England for a year and a half without coming back even for a short visit. It must have been heartbreaking for Maggie to give her up, even to her sister. But why didn't she tell him before that Aisling was her child? Did she imagine that he would think badly of her for having a child out of wedlock?

"Well, you did a damned good job of it."

"The truth is she has given us enormous pleasure. We see her as much our child as Maggie's. She calls us Mum and Dad. Well, she wanted to be like the other children, even though we told her very early on that Maggie was her mother."

"I know it's none of my business, Leonard, and you may not even know, but what's happened to the father?"

Leonard's mouth dropped along with the tongs he was holding. "Christ man! You mean you don't know? You must be the only one in the family who doesn't."

"Should I? I mean it's Maggie's business. No doubt she would have told me if she thought it was important. But she didn't even tell me that she had a daughter."

"Hugh, it's not really my place, but I imagine she was planning to tell you at some point. Perhaps you should take a seat. This might come as a bit of shock."

"I'm not easily shocked, Leonard. And, to be honest with you, I couldn't care less who the father is."

"In that case, Hugh, I have to tell you that you are her father."

Hugh gasped, went deathly white, and felt for the back of the chair to steady himself.

"Hugh, are you all right?" said Leonard, anxiously grabbing him by the arm. "Perhaps you should take a seat."

This time he accepted. "My god, but why didn't she tell me?"

"I expect she had her reasons, but no doubt she'll explain everything later."

At that moment, Deirdre came by and saw that Hugh was looking poorly. "Are you all right, Hugh?"

"Hugh has just found out that Aisling is his daughter. For some reason, Maggie chose not to tell him, and I let the cat out of the bag."

"It must have been quite a shock," she said, putting her hand on his shoulder.

"I'm fine," he said, still holding his head in his hands.

"All he needs is a stiff drink. What is your tipple, Hugh?"

"Em…Just a drop of whiskey, Leonard. Thank you."

Leonard left to get Hugh's drink, and Deirdre sat down on the chair next to him. "It's been quite a day, hasn't it? But you've made one person—no, two people, very happy."

"I'm sorry, Deirdre, for all the trouble I've caused you."

"Trouble? What trouble?"

"I've been an absent father. I mean, I never contributed to her upbringing in any way. I would have, if Maggie had told me."

"She was doing it to protect you, Hugh. She didn't want you to feel obliged to marry her. You had dreams, and she didn't want to destroy them. She was hoping you would come back of your own accord, but when you didn't, she wasn't going to put pressure on you."

"But all these years?"

"It might have ruined your marriage. It might have ruined her marriage. In fact, I think it did, not that that was the only cause. She would never have told you, Hugh, if she hadn't felt that there was still a lot of love between you. She believed that even if you didn't get back together, the time was right for you to meet your daughter. I hope you won't hold it against her."

"For God's sake, no. I just wish I had been able to share the burden of her upbringing."

"Aisling was never a burden. She's been lucky enough to have two mothers and a loving father. And by the look of it, she's now going to have a second loving father."

"I only hope I can live up to her expectations."

"You already have."

"I'm not a learned man, Deirdre, like Leonard. I've read a few books and educated myself as best I can, but I don't want her to be ashamed of me."

"Will you stop that, Hugh Gorman! The truth is, she didn't know what to expect. Her greatest fear was rejection or denial. Otherwise, she didn't give a hoot about your academic qualifications."

"I haven't lost the ould brogue," he said with a smile.

"And why should you be ashamed of that? You're Irish, for God's sake. Have I lost mine?"

"It's a very refined brogue you have now, Deirdre," he said, sketching a smile.

Leonard arrived with two large whiskeys. "Here. This will help buck you up."

"He's fine," said Deirdre. "He's already got over the shock."

Hugh took a sip from his whiskey. "A shock indeed. But I can't say it was an altogether unpleasant one. It's not every day a man acquires a beautiful and highly intelligent daughter. Maggie has a bit of explaining to do, but we can sort that out later."

"Don't be too hard on her, Hugh. She thought it was best for everyone you didn't know."

"Maybe, but I just wish she had allowed me to be the judge of it."

"Her intentions were good, Hugh, if a little misguided. We always said she should tell you but she kept finding excuses. Perhaps it was easier just not to tell you. She had no idea how you would react. Now it doesn't really matter. Just accept that you've acquired a lovely daughter and a new family. At least, I hope you'll see us as that."

"Indeed, I will. It won't be anything new for me. Maggie and Deirdre's mother and father were like second parents to me. Jo was a lovely woman, Leonard. Did you ever meet her?"

"Oh, my goodness, yes, Hugh. She lived with us in her final years when she needed looking after. She was nearly ninety when she died."

Hugh looked around and saw to his surprise that almost everyone had gone. The whiskey had made him slightly light-headed, but it had helped him recover his composure.

Aisling and Maggie said goodbye to the last of the guests and arm in arm came over to the trio by the barbecue.

Maggie could tell at once that Hugh knew. She left Aisling and came over to him. "I was going to tell you, Hugh, but I wanted you to meet her first, to be absolutely sure. I can see, though, that you can love her just as much I do."

"I don't see how anyone could not love her, Maggie."

"Who's exaggerating now? She's not perfect. She has the Gorman temper in her."

"Who said the Gormans have a temper?"

"Well, no one in our family has one."

Though pretending not to, everyone was privy to the "private" conversation Maggie and Hugh were having just feet away.

"They sound just like an old married couple," said Deirdre with a titter.

"Now you two clear off and let us tidy up," said Leonard. "You obviously have things to discuss. I'm sorry, Maggie. I had no idea you hadn't told him."

"We're certainly not going to leave you to clean up this mess, are we, Maggie?" said Hugh.

"Definitely not. We can have our first row later."

"There'll be no row, Maggie. How could there be when you've just presented me with the most beautiful daughter anyone could have wished for? And I don't even have to change her nappies."

Aisling started crying again. Together, Maggie and Hugh went over to comfort her. "It's silly of me, I know," she said, "but I've been longing for this since the day I found out Hugh was my father."

"Well, you're not going to lose me now," said Hugh, "whether in Australia or Ireland, you'll always have a place in my heart."

"Thank you, Hugh," she said and threw her arms around his neck, just like Maggie liked to do.

■

That evening, Hugh decided to stay the night with Maggie. He would explain to Joan and Siobháin the following day about Aisling. He wondered how Joan would take it? Did she know or have any idea that Aisling was his child? *Seeing her*, he thought, *no one could help but see the resemblance.*

The evenings were still quite long and Hugh suggested walking up to the top of Connick to see the sunset. It was a warm peaceful evening, reminding Hugh of those endless twilights as a child when the last of the harvest was being brought in, the apples were ripening on the trees and everything except his parents was perfect. And, on evenings like these, even they seemed tolerable.

They walked hand in hand up a dirt track and across the fields to the highest point where the Forestry Commission had planted a forest of mixed spruce. They sat on Hugh's favourite rock where they had a panoramic view of the countryside. There was nothing, he decided, that could compare to its beauty, not in Australia nor anywhere else in the world.

"I'm sorry, Hugh, for not telling you."

"It's all right, Maggie. Deirdre explained everything. I understand. Maybe it was better. Deirdre and Leonard are lovely people. I don't think she has suffered greatly by not knowing me. Did she say anything?"

"The moment she saw you, she knew you were her father."

"She must have seen photos of me."

"I didn't have any. Her attraction to you was pure filial instinct, Hugh."

"I'm not sure I believe in such things. I was probably the most likely candidate. How many other seventy-year-olds were at the party?"

"Quite a few. You didn't see them. You were too engrossed in conversation with your daughter."

"My daughter. I still can't believe it. I wonder how my sons will take it."

"They'll be delighted to know they have a sister, I'm sure."

"How would Sheila have taken it?" he said absently.

"I didn't want to risk telling you, Hugh, especially when I found out that you were married. I knew you wouldn't have been able to keep it a secret from her, and God knows what the consequences would have been."

"It certainly would have driven a wedge between us. We couldn't have shared Aisling. She'd always have been my daughter, not hers."

"You never know. She might have surprised you."

"Well, we'll never find out now," he said dismissively.

They took a roundabout route back, down narrow paths and boreens he hadn't been in since he was a child. It was pleasing for him to see that some things hadn't changed.

They had a light supper to the sound of Van Morrison. Though they were both tired, they moved the table to the side and turned the kitchen into a mini ballroom. It was not as spacious as they would have liked, but it forced them to keep their moves confined and intimate.

Hugh was happy not to have to rush off, and Maggie was overjoyed that they would be spending their first night together. Nothing was said about Australia and when he'd be going back. Neither of them wanted to broach the subject, though they both knew it had to be faced sooner or later.

Maggie compared Aisling's birthday to a wedding reception and their night together to their honeymoon. Hugh went along with the idea, but he did not applaud it. What was the point of marriage at their age? Did they want to be bound by its restrictions? And it would involve all sorts of legal complications with the inheritance. He didn't want to upset the boat back in Australia. Not that he wished to see his relationship with Maggie as a casual fling, but he felt they were too old to plan too far ahead. Just enjoy the moment for as long as they were both well enough to do so.

Just before she turned out the light, Maggie said, "You told me that Esperance means *hope*. Do you know what Aisling means?"

"I must confess I don't."

"It means *dream*."

"Dream. What a lovely name! The aboriginals have names like that. I had a couple of lads working on the station with beautiful names, Yarramundi, which means deep water, and Jiemba, the laughing star. And the strange thing is their names fitted their character perfectly, Yarramundi was a quiet deep thinker while Jiemba was always laughing and joking. These people are so close to nature. They feel one with it, unlike us in the West, who are moving farther and farther away from the natural world. Virtual reality is more real to children these days than reality itself. So, our daughter's name is dream. Whose idea was that?"

"I liked the sound of the name, but when I found out what it means, I realised it was perfect. Dream has so many connotations, doesn't it? In a dream, you can imagine that things are as you want them to be. In my dreams, I used to see the three of us together, arm in arm, laughing and joking. When I had those dreams, I'd be happy all the next day. But it was always a dream…until today."

"I don't think any of us will forget this day, Maggie. It was a dream I never had, but it seems very much like one now, with a fairy-tale ending." He knew, but did not want to admit it even to himself, that this was not the end, just the beginning. And he had no idea how the story would unfold.

■

They got up late and had a leisurely breakfast. Aisling came over and joined them. He couldn't believe how much at ease he was with her. It was as if they had known each other all their lives. She was immensely affectionate with him and took every opportunity to touch him, putting a hand on an arm or shoulder—"to make sure he was not just an apparition," Maggie said jokingly.

They agreed that during the three days before she returned to England they would do as much as they could together. Hugh suggested going to the sea one day and having a meal at a fish restaurant. Aisling loved gardens like he did. So, they decided to visit some of the large gardens around the country that were open to the public. They all packed into Maggie's big car and set off in the morning, returning just before dark.

Hugh only wished Rory was still around to come with them. He missed their intimate chats. With Rory, he didn't have to choose his words or worry about saying something that might offend. Rory would understand that whatever he said it was without malice. He would have accepted and embrace Aisling unreservedly, deriving as much pleasure as he was from her company.

■

On the morning after the big revelation, Hugh left them at about 11:00, promising to be back for tea. He was dreading having to break the news to Joan and Siobháin, but he knew it had to be done. Both Aisling and Maggie thought Joan would be delighted. Hugh had his doubts. His sister was unpredictable at the best of times, and he had no idea how she would react to yet another of his "follies."

He arrived just as they were setting the table for lunch.

"We didn't expect to see you, Hugh," said Joan in a jolly voice. "But I've made plenty for all of us."

"That was a lovely party yesterday, wasn't it, Uncle Hugh?" said Siobháin.

"It was indeed."

"Aisling is such a lovely girl. Mam says you hadn't met her before."

"No, first time."

"You seemed to get on very well," said Joan. "I couldn't help wondering what a sheep farmer and a distinguished microbiologist had in common."

Hugh wasn't sure whether she was pulling his leg or whether she had genuinely no idea of his connection to Aisling. "You'd be surprised, Joan."

"What did you talk about all the time, Uncle Hugh? She wouldn't let you out of her sight."

"We were just finding out about each other."

"She's certainly a very attractive woman," said Joan. "I'd say now that if you were a few years younger, you'd be asking her out on a date."

"I don't think so, Joan. You see, I need to tell you something."

"Oh, yes, and what's that?" said Joan, emptying some steaming vegetables into a pan.

"Aisling is my daughter."

His announcement resulted in a deafening silence. They were both struck dumb, looking at him open-mouthed, a frozen frame in a film reel.

"What nonsense is this then?" said Joan at last. "How could she be your daughter?"

"Maggie and I…before I left for Australia…"

"God, Hugh Gorman, you were always up to no good. And she never told you all these years?"

"She wanted to protect me, Joan."

"She should have told you, regardless of the consequences. Sure, didn't that poor girl have the right to know who her real father was?"

"Well, she did know, has known for a long time."

"And she never wanted to meet you?"

"She did but the distance didn't help, and I think she was afraid."

"Afraid of what?"

"Of loving Deirdre and Leonard less, of being disloyal in some way."

"Ah, nonsense! If you ask me, it was cruel of Maggie to keep you two apart for so long."

"Didn't you suspect anything?" said Hugh weakly. "I mean, her going off to England like that a few months after I left. Did you believe all that about her having to look after Deirdre in her confinement?"

"I never gave it a second thought, Hugh."

Hugh shrugged his shoulder wearily.

"So, what are you going to do? You have a duty to her now."

"No, Joan, I won't see it as a duty. It's true things are different now. But we both have separate lives. She has her boys and her grandchildren down in Cork. I have mine in Australia. I honestly don't know how the two can be reconciled."

"Are you sure you'll be happy with her, Hugh? You don't have to hook up just because you have found out you have a child together. They've got on grand without you until now."

"Maggie is a lovely woman, Joan, no matter what you say. We understand each other. But the truth is, I don't know what I want. I don't know what she wants. The older you get, the less flexible you become. We'll just have to play it by ear. But I won't leave till I have fixed up the house below. That should give us time to get a better perspective on things. The next two days, though, I want to devote to Aisling. I owe her that at least."

"Of course, Uncle Hugh."

"You won't be able to make it up to her," said Joan grumpily. "You'd better accept that right away."

"I know we can never become like a true father and daughter, but I want to give us a chance to at least get to know each other."

■

For the first time in his life, Hugh had the feeling that he was on holiday. Back in Australia, there was always something happening on the station that wouldn't allow them to take more than a few days off. Sheila had been raised on a farm, so she knew how demanding it was and so never complained. Even if they did go away for a day or two, he was always on the phone to the foreman. Since he'd been in Ireland, he had only called Ron once, and Ron had not felt the need to call him either. By now Brendan would be settling in, and he hoped his presence would keep the boys on their toes.

The two days with Aisling passed very quickly. The trouble was the more he got to know her, the more he grew to love her. He never tired of her company, and it warmed his heart to see Maggie and her together chirping away like two lovebirds. At times, he was almost jealous of the intimate, easy relationship they had together, but he could tell by the way they looked at him and wedged him in between them as they walked along the seashore or around the garden centres that he was far from extraneous. Having now met her and got to know her, he knew he was going to miss her terribly when she had to go back. They talked about whether she could put it off for a few days, but apparently her research team back in Oxford were waiting anxiously for her return.

He wondered how Deirdre and Leonard felt, but they showed no signs of jealousy or resentment. They were happy to tag along and let Hugh and Maggie make up for lost time. Hugh could tell they did not doubt Aisling's deep love for them and they, for their part, understood the importance of a biological father, even one that had been absent all her life.

When the day of her departure came, they all five took her up to the airport in Dublin. Maggie wouldn't let her out of her sight till the very last moment. Hugh was afraid she was going to miss her flight, but Aisling didn't seem worried. He even wondered if perhaps she wanted to miss it.

As she was about to leave to go through the checkpoint, she held Hugh's hands and stared intently at him for a long time as if trying to stamp an indelible image of him on her memory. Did she fear that she might never see him again? He supposed he couldn't blame her if she did. He had deserted her mother all those years ago. So, he could easily desert her too. How could he reassure her that he wouldn't?

"Hugh, you can't imagine how happy I am to have met you at last. I think you two make a lovely couple. Please look after Maggie for me."

"Don't worry, I will," he said without hesitation. While saying it, he meant it, but as she disappeared from sight beyond the barrier, he wondered how easy it would be to keep his promise.

The journey back to Connick was quiet. A chill of sadness hung over them, like the last days of autumn, the harbingers of the winter to come.

That evening, Hugh and Maggie listened to Van Morrison but had no desire to dance. They just sat on the sofa in each other's arms wallowing in their melancholic happiness.

"Enough!" said Hugh jumping to his feet. "We're acting as if we're never going to see her again. Put on your glad rags, Maggie, my dear, we're going to O'Doherty's for a pint. Shall we ask Deirdre and Leonard to come along?"

"O'Doherty's is an awful dive. It's dark and depressing. I'd be ashamed to take Leonard there."

"Okay then. Let's go to the Pig's Ear. Is that more your style?"

"That's a lot more classy, and they often play our kind of music on Sunday nights."

"What are we waiting for then? Shall we call Deirdre and Leonard?"

"No. Hugh, I'd like it to be just the two of us. Do you mind?"

"Of course not."

As it happened, some friends of Joan's were there, and they felt obliged to join them. It was a pleasant enough evening, but Hugh got the feeling that Maggie would have preferred to have had him to herself. Perhaps she too was thinking about the future but couldn't find the right moment to talk about it. Neither wanted to spoil the bliss they were basking in, but they both knew it couldn't last forever. Bitter experience told them that passion quickly burns itself out and life is fraught with disappointments. All they could hope for in the long term was a deep affection and an undying bond that Aisling had cemented between them.

■

The following day, they started work on the lodge. Hugh was not one to stand around and watch. So, while the painters were working on the interior, he worked in the garden pulling up weeds and bringing the flower beds back into shape. He also had to mend the wooden fence and build up the bank of the stream where it had been eroded by winter torrents. Maggie joined them soon after breakfast, and she and Siobháin gave him all the help they could. Soon, the garden was unrecognisable, complete with rose beds, hydrangeas, and a variety of fruit trees including gooseberries and blackcurrants. This required quite a few trips into town to the garden centre.

It was towards the end of the week that he got a call from Ron. He immediately assumed the worst.

"I'm sorry to bother you, boss, but I rang to ask when you're planning on getting back."

"Is there a problem, Ron?"

"Well, it's like this, boss. Everything was hunky-dory until Brendan got back. I know he's your son and all but he's…em… well…kind of interfering in the work. And I don't really know what to do. I had to tell him today that I only take orders from you. It's kind of making us all a bit edgy, like. You understand?"

"Thanks, Ron. I'll have a word with him."

He knew the time would come when he would have to return. The station needed him. What the hell was he going to do with Brendan? He wouldn't have minded if the boy accepted his incompetence, but he was only home a week or two and was already acting the boss. Would he allow himself to be disciplined? Or would he get all worked up and run off in a huff like he did the last time? Perhaps the station was not for him after all. Like it or not, he knew he would have to go back to Australia soon before more damage was done.

For a whole week, he had been riding on a wave of elated oblivion, but like a surfer who knows he will soon be hurtled on to dry land, Hugh was aware that it was only a matter of time before he hit hard reality. Meeting Maggie again had complicated his life but finding out about Aisling had changed it forever. It meant that he was now totally divided between east and west, north and south. He could never be whole again. He would have to sacrifice one half or the other. The question was which?

The builders had nearly finished renovating the house. He no longer had an excuse to stay on. He sat in the new kitchen of the lodge with Siobháin drinking a cup of tea, deep orange rays of evening sunlight streaming through the window, a distinct smell of Ireland wafting through the open window and the gentle sound of flowing water in the background.

"This is a beautiful house, Uncle Hugh."

"It has a lot of potential. Do you think Leonora will like it?"

"She's dying to see it."

"How are things with your mother?"

"I'm dreading the day when she and Leonora meet, but I honestly don't see why they can't be friends."

"It's not as if you're living in the same house. You can see as much of each other as you like. But it will be reassuring for me to know that there will be someone around if she needs help."

"You've been quiet today, Uncle Hugh. Is something the matter?"

"I'm faced with the biggest decision of my life, Siobháin. I feel I must go back to Australia. I can't just abandon a life's work. I love the station, and the truth is, I'm fond of Esperance too. I've been happy there. But now that Maggie and I have got back together and finding out about Aisling, the idea of living here seems attractive. I wish I could put them both on a set of scales and see which side tips, but it's not as simple as that. I don't want to give either up."

"It's the world we live in, Uncle Hugh. I know so many families that are scattered all over the world. Fortunately, international travel is not like it used to be. We aren't completely cut off. I think Maggie is going to be the deciding factor. You have to think how important she is to you. Being separated from someone is not necessarily a bad thing. Leonora and I don't see each other for weeks on end, but when we do meet, we make up for all the time we're apart. You need to have it out with her, Uncle Hugh."

"I know. I need to make a decision. I…we've been putting it off."

◼

As he was walking across the fields to Maggie's house, he remembered she had gone to a dress rehearsal and wouldn't be at home. It would be a good opportunity to ring Brendan.

Maggie had left a salad and cold meat wrapped in Sani on the table for him. He realised how pleasant it was to have someone who cared enough to consider his needs. He was an independent man and had coped well since Sheila died, but it was different knowing that someone was waiting at home for you, willing to exchange tittle-tattle, listen to your plans and ideas, and commiserate with your aches and pains. He missed her and hoped that she wouldn't be too late.

He decided to call Brendan and get it over with. "Hi, mate. How are things on the station?"

"Good, Dad. I'm afraid I don't get on all that well with Ron. I find him a bit of a know-all."

"Yeah, well, maybe you shouldn't take too many initiatives until I get back. You need more time to learn the ropes. He's a good man Ron. He knows his stuff."

"The men respect him, I'll admit, but he doesn't respect me. I think I might have difficulty working with him."

"The thing is, Brendan, he may be an employee, but he can teach you a lot. Try and work with him. When you reach the point when you know the job as well or better than he does, then you can decide whether to replace him or not."

"You know, Dad. I'm not sure my heart's in it. What I'd really like is to do something for myself. The station is yours and Mum's. It'll never be mine."

"I see what you mean. Any ideas?"

"Well, I'd love to have a winery. There's a piece of land to the north on a kind of rise that looks down over the valley. You know the spot I'm talking about. It'd be perfect for a vineyard. I had someone test the soil and he says it's ideal."

"It's not easy starting something from scratch, you know."

"I know. You may think I'm a lazy bum, Dad, but I'm not afraid of hard work, as long as it's something I want to do. You know what I mean?"

"Absolutely, but we're talking about a five-to-ten-year investment here."

"I know, Dad. I worked on a vineyard for two years. I must have told you. I loved it, but I didn't get on with the foreman and it was either him or me."

"Yeah. Well, look, we can talk about it when I get back. I have a few things I need to discuss with you and Niall. There have been some developments."

"What developments? Has Auntie Joan taken Uncle Rory's death badly?"

"No. Well, yeah, but it's not that. Look. I can't tell you on the phone. I'll ask Niall to take a day or two off and fly down with his family. I haven't seen the kids this long while."

"Okay, Dad. I'll try my best to get on with Ron but, Jes', he's such a snooty bastard I feel like punching him in the kisser sometimes."

"Whatever you do, Brendan, don't do that. He's the best foreman I've ever had. We'll sort things out when I get back."

■

Hugh expected Maggie to be back by 10.30 at the latest. He knew the rehearsal was to finish by 9.30 so that the actors could have an early night. He wasn't too worried, although he knew how she hated driving at night. The truth was he missed her. He had got used to spending evenings with her, listening to music, reading and exchanging trivialities. He was also hoping they could talk a little about the future, though he didn't want to upset her with the play opening the next day.

He eyed his cell phone a number of times but resisted calling her. He was surprised, however, that she had not called to say she'd be late. Or had she assumed that he wouldn't be bothered by her lateness?

Just as he was about to give up and go to bed, he heard the car pull up outside. He was relieved but also apprehensive of what might have delayed her. He got up and went to the door to greet her in as casual a fashion as he could.

"I was worried," he said as she entered.

She seemed flustered, not her usual self. He smelt whiskey on her breath.

"You had a party or something. I thought you usually reserved that for after the first night."

"No. Jerry asked me to go with him for a drink."

"I've been expecting you for the last three hours."

"I'm sorry, Hugh. I thought you'd still be working on the lodge."

"At this hour? Besides, the lodge is finished."

"The lodge is finished?" She seemed disappointed.

"Yeah. Siobháin is delighted with it."

"So, there's nothing to keep you here now."

"I thought we might talk about things but it's a bit late."

"No. We should. I'll fix us both a drink."

"If you're not too tired."

Hugh went back to the parlour, but he had lost his desire for discussion.

She laid the drinks down on the table in front of them and sat beside him. She didn't put her hand on his knee as she usually did. Something was up.

"So why did Jerry want to see you so urgently tonight? I thought you were meant to be having an early night."

"He wanted to talk about us."

"You and me? Or you and him?"

"Both. He proposed to me."

"Proposed to you? Just like that, out of the blue?"

"Well, I knew he was going to at some point. But that was before you came."

"I was expecting you home about ten. It took you a long time to say no."

"I didn't."

"What? You said yes?"

"No. Neither."

"But, Maggie, you can't. You deserve so much better than Jerry 'The Real' McCoy."

"You mean I deserve you."

"I didn't say that, but Jerry is such an ass."

"He loves me, Hugh. He's great company. And he's available."

"You mean I'm not."

"Well, are you?"

"Not all the time, but I'd like to spend more time in Ireland."

"You mean you'd come on visits. Two or three weeks a year. I'm too old for that, Hugh. Maybe I was always too old for that. I need someone to share my life with, someone I can rely on, someone who's prepared to devote themselves to me."

"I can't give up everything, Maggie. The station is my life. What would I do with myself here? I would stagnate. Brendan's thinking of starting a new project, and I'd like to be there to make sure he doesn't make a hash of it. I was hoping that you might consider spending some time in Australia."

"Some time, Hugh? Or my whole life? I need to be near my children and grandchildren, Aisling in particular."

"Yeah, well, for a start, I was thinking that once I've sorted things out back home that we'd spend some time in Oxford. I really want to meet my new grandchildren."

"That would be wonderful," she said with restrained enthusiasm. "Aisling would love that too."

"What's happened, Maggie? What's changed?"

She took a long sip from her glass. "I realise that I can't have all of you. I can only have half of you, and I'm afraid that even that might slowly slip through my fingers. I don't want to tie you down, Hugh. I love you dearly. You're the only man I ever truly loved."

"Even more than Jerry."

"I don't love Jerry. I like Jerry. He's good fun. I love you but I can't have you, and it seems you can't have me either. We would both have to sacrifice too much."

"But we have Aisling now. Surely that makes a difference."

"I have always had Aisling. And I thought it would make a difference to us, but I now see it doesn't. It's she who creates a bond between us. The bond doesn't come from us."

"What do you mean, Maggie?"

"I thought…I hoped…that maybe now that Sheila is gone that you'd need me…that you couldn't do without me. I wanted to make myself indispensable. But I realise that no one is indispensable to you."

"These last three weeks have been incredible, Maggie."

"But not incredible enough."

"I haven't been so happy for years."

"It wouldn't last. You'd always be yearning for your other half."

"You mean Sheila?"

"No, Australia."

"Maggie, please don't do anything rash. Give us a little more time."

"What's the point? It'll just prolong the agony."

"Can't you just hold on for a week or two? Till I see the boys? I might be able to work something out. You can't deny we've had a wonderful time together."

"It's been like a dream, Hugh. A perfect dream."

"And so?"

"Dreams don't last. You eventually wake up and have to face an imperfect reality."

"Aisling is a dream, but she's also reality."

"Is she more than just a dream for you, Hugh?"

"Why do you doubt that, Maggie? She and I found an affinity the moment we met. We are so alike, despite never having known each other till last week."

"I'd love to think we'd be a happy family, but we're beyond that. We won't be living in the same continent, let alone the same country or town."

"Please, Maggie. Just give me a little more time."

"When are you leaving?"

"I was thinking I'd get the next available flight. Probably Monday. They'll confirm it tomorrow."

"So, you'll come to the first night of our play."

"Of course, I will. I wouldn't miss it for anything. As long as you want me there…" he added apprehensively.

She didn't answer immediately, just laid her hand on his cheek and looked at him fondly. "Of course, I want you there."

"Will your man want me there?"

"Well, he doesn't have any say in the matter, does he? He'll just have to put up with it." She kissed him longingly on the lips.

"I hope he's a good lover, Maggie," he said with a patronising sneer.

"I doubt it," she said mournfully, "But you can't have everything. And at my age, it's not so important."

"You could have fooled me. Come on. Let's go to bed. I think you're in the mood for a bit of loving. Sex or no sex."

She smiled and let herself be led into the bedroom.

■

Hugh decided to spend the following day with Joan and Siobháin. Leonora was back from Norway, and she needed to go back to London to sort out the flat and decide which things to take back to her new house in Connick. Leonora, it seemed, was tired of London and wanted a change. She was also very excited about the idea of having a garden again.

Hugh broke the news of his imminent departure over lunch.

"I'll be sorry to see you go, Hugh. Will Maggie be going with you?"

"No."

"I expected to hear wedding bells any time soon."

"Not mine anyway, Joan."

"What do you mean?"

"Jerry McCoy proposed to her."

"Don't tell me she accepted?"

"No, but she didn't decline either."

"God, that woman's so fickle. All empty passion and no substance."

"No, Joan. She understands me better than I understand myself. I wouldn't be happy here."

"But I thought you'd rediscovered your roots and were coming home to stay."

"My roots were transplanted, Joan, into different soil a long time ago. It may not be so fertile but I thrived in it, nonetheless. And you can't retransplant an old tree. If I were to come back, I'd slowly wither up and die."

"But sure that Maggie one'd keep you alive. She certainly wouldn't let you stagnate anyway."

"I'd end up resenting it, Joan. Anyway, I haven't entirely made up my mind. She's prepared to give me a few weeks before giving an answer to Jerry."

"Oh, that's very nice of her," she said sarcastically.

"Don't be hard on her, Joan. Both Maggie and Deirdre are good friends. I hope you won't become alienated."

"Oh, I love Deirdre, and Leonard's a real gentleman. I'll definitely make a point of seeing them regular, but if Maggie marries that Jerry character, I'll do my best to avoid her and him."

Hugh laughed. He knew she'd come round in the end. She always did.

■

Hugh and Joan drove Siobháin up to the airport in the morning, which gave them plenty of time to get back in time for the play.

Although Joan had intended to go too, in the end she pleaded fatigue and said she wanted to have an early night. Hugh suspected she didn't want to witness the inevitable meeting between himself and Jerry the Real.

He arrived in good time, but Maggie had already gone backstage to get made up and "collect herself." Deirdre saw him enter the theatre and beckoned him over. "We've kept you a seat, Hugh. Maggie was afraid you mightn't make it."

"It was an early flight."

Hugh sat beside Deirdre but said little. He was anxious, almost as if it was he who was about to go up on stage. He could feel the rising tension and anticipation of the audience. The theatre was full to bursting point. He overheard a couple talking about the actors.

"They say Maggie McQuilty is great."

"But sure, didn't we see her last year in a modern play by that English playwright? What's his name?"

"Oh god, yeah! She was great alright. She reminded me of Jane Fonda."

Deirdre turned to Hugh. "Maggie tells me you're going back to Australia."

"Yeah. I stayed longer than I'd expected."

"Would you ever see yourself living in Ireland again, Hugh?"

Had Maggie primed her to ask him this question? "It's difficult to say, Deirdre. I love Ireland, but I'm not sure it has much to offer me now."

"It has Maggie."

"Apart from Maggie, I mean."

"Leonard and I feel that to have someone you love and respect is the most important thing in life. The rest we can reach a compromise with."

Hugh didn't answer at once. Deirdre and Leonard had been together practically all their adult life. Their present was a continuation of their past. Maggie and he had had a past, once, but with a vast empty hiatus between it and the present. "True. But life is very complicated, Deirdre. If it were only up to us, we might act differently, but we have commitments."

The lights dimmed and silence descended on the theatre.

It got off to a roaring start and quickly the audience got into the mood of the play. Almost every line elicited laughter. Needless to say, Maggie was brilliant. Soon, Hugh was able to relax and enjoy the play. Maggie had gained her stage feet and was in absolute control of the role, playing the audience with her eloquent pauses and subtle facial expressions. When the curtain fell, there was a resounding applause.

When she finally appeared from backstage she was arm and arm with Jerry. Hugh couldn't help feeling a twinge of jealously, but he was beginning to have doubts about whether he was capable of making her truly happy and that she would be far better off with someone like Jerry, who could devote himself entirely to her.

"You're all invited to the party at Jerry's place," she said, unable to contain her elation. "All the girls are dying to meet you, Hugh. You will come, won't you?"

Maggie and Jerry looked expectantly at him, but he couldn't tell whether they really wanted him there or not. "I wouldn't want to be the only nonactor there. If Leonard and Deirdre go, I'll come along too."

"For a short time, Maggie," said Deirdre. "I don't want people to think we're gate-crashing."

"Not at all. Everybody's welcome. We'll meet out front and go in convoy. Jerry's place is about a mile out of town."

∎

Hugh was hoping Maggie would come with him, but she chose to go with Jerry and a crowd of actors, who all tumbled into Jerry's enormous SUV. Maggie sat in front beside Jerry.

For some reason, Hugh was dreading the party. What was it that made him so apprehensive? He didn't want to have to fight over Maggie. He was beyond that. On the other hand, he realised that he was very lucky to have a second chance in life, at an age when many just sit around waiting to die.

Just after he turned off the main road, he pulled over to the side of the road. Should he or shouldn't he go to the party? He knew he had to. He had been many things in his life but not a coward. He had to make sure that he was in possession of all the facts. He needed to get to know Jerry better and make sure that if Maggie were to marry him, she would not be making a terrible mistake. Why he felt so protective towards her he wasn't sure. Maybe he was aware of her vulnerability. Maybe he felt guilty for the life she had had with Tom Kehoe. Maybe she meant more to him than he cared to admit.

Jerry McCoy lived in an elegant old house on the outskirts of town, with a serpentine drive and a perfectly trimmed lawn that sloped down to the river's edge. As he parked on the gravel in front of the imposing entrance, he could make out the dull sheen of light reflecting off the water. He had to admit it was a beautiful location. He wondered how Jerry had made his money. An accountant? A lawyer? Whatever it was, he must have made a fair packet.

Maggie liked men with money, he thought, *but men with money tend to be spoilt and demanding.* On the other hand, Jerry could give her all the material comforts she could desire and possibly the love too.

The house was pulsating with lights and sound. They were playing music from the seventies. Maggie's choice? He was greeted by the large-breasted lady who had played Bettie. She was even more attractive all dolled up for the party.

"Hugh, great you could come. Did you like the play?"

"Brilliant! You and Maggie were fantastic!"

"She's a natural. I have her in mind for the lead in our next play. Come in and let me give you a drink. Maggie and Jerry are putting the finishing touches to the food."

Despite being an oldie, the actors, even the young ones, were happy to chat with him. One of them was convinced that he was Pierce Brosnan's brother incognito. Did Pierce Brosnan have a brother?

Maggie eventually emerged from the kitchen area and came over to be with him. But he felt that she was only half there. People kept coming over to congratulate her. He was introduced with varying labels, from "childhood friend" to "family friend" but no longer "the boyfriend," which was both a relief and a comedown, as he was getting inured to the idea of being the boyfriend. After all, it was the truth, albeit, an aging version of what most people thinks of as a boyfriend.

At one point, she was dragged away by a group of young actors, who wanted her to dance an Irish jig. Hugh had forgotten that as a teenager she had won all sorts of competitions as a Ceilidh dancer. Jerry was there all the time cheering her on and taking every opportunity to fondle her tenderly. It soon became obvious to Hugh that she and the Real McCoy had an intimate, easygoing relationship, which made him both happy and sad. Yet, they behaved more like friends than lovers. Would that be enough for her?

Hugh was about to leave when Jerry came up to him. He was a little tipsy but not drunk. "Hugh, I'm sorry I ignored you. Are you having a good time? You have plenty of female admirers in the company. There was quite a stir when the rumour spread that Pierce Brosnan's brother was in the audience."

Hugh laughed. "I don't think Pierce Brosnan has a brother. If he had, he wouldn't look anything like me. It was a great production, Jerry. Congratulations!"

"Thanks, Hugh. We do our best, which happens to be extremely good, despite our limited resources. Everyone's prepared to chip in, you know. I believe you're heading back to Australia soon."

"That's the plan."

"She's told you I asked her to marry me. I love her dearly, Hugh."

"Isn't she a bit old for you, Jerry?'

"Maggie will never be old. Besides, I've always liked older women. A bit kinky, I suppose you might say."

"As long as she's happy. That's all that matters."

"Absolutely! And I'm sure I can make her happy, give her the good life, which she so craves. We spend a lot of time together. Your arrival put a spanner in the works, but I like to think that I can satisfy her in every way."

"In every way?" said Hugh under his breath. He didn't expect an answer and didn't get one. "You have a grand place here. Were you in business?"

"Good God, no. Much less exciting. Accountancy. But I was good at it and worked for a reputable firm, made good money, and have a sizable pension. And now I'm making the most of it and hope that Maggie will share it with me."

Hugh didn't counter. He didn't want to tell Jerry that he hadn't altogether given up on Maggie. He needed time. Jerry would have to sweat it out a little longer.

"I think I'll be hitting the road, Jerry."

"We're not as young as we used to be," Jerry said with a wry smile.

Hugh wondered whether he considered himself part of the "we."

It was not easy to get Maggie alone. He had to stand for some time on the periphery of a cluster of actors, of which she was the focal point, until he managed to catch her eye.

"You're going, Hugh?" she said with a note of disappointment.

"Yeah. A nice crowd but I've had a long day."

"Will I find you at home when I get back?"

Hugh wasn't sure whether she wanted him to be there or not, but he didn't wish to spoil her moment of glory. "No. You'll be late. I'll sleep in my old bed tonight."

"Will I see you before you leave?"

"I hope so. It'll have to be during the day. You have performances all week."

"Tomorrow is our last chance then."

"I suppose it is."

"Can you come up to the house at around 11:00 and we'll have brunch together."

"I'd love that, Maggie."

She raised herself on tiptoes and kissed him on the cheek. Was it because Jerry was watching that she didn't kiss him on the lips?

As he left the room, Hugh felt sad. He knew it was the end. She, like him, was preparing for his departure. He just couldn't stand the idea of Jerry the Real taking over where he left off.

■

When he arrived at Maggie's place the following day, he half-expected to find Jerry there but she was alone. Her appearance was unusually neglected as if she didn't care anymore if he didn't find her attractive. She looked much older and all the youthful energy she had exuded in the previous weeks seemed to have drained out of her.

"How was the party, Maggie?"

"Great but exhausting. I think I'm getting too old for parties that go on all night."

"Not a bit of it, Maggie."

"Everyone had a good time, I think. Jerry had a bit too much to drink, so I had to put him to bed before I came home."

Hugh wondered whether that was all they had done.

"Bacon and eggs?"

"How did you guess? I'll have to go on a diet when I go back. I've put on a few pounds."

Hugh silently watched Maggie fry the eggs and bacon. From the back, she looked like the same old Maggie. Her slim figure, draped in a slinky silk dressing gown, betrayed nothing of her age. She put the bacon and eggs in front of him and poured them both a cup of coffee. "Why do you have to go, Hugh?" she said wistfully.

"I've told you, Maggie. There's no point in going over it again. I think Jerry can make you much happier than I could. You're number one in his life."

"Not quite. The theatre is number one."

"You come a close second. He has everything you could want, a beautiful house, money, and above all, the time to devote to you."

"I've decided not to marry him, Hugh," she said definitively, looking up to gauge his reaction.

Hugh wasn't surprised. "Because he got a bit drunk last night?"

"No, Hugh. I'd always be comparing him with you. I'd prefer to have nothing than make do with second best. I did that before and regretted it."

"I've told you, Maggie, I can't promise anything. I have to see how things work out when I get back to Esperance."

"I know I can't have you, not all the time, anyway. So, I'll just have to make the most of you some of the time. I will see you some of the time, won't I?"

"Of course, Maggie. I'll be coming and going. We have Aisling, after all."

"Yes, our dream. Hugh, can we make love for the last time? I haven't put on any makeup. My hair is dishevelled. I must look a sight, but I want you to see me as I am. If you can make love to a wrinkled old hag, then I know that we have a future, however limited it may be."

He didn't answer, just took her hand and led her into the bedroom. He did everything in slow motion. He undressed her slowly, aroused her teasingly, and did everything to prolong the pleasure of lovemaking. He wanted to make sure that Jerry would have to try very hard to give her more pleasure than he had.

Hugh had not intended to stay the whole day, but everything was done as if this was their last day on earth. They had lunch with a bottle of wine at around tea time. In the end, it was late evening when he finally left. They walked hand in hand along the road, pretending that it was just a casual evening stroll, but they both knew it would be some time before it happened again, if at all.

At the stile, she held him against her and wouldn't let him go. It brought back their last parting, fifty years ago. Like then, he had to wrench himself free. She cried but did not plead. She must have known it would do no good. Yet, she never stopped smiling, a pale damp smile, sun filtering through a veil of rain.

He did not cry, outwardly at least, though parting from her was like leaving the hospital ward of someone who had only hours to live.

■

Hugh wouldn't let Joan drive him up to the airport. It was a long journey there and back. So, she left him at the bus in town.

On the way in, she turned to him with a remorseful look on her face. "I'm sorry, Hugh. Will you forgive me?"

"For what?"

"For holding a grudge against you."

"It wasn't your fault, Joan. It was that foolish brother of ours that was to blame."

"But I believed *him* and not you."

"It's not surprising. I'd let you down too many times."

"I don't know how to thank you for all you've done."

"At last, I've done a few things right in my life. Siobháin's a lovely girl, Joan. Treasure her. And I'm sure that in time you'll come to love Leonora too."

"I wish you were staying, Hugh. I'm sorry things didn't work out between you and Maggie. I kind of hoped…"

"One of us would have ended up being unhappy. I couldn't have made a new life for myself here, not at my age."

"I know. It was selfish of me to think you could. I can't say she's going to be all that happy with that McCoy character. They say he has a fair ould fondness for the drink."

"Don't mind what people say. He likes a drop but he's no drunkard. Anyway, she's decided not to marry him."

"Really?" Joan exclaimed. "Well, that'll give you greater incentive to come over then so."

"I intend to come back as often as I can. Maggie didn't seem totally against spending some in Esperance either. We have a grand little amateur theatre group there. I may be able to coax her into auditioning for a play. And who knows? She might bring you along with her."

"I'm too old for travelling halfway around the world, but if you stay away too long I might well have to come over and drag you back by the scruff of the neck."

"Nothing changes, Joan. Still the big sister."

The bus arrived exactly on time. He held her for some moments before saying goodbye. He promised to keep in touch. She hadn't figured out how to use Skype or Messenger yet but she would send emails, which was as far as her electronic skills extended.

The bus had not gone more than a few miles when he began to feel in limbo. The towns he passed through, the fields that whizzed by, and the people he observed in the seats around him were at once familiar and foreign. They were no longer his towns, his fields, his people. They neither belonged to his past nor his present, and it was unlikely they would ever belong to his future.

On the long journey back to Esperance, he had plenty of time to think. How differently things had worked out. Only six weeks earlier, he had no idea Rory was going to die nor that he would hook up again with Maggie. As for Aisling, her existence would never have entered his wildest dreams.

He thought of those last days with Rory and cried, not out of sadness but joy. They had had the opportunity to say things that would never otherwise have been said. Above all, he had been there at the end. He had held his hand as he passed through the thin wall that divides life from what is beyond. Now that things with Joan were better, he would be able to laugh at Rory's gullibility or big-heartedness, depending on how you see it. In a way, it represented his finest hour. He was able to perform a ridiculous act of generosity that would define his life for as long as he remained in people's memories.

He knew how the boys would take the news that they had a sister. They would initially be shocked. Their shock would turn to anger, their anger to fear that they might have to divide the inheritance three ways. He would propose an extended family meeting, but they would find excuses not to go. They would show indifference, feigned or real, to the spurious sister their father claimed to have in another hemisphere. Aisling would be nothing to them but a hibernating worm that had crawled out of the woodwork in search of sustenance.

No. Aisling was his alone, his and Maggie's. She was from his other life. Yet, for him she was the link that would forever connect his past with his present. She would bridge the fifty-year hiatus. Together or parted, Maggie and he would be joined inextricably for as long as they lived. This thought was a comfort to him. Home would no longer be either Australia or Ireland but somewhere in between.

Despite all that had happened, despite reliving his childhood a hundred times, he had that feeling of hope, of rejuvenation, as the plane began to dip towards the Australian dawn. Was he coming home or coming from home? He wasn't sure anymore and never would.

As he stepped off the plane, he felt invigorated by the familiarity of it. In many ways, these people were more his people than the Irish now. Yet, they would always see him as Irish. In the same way he could never lose the ould brogue, he could never lose his love for his homeland. As he walked towards the terminal at Esperance, he realised how much he loved his adopted land too. It was spring down under, and nature was resurgent with soft green leaves and blossoming trees. He decided to treat himself and take a taxi home.

He was looking forward to seeing Brendan and working with him on his project. Above all, he was looking forward to seeing the familiar, to be able to spend some time in the presence of Sheila's spirit, and to walk for miles across the station until he was too exhausted to continue and then return to the home Sheila and he had made together.

He knew why he had fallen in love with Esperance. It was, as the name denoted, hope. Now, he not only had hope but a dream as well, Aisling. Two dreams, in fact. He had Maggie too. As soon as he was settled in, he would call her, and they would arrange to spend a real honeymoon in Oxford. He had heard it was a beautiful city, but even more so now that it contained his wonderful daughter. His three newly-discovered grandchildren were scattered over the country but no doubt Aisling would arrange for them to be there to meet their second granddad. He found it hard to believe that at seventy-three, having just lost a beloved brother, life could hold out so much promise.

There would be no official marriage, no hullabaloo, no public celebration. They would relish each other's company for as long as it gave them pleasure. They would be united not by any social bonds, but by the only bonds that really mean anything, love and understanding, for he could now see that they had always had both. It simply required a number of deaths and fifty years for him to realise it.

As they were leaving the vicinity of the airport, Hugh had a sudden urge to see the sea. He wasn't quite sure why. Was it because it was common to both his homes? The sea was the same the world over, the constant ebb and flow, the infinite pounding of the waves, the break, break, break.

Hugh leaned towards the taxi driver. "Would you mind if we took the long route by the coast?"

"It's up to you, mate. You're paying. Feel like a swim, do you?"

"No. It's been a long journey. I need some fresh air."

"Where did you fly in from?"

"Ireland."

"Been back to the homeland, eh?"

"Yes." He didn't wish to elaborate.

"Where do you want us to go then, boss?"

He thought for a moment, but not for long. "Twilight Bay." It too held memories. Australian memories, of the children growing up, of Sheila in her prime.

The taxi driver parked as close as he could to the beach and Hugh got out and breathed in the revitalizing air. There was the odd stroller, the wind ruffling their hair, and one or two dogs running helter-skelter along the beach, retrieving a ball or chasing a loan seagull. He walked down to the water's edge and lay on the cool sand. There was a strong wind and the waves crashed on to the beach with a deafening thrashing of tumbling water. He was sitting too close the sea, and his face was sprayed with water. He made no attempt to wipe it off, just ran his tongue over his lips relishing the sharp tang of salt.

Suddenly, he was overcome by fatigue. He closed his eyes and allowed the sound of the waves lull him into a slumber. Break, break, break. What surprised him was that the sound of the crashing waves did not crush him as they had in Ireland. He no longer felt pummelled by the act of living. On the contrary, the waves reminded him of the perpetuity of life, not of his life, but of life in general. He would live the rest of his as best he could and his children and their children would carry it on, happily or unhappily, in the manner chance decided. As he listened to the waves, he realised that life can be interpreted in so many ways. He would choose to interpret it optimistically. Things would work out between him and Maggie. Providence had given her back to him, and it would be foolish of him to turn down such an undeserved gift.

He became aware of someone standing over him, blocking out the morning sun. He looked up at the dark figure and wondered what they wanted, standing so close. Then, he realised it was the taxi driver.

"How long are you planning to stay here, boss? The clock's ticking."

"I know but I've chosen to ignore it."

"Suit yourself. We can stay here till the cows come home for all I care."

"I suppose I ought to get home. My son will be expecting me. I have to break some news to him."

"Is it bad?"

"No, well, it depends on how you see it."

"I suppose nothing's black and white in this world."

"Very true."

As they walked back up the beach, Hugh was no longer thinking. He had done too much thinking in the past six weeks. Besides, all thoughts were drowned out by the break, break, break of the sea, as it proclaimed its age-old message over and over again; life goes on, for better or for worse, and you've got to make the most of it while you can.